T0293579

Guide to Disability and Inclusion in the Workplace

This book is dedicated to Em, who saw me and changed everything.

Guide to Disability and Inclusion in the Workplace

Katherine Breward, MBA, PhD
University of Winnipeg

S Sage Reference

FOR INFORMATION:

2455 Teller Road
Thousand Oaks, California 91320
E-mail: order@sagepub.com

1 Oliver's Yard
55 City Road
London, EC1Y 1SP
United Kingdom

Unit No 323-333, Third Floor, F-Block
International Trade Tower Nehru Place
New Delhi – 110 019
India

18 Cross Street #10-10/11/12
China Square Central
Singapore 048423

Printed in the United States of America

Library of Congress Cataloging-in-Publication Data: 2023949309

ISBN: 9781071902721

Acquisitions Editor: Kaitlin Ciarmiello
Development Editor: Laura McEwan
Production Editor: Syeda Aina Rahat Ali
Copy Editor: Deanna Noga
Typesetter: Hurix Digital
Proofreader: Ellen Brink
Indexer: Integra
Cover Designer: Dally Verghese
Marketing Manager: Gabrielle Perretta

24 25 26 27 28 10 9 8 7 6 5 4 3 2 1

Brief Contents

Detailed Contents

Preface

This book is designed to inform and support both students and practitioners in appropriate, respectful, and productive inclusion of workers with disabilities in a wide range of employment settings. It includes background context on the legal environment for diversity programs and the underlying psychology of inclusion. The bulk of the book, however, is dedicated to practical how-to strategies for accommodation of unique individuals with specific types of disability throughout the employment cycle as well as real-world examples. As such, it can help readers not only understand disability accommodation in abstract terms, but also implement best practices in inclusion in their own workplaces.

Chapter 1 introduces the topic by addressing why inclusion of workers with disabilities is important and discussing the legal landscape and legislative environment. Important legal terms such as *reasonable accommodation* are defined in this chapter, helping employers and managers better understand their responsibilities and helping workers with disabilities better understand their rights. In Chapter 2, the entirety of the employment cycle is considered, with attention paid to disability-related barrier removal at each stage of the cycle. For example, common barriers that occur during recruitment, selection, onboarding, training, and safety plan execution are covered alongside barriers related to completion of job tasks. (The individual nature of disability accommodation and the need for respectful collaboration with each worker with a disability is emphasized in this chapter and throughout the book.) Chapter 3 addresses some of the cultural, social, and psychological aspects of inclusion. In this chapter, readers will learn more about the nature of nonconscious bias and prejudice, as well as how to minimize it. The impact of peer attitudes and organizational culture on inclusion outcomes is also considered alongside tips for fostering positive attitudes and cultures. The next four chapters (Chapters 4 through 7) each examine common strengths, functional limitations, barriers, and accommodations for specific types of disability. Chapter 4 considers people with mobility impairments, such as a wheelchair users, amputees, and people who are quadriplegic, as well as people with sensory impairments such as vision or hearing loss. Chapter 5 discusses people with neurodiversity, including autism, attention deficit hyperactivity disorder, and learning disabilities. Chapter 6 examines the needs of people with psychiatric conditions, such as mood disorders, anxiety, and schizophrenia, as well as developmental disabilities and brain injuries. Chapter 7 considers a wide range of intermittent disabilities, which are conditions that come and go at unpredictable intervals. Examples include people with digestive- and pain-related disorders as well as arthritis. Addictions are also covered in this chapter, and disability management plans are discussed. Chapter 8 addresses inclusive design, a philosophy that looks at how to create workplaces with fewer inherent barriers rather than focusing on post-hoc accommodation. The chapter includes a range of inclusive suggestions for office building construction, physical workspace design, tool design, work process design, software design, team building and training, and even the managing of the social environment. In Chapter 9, readers can practice their newly acquired skills and understanding by working through nine real-world cases featuring different accommodation scenarios. In Chapter 10, some further suggestions for moving forward are offered. Areas that are currently evolving (either legally or as relates to our understanding of best practices) are discussed, including disability management plans, inclusion of people who are neurodiverse at work, and story-telling–based diversity training. Extended examples of companies addressing the needs of workers with disabilities are offered. Finally, the appendix offers helpful checklists and forms to ensure practitioners address disability-related inclusion effectively throughout the employment cycle. These checklists are useful tools to use when going through diversity audits and individual accommodation planning, helping ensure key considerations are not overlooked.

Should a qualified student require a book hosted on Sage Knowledge as an ePub or fully typeset PDF, contact your campus Accessibility Services or Disability Services Office. If you need further assistance, you can send an inquiry to accessrequest@sagepub.com. Sage replies to all inquiries promptly, typically within five working days. If it does not have the file in-house, it shall exercise reasonable efforts to have the file produced at no cost to the requestor. Sage is not able to provide books in Word, HTML, or XML format. PDFs obtained from Sage directly are DRM-free (no print or copy restrictions) and permit magnification by the rendering application. Accessible copies are issued for use by qualified students only.

Sage's publications are designed to follow a logical reading order and semantic structure rather than work with any specific screen reader. However, Sage tests its products with the following combinations:

- JAWS and Chrome

- NVDA and Firefox

More information on accessibility features for this text can be found in the Sage Knowledge Accessibility Guide, https://sk.sagepub.com/accessibility. If you have any comments, questions, or feedback about the accessibility of Sage Knowledge, Sage's accessibility team would love to hear from you. You can contact them at online.accessibility @sagepub.com.

Acknowledgments

No author gets a book to print alone, and this work would not have been possible without the help of an entire team at Sage. I especially want to thank forward-looking acquisitions editor Kaitlin Ciarmiello and my fantastic developmental editor Laura McEwan, whose suggestions improved the book in innumerable ways. I would also like to thank the many workers with disabilities who have shared their stories with me over the years in research interviews, surveys, and informal conversations. Your willingness to share a small part of yourself has been instrumental in my developing understanding of issues around disability inclusion, and I am grateful for your trust. Thank you also to my Facebook tribe—the other "lost women" who, like me, were diagnosed as autistic only in mid-adulthood—and to my husband Michael, who waited 60 years for his diagnosis. Your combined support and perspective have given me the strength to unmask, be openly autistic, and advocate to remove my own barriers as well as those of others, and that has made all the difference.

Disability at Work

Introduction and Legislative Framework

M ost people with disabilities are able to make valuable contributions to organizations. They want to work. Employment provides not only income and associated financial independence, but also a sense of challenge, accomplishment, satisfaction, and self-esteem. It provides a means to contribute to the community in a visible way that is acknowledged and respected. Despite strong preferences for working and clear benefits associated with doing so, many people with disabilities find themselves unemployed or underemployed. The following quotes extracted from unpublished interviews with job candidates with disabilities that were conducted by the author in 2020 begin to explore why:

> I feel like employers won't even look at what I can offer. When they hear "disability" they focus on their own ideas about problems and limitations, most of which aren't even accurate based on my condition. But all they see is inconvenience and even the well-intentioned ones—honestly, sometimes I think they are so afraid of doing something wrong or it being awkward that they just prefer to avoid hiring me. (33-year-old female with cerebral palsy who uses lower body mobility and upper body agility aids and has been seeking teaching and training roles for 4.5 years)

> I've almost given up even looking for work. It seems pointless. I would be great at safety assessments but getting past a job interview is just impossible for someone like me. I always seem to answer wrong. I don't know what they expect from me. (24-year-old nonbinary engineering graduate with autism, has been job-seeking for 2 years)

> I'd love to go for a promotion but because sometimes I get flare-ups, they won't even consider me. It's not fair; other people sometimes miss a shift, too. (47-year-old female healthcare worker with rheumatoid arthritis who has worked for the same employer for 11 years)

Now that I've sorted out meds, if I could change just one thing about my life I'd want to work, but with no prior job experience it is really tough to just get in the door. Especially when you have to explain why you haven't worked until now. (29-year-old male with bipolar disorder seeking entry-level retail and customer service roles)

Unemployment and Underemployment by the Numbers

The U.S. Bureau of Labor Statistics (2022) reported that in 2021 only 19.1% of people with disabilities were employed, compared with 63.7% of the general population. When considering only the people who are actively looking for work, 10.1% of people with disabilities were unemployed, compared with 5.1% of the general population. This statistic does not include people who have stopped actively looking for work, a group in which people with disabilities are also overrepresented. For example, in 2021, 8 out of 10 American residents with disabilities reported not being in the labor force, compared with only 3 out of 10 in the general population. Significant disadvantage remains even when age and education are controlled for, so clearly these results are not merely due to people with disabilities being older on average than the general population (although that does contribute somewhat to the higher *not in the labor force* rates) or less well-educated. Furthermore, there is evidence of complex intersectional forms of disadvantage that replicate other biases. For example, among people with disabilities in the United States, the jobless rate varied significantly by race, with Black people having a jobless rate of 15.1%; Hispanics, 13.3%; Whites, 9.3%; and Asians, 8.5%. In addition, employment rates varied by the nature of the disability, with mental, psychiatric, and neurological disabilities especially likely to trigger disadvantage and discrimination.

There is also evidence of underemployment. For example, the same U.S. Bureau of Labor Statistics report indicated that 29% of workers with disabilities work part time, while only 16% of workers without disabilities do so. While some of these part-time placements will be the preferred mode of work, many people with disabilities find themselves in part-time work involuntarily. This limits both their income and access to benefits, which are generally offered only to full-time workers. There is also evidence that people with disabilities have more trouble climbing the career ladder. For example, 36.5% of people with disabilities work in more senior management and professional occupations; however, in the nondisabled population, that number goes up to 42.7%. People with disabilities are also overrepresented in lower paying service jobs.

These patterns of disadvantage are similar in other nations. In Canada, one in five adults report having a disability. In the most recent Statistics Canada report available (consisting of data collected in 2017), the unemployment rate for the general population was 5.8%, for people with mild disabilities it was 35%, and for people with severe disabilities it was 74%. In the European Union (EU), quality of life surveys from 2017 indicate that 28% of the population has some form of disability. Despite the high prevalence of disability, employment figures from the same year showed that only 50.6% of adults with disabilities were employed compared to 74.8% of the people without impairments. The European unemployment rate (which, again, includes only those looking for work, and not those who have given up), was 17.1% for people with disabilities and 10.2% for the rest of the population.

In Japan, only 6% of the population is defined as disabled, a much lower number than in most nations, which is a result of limited legal definitions of disability. Among that group, participation in employment is much lower than for the rest of the population. Formal Japanese government census results from 2006 (the latest available with disability-related numbers) indicated that 60.4% of the nondisabled population was employed, but only 52.7% of adults with intellectual disabilities were employed. That number went down to 43% for physical impairments and 17.4% for mental impairments. Among workers with disabilities in Japan, 59.4% worked in noncompetitive "welfare-oriented employment," meaning government-mandated vocational aid centers and supervised workshops with limited opportunities.

In a final example, data that was collected and collated from 18 Asian-Pacific member states in 2020 indicated that there are approximately 472 million people of working age with disabilities in the geographic area, and persons with disabilities are between 2 to 6 times less likely to be employed. (There is considerable variation between nations.) In addition, women with disabilities in Asia Pacific were half as likely to find jobs when compared to their male counterparts. People with psychosocial and intellectual impairments also experienced heightened disadvantage.

The Costs of Lack of Inclusion

This lack of inclusion costs communities in both direct and indirect ways. Businesses are negatively impacted since they are not fully utilizing the labor force. At the time of writing this book, the United States, Canada, and Europe were all experiencing severe labor shortages. On June 3, 2022, Stephanie Ferguson, the senior manager of employment policy at the U.S. Chamber of Commerce, reported that the United States had 11.4 million job openings but only 6 million unemployed workers to fill them. Financial analysts expect these shortages to last years, potentially decades, due to a combination of slower population growth and reduced migration. These labor shortages impact many aspects of day-to-day life. In 2022, chaos at airports, particularly in North America, was one of the most visible and newsworthy indicators. A shortage of flight attendants, security personnel, baggage handlers, and ground crew led to thousands of flight cancelations and delays with widespread negative impacts. Similarly, news reports at the time mentioned restaurants and retail businesses being forced to close completely due to lack of staff, while goods languished due to a shortage of customs agents, dockworkers, and truck drivers. The supply chain issues caused in part by these labor shortages contributed directly to extremely high inflation rates that negatively impacted many households and businesses. With these dire examples of the impact of labor shortages, the imperative to fully utilize existing workers is clear. Many potential workers with disabilities, however, do not appear in unemployment statistics because such statistics only include those actively looking for work, and many people with disabilities have given up on job-seeking due to the discrimination and barriers they have faced.

In addition to negative impacts on businesses and the market economy, individuals and communities in general are also damaged by lack of inclusion. The lack of financial independence and poverty that accompany unemployment and underemployment are only the beginning. In a society in which people are often measured based on their jobs and productivity, unemployment can lead to feelings of hopelessness, worthlessness, depression, and poor self-esteem (Mousteri et. al., 2018). These feelings themselves can further compromise health and act as a trigger for stress-related medical conditions (Pietrangela, 2019). For example, a meta-analysis from 2018 representing 25 years of medical research and led by Marc De Hert indicated that depression increases the risk of coronary mortality (fatal heart attacks) by 36%. As a result of these sorts of effects, when people who are able to work cannot find suitable employment, the community bears a range of direct and indirect support, social service, health-, and well-being–related costs (Beja, 2020). For example, demand for services ranging from mental health interventions to food banks and job placement programming all increase. Tax revenues decrease, both due to lessened spending and the direct reimbursement of certain types of taxes that are based on income. By contrast, inclusive communities tend to be strengthened. When workers feel included and respected, mental health needs are lessened and well-being, resilience, and productivity are increased.

Why Barriers Persist

With the personal and community benefits of inclusion clear, asking why there is still so much discrimination and discounting in the labor market, particularly in times of severe labor shortages, is useful. Some employers still act in biased ways. One reason their complacency is successful is that available legal interventions for discrimination tend to be time-consuming, bureaucratic, and, in some jurisdictions, costly to access. For example, it can take more than 2 years for a case to reach resolution in Canada's provincial Human Rights Tribunals, and according to its website, the formal Equal Employment Opportunity Commission (EEOC) process in the United States takes an *average* of 10 months—meaning half the cases take longer to resolve. Remedies may take years, requiring significant time, energy, and expertise navigating the legal system. Vulnerable workers who are focused on survival may not be in a position to invest their resources in justice, or they may not have confidence that they will achieve a positive outcome. Addressing these deliberate and intentional forms of discrimination requires not only public education and myth-busting but also more effective, less onerous legal tools.

While a small minority of employers are deliberately discriminatory, a great deal of prejudice occurs on a nonconscious level, meaning that it occurs without the active awareness or endorsement of the parties involved. This occurs due to a combination of attribution error, in-group effects, and stereotyping, which causes employers to perceive (in some cases nonexistent) limitations and barriers rather than skills and competencies. To use the language of public service messaging, they perceive only the disability, not the many abilities that the job candidate brings to the table. I, the author of this book, am neurodiverse and a respected, award-winning educator and have experienced this personally when professional colleagues, not realizing they are speaking to a person with autism, have sincerely and adamantly voiced faulty assumptions that people with autism cannot work in roles that involve interactions with people or teaching (Chapter 3 delves more deeply into the underlying psychology of nonconscious bias and how to reduce it).

Many of the barriers experienced by workers with disabilities are accidental or inadvertent, created by a lack of forethought and insight about needs. Barriers that are obvious to people who are disability-aware may be completely invisible to employers without that awareness in much the same way that common forms of systemic racism are often invisible to those with White privilege and limited diversity in their social circles. For example, many people using online job boards to post jobs are not aware that such boards are not always equally accessible for the vision impaired. In another example, many online selection tests are time limited with no clear option to request extra time due to conditions such as dyslexia. These sorts of barriers, while inadvertent, still constitute discrimination under law. (The section on Legislation and the Legal Context for Disability Accommodation in this chapter discusses direct versus indirect discrimination in more detail.)

Biomedical and Social Models of Disability

Biomedical models focus on disability as the result of physical or mental deficits or defects. As a result, the focus for interventions is the person with a disability and medical techniques that cure or manage illness and increase quality of life. While these are laudable goals, this focus tends to pathologize differences, some of which may simply represent normal human variation. For example, neurodiverse people with conditions such as dyslexia and attention deficit hyperactivity disorder (ADHD) often argue that they think differently but not wrongly, but their differences and strengths are not appreciated by many neurotypical people. Problems with the biomedical model of disability include its tendency to result in (often nonconscious) perceptions that people with disabilities are less than others. It also encourages a focus on medical interventions. As such, resources are poured almost exclusively into medical advances when adapting the environment could, in many cases, result in wider benefits.

The social model of disability, by contrast, states that disability is the outcome of the barriers society has raised by excluding groups of people when designing policies, laws, infrastructure, and overall human environments. For example, wheelchair users often experience undue mobility impairments because streets are often designed without lowered curbs and store aisles can be too narrow. People with Crohn's disease or similarly unpredictable digestive issues may not be able to access public spaces such as parks due to a lack of suitable washroom facilities. The stimming, or self-stimulating, behaviors commonly used by people with autism to self-sooth, such as hand flapping, are usually completely harmless but are considered *weird* and *unprofessional*, resulting in social judgment that magnifies communication and social barriers. In a final example, people with sight impairments are often disadvantaged in public spaces due to challenges such as a lack of sound-based traffic signals and the lack of braille (not to mention the lack of tactile exhibits) in educational spaces such as museums. The main idea behind the social model of disability is an acknowledgment that impairment is often socially and structurally created rather than being inherent. Communities can, collectively, choose to lessen the degree to which that is true by designing more thoughtful and inclusive spaces. (Chapter 8 discusses information about inclusive design in more depth.)

Legislation and the Legal Context for Disability Accommodation

Awareness that both direct and indirect discrimination are prohibited by law in most nations, including the industrialized Western democracies, is important. Discrimination does not have to be intentional to result in legal, financial, and reputational damage. Direct discrimination occurs when a person is treated differently due to a protected characteristic. Protected characteristics include aspects of identity for which discrimination is prohibited under law. While they may vary by jurisdiction (e.g., gender identity and sexual orientation are formally protected in some countries and states but not in others), they generally include gender, ethnicity, race, and disability. Indirect discrimination occurs when a job requirement that appears to be neutral for everyone has the effect of disadvantaging a group of people due to a protected characteristic. For example, having a rule that employees with more than two absences a month cannot share in a group-based productivity bonus may be well intended but significantly disadvantage people who have episodic disabilities with unpredictable flare-ups or workers who need scheduled time off for medical appointments. Similarly, having strict rules about when employees may take bathroom breaks (and for how long) can create both disability and gender-related disadvantages due to symptoms associated with specific disabilities and menstrual hygiene needs.

Within that broader context of prohibitions against both direct and indirect discrimination, there are further equity and legal rights granted specifically to persons with disabilities. While legislation is emerging throughout the globe, Western democratic, industrialized nations have had a historic cultural focus on individual rights and economic productivity. Unsurprisingly, these nations have been policy leaders in this area, developing some of the first formal legislation granting people with disabilities rights to participate fully in society in general and labor markets in particular. The United Nations has also developed its own guidelines to inspire and direct the efforts of the global community. Let's begin by examining the United Nations directives and then legislation from the United States, Canada, European Union, and Australia.

The United Nations Convention of the Rights of Persons with Disabilities

The United Nations Convention on the Rights of Persons with Disabilities (CRPD) is an international treaty that first took effect on May 3, 2008. As of 2022, it has been signed by 164 nations. The treaty strives to ensure equal rights and unencumbered access to services for persons with disabilities across a broad range of areas (i.e., housing, education, and work). It also explicitly prohibits direct and indirect forms of discrimination. It contains 50 articles. For the purposes of this text, let's consider Article 27, which is directly related to employment. The Article in full states:

1. States Parties recognize the right of persons with disabilities to work, on an equal basis with others; this includes the right to the opportunity to gain a living by work freely chosen or accepted in a labour market and work environment that is open, inclusive and accessible to persons with disabilities. States Parties shall safeguard and promote the realization of the right to work, including for those who acquire a disability during the course of employment, by taking appropriate steps, including through legislation, to, inter alia:

   a) Prohibit discrimination on the basis of disability with regard to all matters concerning all forms of employment, including conditions of recruitment, hiring and employment, continuance of employment, career advancement and safe and healthy working conditions;

   b) Protect the rights of persons with disabilities, on an equal basis with others, to just and favourable conditions of work, including equal opportunities and equal remuneration for work of equal value, safe and healthy working conditions, including protection from harassment, and the redress of grievances;

c) Ensure that persons with disabilities are able to exercise their labour and trade union rights on an equal basis with others;

d) Enable persons with disabilities to have effective access to general technical and vocational guidance programmes, placement services and vocational and continuing training;

e) Promote employment opportunities and career advancement for persons with disabilities in the labour market, as well as assistance in finding, obtaining, maintaining and returning to employment;

f) Promote opportunities for self-employment, entrepreneurship, the development of cooperatives and starting one's own business;

g) Employ persons with disabilities in the public sector;

h) Promote the employment of persons with disabilities in the private sector through appropriate policies and measures, which may include affirmative action programmes, incentives and other measures;

i) Ensure that reasonable accommodation is provided to persons with disabilities in the workplace;

j) Promote the acquisition by persons with disabilities of work experience in the open labour market;

k) Promote vocational and professional rehabilitation, job retention and return-to-work programmes for persons with disabilities.

2. States Parties shall ensure that persons with disabilities are not held in slavery or in servitude, and are protected, on an equal basis with others, from forced or compulsory labour.

The U.S. Legislation Environment

In the United States, the legal definition of disability is enshrined in the Americans with Disabilities Act (ADA). The ADA defines disability as a physical, mental, or neurologic impairment that substantially limits one or more major life activities. This definition includes people who have a history of such an impairment, even if they do not currently have functional limitations. Key legal concepts within ADA legislation include the duty to reasonably accommodate undue hardship and bona fide occupational requirements.

Duty to reasonably accommodate means that an employer must take all *reasonable measures* to enable an employee with a disability to keep working. These rights extend to job candidates, who must not be discriminated against due to disabilities that can be accommodated. Reasonable measures can include a broad range of accommodations. Common accommodations include the following categories, although this list is not comprehensive because accommodations vary widely and are limited only by the creativity of the people involved:

- Structural changes (e.g., installation of wheelchair ramps, accessible bathroom facilities)

- Workstation adjustments

- Provision of technical devices and software (e.g., braille readers, voice-to-text software)

- Changes to secondary aspects of the job and amended job descriptions

- Adjustments to processes (e.g., recruitment, training practices)

- Adjustments to supervisory practices (e.g., providing written task lists and explicit guidance on task prioritization)

- Social consideration (e.g., ensuring peers use appropriate forms of communication and respect sensory sensitivities).

- Direct human support (e.g., an assistant, a social coach for some types of social and communication impairment)

- Flexible scheduling

- Permission to work from home as needed

- Transportation assistance

Correctly defining the primary and secondary aspects of a job is critical when accommodating an employee involves amending secondary aspects of the job. The primary aspects of a job will establish the bona fide requirements (BFORs), which are the knowledge, skills, abilities, and other traits

(KSAOs) without which a person simply cannot perform the role. For example, a person with severe vision impairment would not be able to meet the BFORs to drive a truck or fly a plane because vision is necessary to complete those tasks safely. The information related to BFORs should come from a scientifically derived job analysis—a formal human resources process that is used to identify job tasks and the needed KSAOs to achieve them. The result of the process is a job description. Conducting the job analysis process properly is critical; practitioners must use objective scientific methods rather than basing it on indefensible subjective impressions or *gut feel*, because courts may require employers to explicitly defend the job requirements should a complaint arise.

Employers are not able to deny accommodations for disabilities without proving undue hardship. In some cases, to prove undue hardship, a detailed medical assessment may be required that proves an individual cannot complete essential operational requirements of the job. Secondary aspects of the job are less relevant, because employers are expected to reconfigure or redistribute these tasks. The EEOC, in its role as the federal agency responsible for enforcing the ADA, lists factors that determine whether a particular accommodation presents an undue hardship to the employer or service provider. They include, in summary

- the nature and cost of the accommodation;
- the financial resources of the employer;
- the nature of the business, including size, composition, and structure; and
- accommodation costs already incurred in a workplace.

Financial difficulty for the employer alone is not usually sufficient to reject accommodation requests. Courts will look at tax credits and deductions available and at the employee's willingness to pay for part of the costs. In addition, the definition of *excessive costs* varies depending on the size of the organization. A very small operation may not, for instance, be required to install an elevator in their building, the cost of which may exceed their annual revenues. However, larger and better resourced companies would be required to do so.

Let's consider *EEOC v. Walmart* (Dorrian, 2021), an example of ADA legislation enforcement. Paul Reina, who is deaf and has a visual impairment, had successfully worked as a cart pusher at Walmart for 16.5 years with the occasional assistance of a job coach who was provided by Walmart. A newly assigned manager rescinded his access to the job coach and argued that Paul was unable to do his job tasks since he could not readily answer customer questions. As a result of this combination of withdrawal of support and adding job duties, Paul was no longer considered a suitable employee and termination was attempted. Paul's legal representatives successfully argued that there was no merit to the decision to take away the job coach and that a job coach was a reasonable accommodation. It was also determined that answering customer questions was not a core part of the cart pusher job and therefore was not a BFOR. Walmart was required to reinstate Mr. Reina's employment and pay damages of $300,000.

International Legislative Environments

Most Western industrialized nations have legislation that is very similar to the ADA. The core concepts of reasonable accommodation and undue hardship appear in all legislation, although some details differ. Many nations also have more specific definitions of disability. Let's evaluate a sampling of international legislation from Canada, the European Union, and Australia. Employers need to be aware of laws in all jurisdictions within which they operate because they are beholden to the rules in the nations in which they have employees, regardless of the location of their company headquarters.

In the Canadian Human Rights Code, disability is defined as:

1. Any degree of physical disability, infirmity, malformation, or disfigurement that is caused by bodily injury, birth defect or illness and, without limiting the generality of the foregoing, includes diabetes mellitus, epilepsy, a brain injury, any degree of paralysis, amputation, lack of physical coordination, blindness or visual impediment, deafness or hearing impediment, muteness or speech impediment, or physical reliance on a guide dog or other animal or on a wheelchair or other remedial appliance or device,

2. A condition of mental impairment or a developmental disability,

3. A learning disability, or a dysfunction in one or more of the processes involved in understanding or using symbols or spoken language,

4. A mental disorder, or

5. An injury or disability for which benefits were claimed or received under the insurance plan established under the *Workplace Safety and Insurance Act, 1997.*

The Canadian Human Rights Commission uses effectively the same definition of reasonable accommodation as the ADA. The Supreme Court decision *Alberta Dairy Pool v. Alberta (Human Rights Commission)* (1990, 2.S.C.R. 489; Baker, 1991) established the criteria used to determine undue hardship, which includes the following in summary:

- Excessive expenses will be incurred,

- Disruption of existing collective agreements will occur,

- Existence of highly interchangeable work force or facilities,

- Being a very small operation,

- Safety concerns, and

- Creation of morale problems with other employees.

The creation of morale problems with other employees is the most difficult criterion to justify and, as a result of case precedents occurring after the Supreme Court's 1990 decision, is seldom accepted in courts. The common legal understanding that has developed since 1990 suggests that morale is relevant only if an accommodation significantly interferes with the rights of other employees. Similarly, disruption of collective agreements has received inconsistent support in subsequent court cases and is not a reliable criteria to lean on to deny accommodations.

In one famous Canadian case that went all the way to the Supreme Court, a man by the name of Keays was dismissed by Honda after 14 years of service. Honda used a progressive discipline system related to attendance, and Keays was perceived as having excessive absenteeism due to symptoms associated with chronic fatigue syndrome. While initially supportive, his manager grew impatient after a lengthier disability leave and terminated his employment. Keays was ultimately awarded 24 months' salary (15 months to meet the legal requirement for reasonable notice of termination and another 9 months for damages), as well as an additional $100,000 in damages. The judge called Honda's behavior related to the termination "egregious bad faith."

Turning now to the European Union, the European Charter of Fundamental Rights has two articles relevant to disability. Article 21 lists disability as a ground on which discrimination is prohibited, and Article 26 calls for the integration of persons with disabilities. The definition of disability, however, is derived from Council Directive 2000/78/EC, which became active on November 27, 2000. It states:

> As with other grounds specified in the framework directive, no definition is provided of the term disability . . . . EU-wide definitions will evolve as cases reach the Court of Justice. This will be a long process, and there will inevitably be a period of uncertainty as cases are taken through the courts.

Subsequent court decisions, however, have supported defining physical, sensory, mental, and psychiatric conditions as disabilities in a manner compatible with the North American definitions presented.

The Council Directive 2000/78/EC, Article 5, also states:

> In order to guarantee compliance with the principle of equal treatment in relation to persons with disabilities, reasonable accommodation shall be provided. This means that employers shall take appropriate measures, where needed in a particular case, to enable a person with a disability to have access to, participate in, or advance in employment, or to undergo training, unless such measures would impose a disproportionate burden on the employer.

Worth noting is that the term *disproportionate burden* is equivalent to the concept of *undue hardship* that is used in America and Canada.

The European Union also subscribes to a legal concept known as *positive action*, laid out in the Council Directive 2000/78/EC Article 7.2. It states that

> with regard to disabled persons, the principle of equal treatment shall be without prejudice to the right of Member States to maintain or adopt provisions on the protection of health and safety at work or to measures aimed at creating or maintaining provisions or facilities for safeguarding or promoting their integration into the working environment.

Furthermore, the directive

> does not require the recruitment, promotion, maintenance in employment or training of an individual who is not competent, capable, and available to perform the essential functions of the post

concerned or to undergo the relevant training, without prejudice to the obligation to provide reasonable accommodation for people with disabilities. Appropriate measures should be provided, i.e., effective and practical measures to adapt the workplace to the disability, for example adapting premises and equipment, patterns of working time, the distribution of tasks or the provision of training or integration resources. To determine whether the measures in question give rise to a disproportionate burden, account should be taken in particular of the financial and other costs entailed, the scale and financial resources of the organization or undertaking and the possibility of obtaining public funding or any other assistance.

The Council Directive was enforced in a case that came out of Estonia in 2021. Tartu Vangla, a prison official, was dismissed from his role due to a worsening hearing impairment. The organization had a rule that all employees "must have hearing acuity that meets minimum sound perception thresholds." This requirement was rejected by the courts since it was too absolute. There was no assessment of requirements associated with individual job roles and therefore no legitimate evidence that full hearing was a BFOR.

Similarly, Australia has two relevant pieces of legislation. The Disability Discrimination Act (DDA) of 1992 prohibits discrimination against people with disabilities. In 2014, this protection was enhanced with the introduction of the Disabilities Act, which mandates full inclusion in all aspects of life including education, training, and employment (NSW, 2022). Australia defines disability as any physical, intellectual, psychiatric, sensory, learning, or neurological limitation. Its definition explicitly includes physical disfigurement and the presence in the body of disease-causing organisms (such as HIV). Australian legislation also specifically mentions that the relevant disability could be in the past, anticipated in the future, or may be believed to exist now. It uses similar definitions of reasonable accommodation and undue hardship as the United States, although it substitutes the term *unjustified hardship*. Unjustified hardship may include major difficulties in accommodation or unreasonable costs. Employers claiming unreasonable costs must have attempted to use the Australian government's Workplace Modification Scheme, a formal government program that funds disability-related workplace modifications or equipment purchases, prior to making such a claim.

The following example from Australia highlights the fact that disabilities do not have to be active for discrimination to occur. In one case from 2014, according to the Australian Human Rights Commission, a woman named Kimberly was offered a part-time receptionist job at a medical clinic. A few weeks after starting her new job, her employer discovered that she had previously made worker's compensation claims for repetitive strain injuries to her wrists and hands. While she was not currently experiencing symptoms and was performing well, her employer dismissed her due to fears that future flare-ups would interfere with her work. The complaint was ultimately resolved in favor of Kimberly, with her former employer being required to pay significant financial compensation.

While there are minor differences in the details, most industrialized Western nations have roughly similar legislation. The inclusion of workers with disabilities has become a priority throughout these nations and in much of the rest of the world. Remembering that this is not a legal issue— at the end of the day, it is a human issue— is important. When inclusion becomes about more than strict legal compliance, amazing things can happen. Hiring workers with disabilities can create meaningful competitive advantage, and employers have access to a wider pool of talent who bring their individual KSAOs to their work, including people with rare and hard-to-find skills. Additionally, it could be inferred that workers with disabilities tend to be more loyal to accommodating employers, reducing turnover.

Finally, employers benefit from having an alternate perspective. Industries from food service to consumer-packaged goods, software to finance, can benefit from having employees who have heightened personal awareness of the needs of the portion of their customer base with disabilities. Their insights can be used to build better processes, products, and services and capture more market share. Having workers who are neuro-diverse, such as people with autism, dyslexia, and ADHD, can also confer an innovation advantage because they tend to view the world through a different lens than neurotypical people. That means they ask different questions that can productively challenge stale, unhelpful assumptions. All these advantages make inclusion profitable for the bottom line as well as the soul.

FURTHER READINGS

Department of Economic and Social Affairs. (2022, May 6). *Convention on the Rights of Persons with Disabilities (CRPD)*. United Nations. https://www.un.org/development/desa/disabilities/convention-on-the-rights-of-persons-with-disabilities.html

Goering, S. (2015). Rethinking disability: The social model of disability and chronic disease. *Current Reviews in Musculoskeletal Medicine, 8*(2), 134–138. https://doi.org/10.1007/s12178-015-9273-z

Tompa, E., Samosh, D., & Boucher, N. (2020). *Skills gaps, underemployment, and equity of labour-market opportunities for persons with disabilities in Canada.* Future Skills Centre. https://www.torontomu.ca/content/dam/diversity/reports/Skills-gaps-underemployments-and-equity-of-labour-market-opportunities-for-person-with-disabilities.pdf

U.S. Equal Employment Opportunity Commission. (n.d.). *The EEO status of workers with disabilities in the federal sector.* https://www.eeoc.gov/federal-sector/reports/eeo-status-workers-disabilities-federal-sector

REFERENCES

Australian Human Rights Commission. (2012). *Know your rights: Disability discrimination.* https://humanrights.gov.au/our-work/disability-rights/know-your-rights-disability-discrimination

Baker, D. (1991, September). Alberta Human Rights Commission v. Central Alberta Dairy Pool. *McGill Law Journal, 36*(4). https://lawjournal.mcgill.ca/article/alberta-human-rights-commission-v-central-alberta-dairy-pool/

Beja, E. L., Jr. (2020). Subjective well-being approach to valuing unemployment: Direct and indirect cost. *International Journal of Community Well-Being, 3,* 277–287. https://doi.org/10.1007/s42413-019-00053-7

De Hert, M., Detraux, J., & Vancampfort, D. (2018). The intriguing relationship between coronary heart disease and mental disorders. *Dialogues in Clinical Neuroscience, 20*(1), 31–40. https://doi.org/10.31887/DCNS.2018.20.1/mdehert

Department of Economic and Social Affairs. (n.d.) *Convention on the Rights of Persons with Disabilities: Article 27—Work and employment.* United Nations. https://www.un.org/development/desa/disabilities/convention-on-the-rights-of-persons-with-disabilities/article-27-work-and-employment.html

Directorate-General for Communication. (n.d.). *EU Charter of Fundamental Rights.* European Commission. https://ec.europa.eu/info/aid-development-cooperation-fundamental-rights/your-rights-eu/eu-charter-fundamental-rights_en

Dorrian, P. (2021, September 24). Walmart, EEOC renew fight over coach as disability accommodation. *Bloomberg Law.* https://news.bloomberglaw.com/daily-labor-report/walmart-eeoc-renew-fight-over-coach-as-disability-accommodation

European Disability Forum. (2021). *Court of Justice of the European Union stands against disability-based discrimination at work in Estonia.* https://www.edf-feph.org/court-of-justice-of-the-european-union-stands-against-disability-based-discrimination-at-work-in-estonia/

European Union. (2000). Council Directive 2000/78/EC of 27 November 2000 establishing a general framework for equal treatment in employment and occupation. *Official Journal L, 303,* 16–22. https://eur-lex.europa.eu/legal-content/EN/TXT/?uri=celex%3A32000L0078

Ferguson, S. (2022, August 5). *Understanding America's labor shortage.* U.S. Chamber of Commerce. https://www.uschamber.com/workforce/understanding-americas-labor-shortage#:~:text=Right%20now%2C%20the%20latest%20data,have%205.4%20million%20open%20jobs

Government of Canada. (2022). *Rights in the workplace.* https://www.canada.ca/en/canadian-heritage/services/rights-workplace.html

Kudo, T. (2010). Japan's employment rate of persons with disabilities and outcome of employment quota system. *Japan Labor Review, 7*(2), 5–25. https://www.jil.go.jp/english/JLR/documents/2010/JLR26_kudo.pdf

Lecerf, M. (2020). *Employment and disability in the European Union.* European Parliamentary Research Service. https://www.europarl.europa.eu/RegData/etudes/BRIE/2020/651932/EPRS_BRI(2020)651932_EN.pdf

Lynk, M. (2008, February 12). Keays v. Honda Canada: *The scope of the Disability Accommodation Duty in Canadian Employment Law.* TheCourt.ca. http://www.thecourt.ca/keays-v-honda-canada-the-scope-of-the-disability-accommodation-duty-in-canadian-employment-law/

Morris, S., Fawcett, G., Brisebois, L., & Hughes, J. (2018, November 28). *A demographic, employment and income profile of Canadians with disabilities aged 15 years and over, 2017.* Statistics Canada. https://www150.statcan.gc.ca/n1/pub/89-654-x/89-654-x2018002-eng.htm

Mousteri, V., Daly, M., & Delaney, L. (2018). The scarring effect of unemployment on psychological well-being across Europe. *Social Science Research, 72,* 146–169. https://doi.org/10.1016/j.ssresearch.2018.01.007

New South Wales (NSW) Legislation. (2022). *Disability Inclusion Act 2014 No 41.* https://legislation.nsw.gov.au/view/whole/html/inforce/current/act-2014-041

Pietrangela, A. (2019, October 22). The effects of depression on the body. *Healthline.* https://www.healthline.com/health/depression/effects-on-body

Social Development Division. (2020, December 23). *Employment of persons with disabilities in Asia and the Pacific: Trends, strategies and policy recommendations*.https://www.unescap.org/kp/2020/employment-persons-disabilities-asia-and-pacific-trends-strategies-and-policy

U.S. Bureau of Labor Statistics. (2022, February 24). *Persons with a disability: Labor force characteristics—2021*. https://www.bls.gov/news.release/archives/disabl_02242022.htm

U.S. Department of Justice. (n.d.). *Introduction to the ADA*. ADA.gov. https://www.ada.gov/ada_intro.htm

Inclusivity and Organizational Processes

I n this chapter, we explore the multifaceted roles of human resources (HR) departments, managers, and supervisors in supporting workers with disabilities. We take a comprehensive look at the ways in which, to prioritize inclusion, disability must be considered when planning workplace policies, procedures, processes, and resource allocation at all stages of the employment relationship.

The Role of Employers in Identifying and Responding to Accommodation Needs

Supervisors, managers, and HR all have important roles to play in supporting workers with disabilities. As the people with the most day-to-day contact with individual workers, managers and supervisors can help identify when someone may be struggling and need additional supports or accommodations. These leadership roles can, over time, develop the kind of trusting and mutually respectful relationships that encourage disclosure of needs. Supervisors and managers are also the best positioned to identify and mitigate problems with peers such as stereotyping, discounting, harassment, or bullying related to their disability. HR, on the other hand, is usually the department with the most practical knowledge about legislative requirements, processes, and procedures related to accommodation. It, in collaboration with the employee, is generally the best positioned to propose specific accommodation strategies. HR is also the department that would handle confidential medical information such as doctor recommendations, and when needed, it would develop formal disability management plans. HR generally acts as a coach or advisor for managers and supervisors, providing guidance to ensure that they handle matters appropriately and legally, while managers and supervisors are most often the ones directly implementing accommodation strategies. Both parties have formal legislated responsibilities to ensure accommodations are handled such that direct and indirect discrimination does not occur.

Recognizing that managers, supervisors, and even HR personnel are not entitled to know details of a worker's medical diagnosis due to privacy is important, although the worker can choose to share that information if they wish. Nor can HR, managers, or supervisors share any diagnostic or medical information that is provided with other parties, such as coworkers, without the express permission of the worker who is impacted. They are, however, entitled to know what functional limitations a person has and how those functional limitations can be mitigated and accommodated. This is the usual focus of doctor's notes and related communications with healthcare providers.

Hurdles to Requesting Accommodations

Many people with invisible disabilities report an extreme reluctance to reveal their disabilities, which precludes them from asking for and receiving accommodations. This negatively impacts work performance. The most common reasons for this attitude include fear of stigma and discrimination (including concrete negative career impacts such as not being considered for new assignments or promotions), not wanting to be a nuisance, and the belief that accommodations would not be forthcoming. Fears of stigma are especially high among those who have psychiatric and mental disabilities. Their fears are valid. Experimental studies conducted in 2008 by Spirito Dalgin and Bellini indicated that decision makers' employability perceptions about candidates were heavily influenced by disability type, with applicants with psychiatric impairments receiving significantly lower ratings that comparably qualified candidates with physical impairments. Even people with visible disabilities often report that they just get by instead of asking for needed accommodations due to fears of increased discrimination and discounting. These fears are valid since these negative outcomes still happen all too frequently. For example, the Canadian Human Rights Commission reported that out of all discrimination complaints received between 2016 and 2021, 37% involved disability-related discrimination. The American Equal Employment Opportunity Commission (EEOC) reported that out of 61,331 complaints filed in 2021, 37.2%, or 22,815, involved disability-related discrimination. Furthermore, in 2022 the EEOC reported that in the preceding 5-year period complaints related to physical disability discrimination had increased 22% while those involving mental disability-related biases had increased 72%. Unfortunately, the legal mechanisms that provide recourse can be onerous and time-consuming. For example, taking a year or two—or more—to resolve Human Rights

Tribunal and EEOC complaints or fight wrongful dismissal cases in court is not uncommon.

For workers who are considering disclosure, there are several variables to consider. Recognizing that disclosure can happen at any time without any loss of rights is critical. For example, failure to identify a disability during recruitment and selection or initial orientation has no bearing on the employer's subsequent obligations to provide reasonable accommodations to the point of undue hardship. This means that workers who are uncertain whether or not they may require an accommodation in a given job can take a wait and see approach and assess the situation once they have started working. That said, failure to acquire needed accommodations as quickly as possible can negatively impact performance during an initial probationary period, which also creates career risk. There is no easy solution to this dilemma, and individuals making a personal decision about disclosure often find making their decision highly stressful. According to a thorough research review conducted by Sarah von Schrader, Valerie Malzer, and Susanne Bruyère in 2014, the factors such workers consider include the inherent visibility of their disability, the employer's reputation for inclusion, the effectiveness of employer's formal policies and procedures related to accommodation, the labor market and personal economic vulnerability, and the nature of their disability. Unfortunately, mental, neurological, and psychiatric impairments are still much more heavily stigmatized than physical impairments due to persistent myths and stereotypes surrounding these conditions, as well as the faulty assumption that people can control mental and psychiatric illness through willpower alone. Attitudes are evolving, but the process is slow. Since these stigmatized conditions are also invisible, the rates of disclosure, and hence support, remain low.

Managers and HR personnel can help make workers more comfortable revealing their disabilities by behaving proactively and normalizing accommodation. Some effective ways to do this include preemptively asking each new hire about accommodation needs, asking again during performance reviews, and including questions about unmet accommodation needs on annual employee surveys. If a senior executive within the organization has a disability and is comfortable doing so, openly discussing their disability and associated accommodations can send a strong cultural message of inclusion. In addition, positive supervisory practices, which include knowing employees well and actively monitoring their well-being in everyday conversations, can create a level of trust and comfort that encourages openness. Remember, trust is based on perceptions of benevolence, integrity, and competence. For an employee to trust their manager with their disability-related information, they need to believe that their manager has their best interests at heart, will follow through on commitments and promises, and has the basic knowledge and resources to address their concern. The absence of any one of these will impair trust enough to inhibit accommodation requesting. (For more tips on fostering a broadly inclusive organizational culture, delve into the discussion in Chapter 3.)

Common Disability-Related Issues and Barriers at Each Stage of Employment

Disability-related barriers can occur at any stage in the employment relationship, including before hiring even occurs! In this section, we explore the most common issues and barriers that arise at varied stages in the employment relationship.

Job Analysis

Before hiring anyone, companies need to determine the job description and the knowledge, skills, abilities, and other traits (KSAOs) needed for the job. To avoid errors and nonconscious discrimination, job analysis processes should be conducted objectively, using scientific methods that ensure the validity and reliability of the data. Common techniques used include interviews with current job incumbents, observation, journaling, questionnaires, and assessments of the traits of workers who are successful in the role. (More information about each method can be found in any introductory HR textbook.) A poorly done job analysis can bake in discriminatory disability-related barriers if the KSAOs identified are not valid. That is most likely to happen when people make assumptions and develop a job description based on gut feel rather than studying the particulars of a given job. For example, clear speech may not be required for a customer service agent if they are responding primarily to text and email-based inquiries rather than phone inquiries.

Problems also arise when job descriptions are not updated regularly. For example, voice-to-text software may render requirements related to typing speed (words per minute) irrelevant. Also, distinguishing between primary and secondary aspects of the job, since that is relevant to determining whether a candidate can meet the bona fide occupational requirements (BFORs), is important. Employers may be asked to adjust secondary aspects of the job. In one instance involving a colleague of the author, an employer was required to eliminate internal mail delivery from the job description of a receptionist after she acquired a mobility-related disability because of a car accident. Since the century-old building that housed the offices had five floors with no elevator, another employee was assigned the mail delivery task, which generally took 30 minutes out of an 8-hour workday.

Recruitment and Selection

Employers are prohibited by law from asking directly about disabilities during hiring processes. Asking if people can complete primary aspects of the job is legal, though. For example, it would be illegal to ask, "Do you have a disability that prevents heavy lifting," but it would be acceptable to inquire, "This job requires you to lift bags weighing up to 40 pounds repeatedly throughout the day; is that something you are able to do?" Similarly, it would be illegal to ask, "Do you have a medical condition that renders travel difficult," but it would be acceptable to ask, "This job requires regular overnight travel; is that something you are willing and able to do?" Note that the job requirements asked about must represent legitimate, primary job criteria. Such requirements are generally derived from a formal, scientifically sound job analysis process to ensure they are valid and represent legitimate job requirements rather than subjective impressions of the KSAOs needed.

There is one limited exception to this "don't ask" rule. In most jurisdictions in the United States, Canada, and the European Union, asking about disability status for the purposes of compliance with formal employment equity and affirmative action programs is unacceptable. (Managers and HR personnel should always check regulations within their specific state, province, or nation.) For example, in Canada, seeing checkboxes on application forms that ask people to voluntarily identify whether they are female, a visible minority, Indigenous, or have a disability as part of compliance with federal level employment equity programs is common. Importantly, recognize that these disclosures do not, however, give the employer permission to ask about details of the disability. At most, they can ask if the candidate is able to meet legitimate job requirements.

Barriers to full participation in the workforce start early: during recruitment, selection, and job-seeking. Although jobs are advertised in many ways, surveys conducted by firms involved in professional job placement services, such as TopResume and TopCV, consistently indicate that most jobs are currently found either through personal networking or online ads. Personal networking can pose challenges for people with disabilities that impact social behaviors, such as anxiety and autism, and for people with communication-related impairments. For example, networking with strangers at a busy, loud cocktail party is difficult for the hard-of-hearing, uncomfortable for many people with speech impairments, medically hazardous for people recovering from alcoholism, and potentially impossible for someone with sensory sensitivities that are triggered by crowds. (Such events have also been demonstrated to directly disadvantage people who are less physically attractive and people who are introverted. Although those are not disability-related issues per se, they still represent notable equity issues.) Employers who use methods such as mass recruiting at large job fairs and on-campus cocktail party networking events for students should consider complimenting these methods with something more accessible for people who need quieter and less busy environments to engage effectively.

Some companies recruit solely from their own company websites, but the overwhelming majority use job-posting services such as Indeed, Glassdoor, and ZipRecruiter. Not all job-posting services and company websites are equally accessible, particularly for vision-impaired people or people who struggle with using a mouse, so simply accessing and responding to employment listings may be problematic. The most common issues encountered include the following:

- Reliance on color to signal key requirements (such as using red to denote fields that need to be completed before submitting an application). This disadvantages vision-impaired and color-blind people

- Websites that cannot be navigated by screen readers that convert text to speech

- Websites that require the use of a mouse instead of the keyboard. Many commonly used assistive devices such as screen readers rely on keyboard commands to function

- Video instructions that lack captions for hearing impaired people

- Lack of information about whom to contact for assistance and accommodations

There is a standard that has been developed to assist employers with their online job ad strategy. The World Wide Web Consortium has published Web Content Accessibility Guidelines (WCAG in version 2.1 at time of writing). This standard has been applied in court cases and is increasingly understood as the ADA legislative standard. Employers are advised to ensure that the sites on which they choose to post ads are compliant with this standard.

Artificial intelligence (AI) is increasingly being used to prescreen candidates' application forms and résumés. AI may also be involved at later stages in the hiring process, such as selection testing and conducting interviews. AI relies on human generated algorithms and machine learning, both of which have been demonstrated to replicate conventional human biases. For example, AI may learn to dismiss résumés with employment gaps (which could potentially be health-related) or may evaluate candidates during interviews based on body posture and facial expression, disadvantaging those whose disabilities impact these areas. Researchers including Selin Nugent and Susan Scott-Parker (2022) have published cautions about the potential for AI to result in as-yet undetermined indirect forms for discrimination. This is an area for ongoing assessment, research, and vigilance.

Employment testing poses another barrier in the recruitment and selection process. Many companies now require candidates to complete online tests such as aptitude tests, job knowledge tests, and even personality profiles. These tests suffer from many of the same issues as job listings themselves, including lack of accessibility using a keyboard versus a mouse and lack of ability to use screen readers. Furthermore, the tests are generally time limited, which poses an additional and significant barrier for people with conditions such as dyslexia, ADHD, and cognitive impairment, and people who are lacking fluency in a given language. Locating instructions for getting extra time is generally difficult or impossible, and many candidates fear being stigmatized because of making such a request. Furthermore, the tests often require literacy skills at a level that exceeds the requirements of the job, creating indirect discrimination. People with autism also frequently report confusion about questions that seem to lack precision, especially as related to personality tests. For example, some questions in commonly used extraversion scales ask how other people perceive the individual taking the test, which can be very difficult for people with autism to answer because it requires a certain degree of mind reading about the social perceptions of others. Similarly, "Are you a good communicator" is a situational question that would lead many people with autism to ask, "In what context?" They would feel unable to answer until further details about context were revealed, and such guidance is seldom available within an online test.

To mitigate these problems, employers are strongly encouraged to scientifically assess the validity and relevance of employment tests, especially personality tests. They should offer alternate test formats, including the ability to print them, complete them at home in writing, and scan them back, or the opportunity to do the tests verbally. Extra time should be offered, and the way candidates can request that extra time (or other available accommodations) should be made clear. Having a formal policy and a dedicated staff member assigned to manage such accommodations to ensure consistency across candidates is helpful.

The interview process is also fraught with unintentional barriers. First and foremost, employers may find it difficult to resist their own nonconscious stereotypes about disability, which often leads to undervaluing candidates with visible disabilities. (Chapter 3 discusses further how to address this problem.) Some other considerations include ensuring that the physical space that interviews are held in is fully accessible for people with mobility, agility, and vision impairments and is free from excessive visual, auditory, or scent-based distractions, which will help candidates with autism and ADHD perform at their best. And if the interview is being held online, the meeting software must allow for closed captioning for the hearing impaired.

Interviewers should also be trained to actively avoid bias. They should be aware that eye contact and body language can be heavily influenced by disability-related factors, and they need to be careful about making attributions based on those criteria. For example, people with vision impairments or autism may make very little eye contact but still be excellent candidates. Among people with autism, a lack of eye contact is due to sensory issues rather than a lack of trustworthiness or interest. Many people with autism find that they are able to focus on what another party is saying, or they can look them in the eye, but not both at once. So looking away is actually a sign that they are paying careful attention! Similarly, people with multiple sclerosis (MS) may sit in positions that seem unusual or shift their position often. This is not a sign of impatience or inattention but is merely due to symptoms associated with MS.

Structured interview protocols should also be used, and there should be a formal scoring guide for interview questions. Structured interviews minimize nonconscious bias—both the more common discriminatory biases against people with disabilities, and, interestingly, also leniency biases in which people with disabilities are given higher ratings than similarly qualified people without disabilities. The latter was demonstrated in research conducted by Ellyn Brecher, Jennifer Bragger, and Eugene Kutcher in 2006. (Want more guidance on structured interviews, question design, and scoring? See the recommended reading list at the end of this chapter and the interview checklist found in the Appendix.) Additionally, interview questions and scoring guides should be free from hidden biases against people with disabilities. For example, recreational participation in team sports should not be interpreted as a sign of leadership ability and awarded extra points, nor should taking an extra year or two to complete a degree be penalized, or breaks in employment judged harshly.

In the final decision-making phase of recruitment and selection, using a banding strategy to improve equity-related outcomes is common. Banding acknowledges that we can never eliminate nonconscious bias and that our scoring systems for things such as interview question responses are imperfect, prone to both unrecognized systemic and random error. To use banding, HR personnel must also be using a formal, numerical scoring system for each candidate. They would receive scores based on their résumé, interview performance, selection test scores, and any other relevant predictors for job performance. When banding, rather than hiring the top-ranking candidate based on a numerical score, hiring agents establish an acceptable range of scores and then pick a candidate from within that group with an eye to inclusion imperatives and priorities. For example, an organization may determine that any candidate who scores 95 out of 100 or higher would be an acceptable hire. If people with disabilities were not equitably represented within the organization, hiring agents may then decide to give the job to a candidate with a disability who scored 96.5 rather than a candidate without a disability who scored 97. Such decisions should be taken with full information about current organization demographics to avoid assumptions. Banding has been shown to improve equity outcomes across a wide variety of hiring contexts without sacrificing the caliber of employees hired.

Onboarding and Training

The initial orientation process when someone is newly hired is referred to as *onboarding*. Training occurs during the onboarding process and often continues at intervals throughout the employment relationship. Training needs to be equally accessible to all qualified employees to avoid indirect discrimination. This is particularly true for developmental training that contributes to promotion potential.

The most common barriers encountered during training include lack of accessible materials for the vision impaired and a lack of attention to the needs of hearing-impaired individuals. Materials, including policy and procedure documents, need to be provided in formats that are accessible to both groups. This may include ensuring that file formats can be read by screen readers, using closed captioning in training videos, making sure websites include image descriptions, and employing similar initiatives that translate visual input into auditory or tactile input and translate auditory input into visual input. Written materials should use uncluttered, clean fonts such as Arial and Verdana, to maximize readability for people with dyslexia. Consideration can also be given to licensing some of the emerging specialized fonts developed specifically for dyslexic readers, although the merits of such fonts are still controversial, with some studies citing improvements in reading with their usage and others not. Increasing the space between words and the space between lines as well as avoiding underlining and italics also improve read-ability for the dyslexic community. Workers with conditions that impact attention and information processing, such as ADHD and autism, may also appreciate receiving materials in advance so they can review them early and have them readily at hand during lectures and lessons.

If training is delivered in a traditional classroom format or involves group discussion, then both the instructor and classmates should ensure they face people who are hard of hearing when speaking to maximize what is heard and permit the reading of lips. A failure to ensure that class-mates do this can result in the individual with the hearing impairment missing key information, being unable to contribute to discussions, and feeling disrespected and devalued. There should also be a strategy for learners with severe social anxiety. For example, if classroom discussion is a big component of learning, could those learners submit their thoughts and views to the instructor in writing? Maximizing options helps not only learners with disabilities but also helps embrace the wide variety of learn-ing styles and preferences in the broader community. This improves learn-ing for all.

In addition to a lack of accessible materials and communication chal-lenges, people with disabilities may also struggle with training length and intensity. For example, there are many medical conditions that make it difficult to sit still in a seat for 3 hours in a row (a typical amount of time for a morning or afternoon training session). Some people will also need to be able to eat, drink, and use the bathroom on their own schedule with-out negative repercussions. Frequent breaks and minimal rules centered on controlling and regulating the behaviors of others at an unreasonably micro level (such as dictating bathroom break times) can minimize the fear of negative social repercussions for self-care that is often felt by peo-ple with disabilities, who sometimes find that they are forced to choose between attending to their most basic physical needs and being perceived as a responsible, contributing, and engaged employee.

Offsite training often poses a problem for people with disabilities, particularly those with hidden disabilities. If travel is not required for the job itself, requiring travel for training may create an unnecessary and serious barrier for people with health conditions that make travel unsafe or unusually inconvenient. Many corporate employers, for example, might assume all their employees have cars and are able to drive to offsite training locations. They should consider whether venues are accessible by public transportation and whether the public transportation is available during the required hours. Difficulties with air travel are also common and can occur because of a broad range of disabilities, ranging from mobility and vision impairments to autism and social anxiety. Since wheelchairs and similar devices need to be loaded into the baggage compartment, hearing about them getting damaged or even lost is not unusual, sometimes with humiliating results. Some disabilities, such as irritable bowel syndrome, require near constant access to bathrooms and a modicum of privacy to maintain personal dignity. In the United States and between nations, there is also considerable variation in the legal status of medical marijuana and potentially some other medications, such that travel across state or national borders may force people to choose between their health and their job.

Offsite team building and leadership training that is based on vigorous outdoor activity also poses a special problem. Many people with disabilities find it difficult to participate in initiatives such as adventure training, leading to feelings of exclusion. In any large group there will almost always be people with invisible disabilities who risk either being outed by having to reveal their limitations or appearing to not be a team player if not fully participating. In a personal example, an acquaintance of the author was horrified to discover upon arrival at a company retreat that they were all expected to hike 10 kilometers into the mountains as a team to locate a hidden object. The worker involved had a congenital defect in their hip socket that completely precluded participation in this activity, even though she appeared to walk normally. Having no desire to discuss her medical information with coworkers, she discussed her dilemma privately with her manager. Her subsequent lack of participation was poorly understood by coworkers and was misinterpreted as an indicator of a lack of seriousness about her career, which negatively impacted her workplace relationships and perceived promotion potential for the duration of the employment relationship. These same types of intensive physical activities also tend to out workers who are pregnant and have chosen not to reveal their pregnancies yet, which creates a gendered equity issue. They are best avoided unless HR takes enormous care ahead of time to ensure there will not be these forms of exclusion and associated negative repercussions.

Promotions and Employee Development

Promotion and employee development processes share many of the same vulnerabilities and potential for bias that were explored in the sections on recruitment, selection, and training. Promotions are, in essence, an internal recruitment and selection exercise and the same tips about posting jobs, conducting interviews, testing, and decision making are all applicable. In addition, participation in internal training is often a requirement (or significant advantage) for promotion, so ensuring equitable access to training should naturally increase the equity of promotions as long as active biases do not render the training irrelevant.

One common barrier encountered in traditional corporate settings is that promotions are awarded based on supervisor recommendations. Supervisors, unless specifically trained to avoid it, may engage in nonconscious bias about who makes for suitable promotion material. This is especially likely to happen when the promotion involves moving into a leadership role. It is well documented that nonconscious stereotypes about who makes a good leader are often informed by completely irrelevant criteria, such as being physically powerful or dominant—or even just being tall and having nice hair! The emphasis on physical prowess, while it may have made sense in earlier historical eras when conflicts were routinely resolved through battle, makes no sense in contemporary business settings. It has no bearing on relevant leadership skills yet remains a persistent part of the leader stereotype. To avoid such stereotyping, organizations should train supervisors, have multiple people rating each candidate (preferably a diverse group), and use objective, measurable promotion criteria.

Importantly, investigate the validity of any underlying assumptions about what is needed for the role. For example, in one documented case (Breward, 2010), a very talented worker was initially denied a promotion to accounting manager since their Crohn's disease required them to work from home occasionally at unpredictable intervals, especially when under stress. Management assumed that the individual involved would be a poor fit for the promotion because they would not be physically present in the office to answer the questions of junior accounting staff. After a disastrous outside hire (who sexually harassed numerous members of the accounting staff and then quit within 4 months), they decided to give their internal candidate the promotion despite their concerns. It turned out that they excelled in the role, and the junior accountants had no problem just contacting them by phone, text, or Zoom when they had questions if they were working from home. Nobody had bothered to ask the junior staff if they actually needed in-person support; management had assumed it would be an issue without doing any investigation.

Job Sites

Workplaces need to be physically accessible to the workers using them. Accessibility, however, means more than simply having wheelchair ramps leading into the building, although that is important, too. For people who use wheelchairs, hallways, meeting rooms, cafeterias, and washroom facilities also need to be accessible. Office and workstation allocations need to consider the location of accessible washrooms and the degree to which nearby hallways are navigable. One common problem that frequently goes unrecognized relates to the scooters used in lieu of wheelchairs by many people with disabilities. The scooters are longer than an average wheelchair. Many office buildings have a double set of doors upon entry, particularly in cold climates. This requires a person in a wheelchair to push two different buttons, one to open each set of doors. The problem arises when the space between doors is too narrow to position the scooter in a manner that makes the second button accessible. One student at a university in Manitoba, Canada, reported getting stuck between doors for almost 40 minutes before another party happened along who could help.

While the needs of wheelchair users tend to come to mind first when considering job site accessibility, there are many other forms of disability that benefit from special attention to accessibility. For example, braille signs and elevator buttons are helpful for the visually impaired, as are uncluttered hallways and rooms. People with ADHD and autism are often easily distracted or experience sensory overload as a result of visual, auditory, and olfactory distractions. Placing their workstations in quieter areas with minimal distractions improves mental well-being, focus, and performance. People with chronic pain may benefit from being placed near a window that looks out onto a natural setting including trees. Research has demonstrated that people are better able to manage their pain when exposed to a view that includes nature as compared to, for example, a parking lot or brick wall. When allergies are not an issue, allowing a well-behaved pet into the workplace can also be highly beneficial for workers with mental health conditions such as depression and anxiety. The resulting mental health boost makes the affected employee feel that being present on the job site is more tolerable, perhaps even enjoyable. As a side benefit, pets in the workplace also decrease stress levels and improve mental well-being among workers without disabilities, too! Some of these strategies, such as getting quieter office space or a spot with a window, may be perceived as perks by coworkers. It is important to carefully manage any social consequences that may arise as a result. (For more information on this topic, refer to Chapter 3.)

Supervisory Practices

The relationship a worker has with their direct supervisor has a significant influence on job satisfaction and organizational commitment. Positive supervisory practices are strongly associated with healthy, functional relationships between workers and their supervisors. These practices emphasize knowing employees as individuals and focusing on strengths rather than deficits. Supervisors who are using this method not only correct problem behaviors, but they also notice and celebrate the positive and highlight what is working well. Often this recognition takes place very publicly.

Many people describe positive supervision as "treating others as you would like to be treated." However, this is not always a useful characterization. For some people with disabilities, being treated as others would like to be treated may not be helpful. For example, people with autism do not benefit from being treated as if they were neurotypical; in fact, having someone do so is often frustrating and isolating. Instead, supervisors should focus on treating their direct reports the way those reports want to be treated. This means adjusting approaches, such as communication style, to take into account worker preferences. A positive supervisor respects and supports work style differences. They listen to their workers, know their unique needs and preferences, and acknowledge those preferences in their behavior. For example, supervisors may communicate an important change to one employee in person and another may receive a detailed email. Similarly, one employee may be provided very direct feedback while another may be corrected more indirectly or may have constructive criticism sandwiched in between praise. Additionally, positive supervisors are willing to demonstrate trust by delegating work and decisions to employees, along with appropriate support.

Positive supervision is enormously beneficial for all employees, but especially so for employees with disabilities. Many workers with disabilities fear stigma, discounting, and discrimination. Positive supervisory practices minimize this risk for several reasons. First, supervisors know their individual workers better and so are less likely to make stereotype-driven attributions about them. (It is well established in the psychology literature that familiarity and positive contact lessen nonconscious stereotyping.) In addition, positive supervision increases trust, so employees are more likely to believe that their supervisor is benevolent and has integrity. This also lessens fears about stigma. Positive supervision explicitly does *not* use a one-size-fits-all model, which gives the supervisor the flexibility needed to address individual needs. The inherent focus on strengths rather than limitations is empowering and helps both workers and managers fully appreciate the value of their efforts and contributions.

Workplace Health and Safety Planning

Workplace health and safety planning is, at its heart, all about prevention. Foresight and planning can prevent emergencies; eliminate, control, and contain workplace hazards; and ensure that when an emergency does arise, the response is effective. Consideration of disability-related needs has to occur in all these areas.

The best way to reduce accidents, injuries, and occupational disease is through careful assessment and reduction of workplace hazards. This occurs (or should) in every organization and is overseen by occupational health and safety committees. These committees are legally mandated for all but the smallest organizations in most jurisdictions, including a significant number of U.S. states, the European Union, and all of Canada. (The exact number of employees you can have before a safety committee is required ranges from 10 to 50 by jurisdiction, so check local regulations.) When performing their normal duties, committee members should be attentive to the following needs related to disability:

- Ergonomic workstations are optimized for the unique needs and limitations of employees with hearing, sight, agility, or mobility impairments. This can help prevent workplace injuries such as eyestrain, muscle tension and soreness, and carpel tunnel syndrome. Workstation optimization is very individual, and what works well for one employee will not for another, so having qualified experts conduct ergonomic assessments is important.

- Have safety inspectors take wheelchairs and other mobility aids into consideration when ensuring paths are reasonably free of barriers and hazards, such as boxes stacked in hallways and placement of electrical cords. It can be useful to have a member of the safety committee conduct safety inspections using a wheelchair and crutches on occasion to highlight barriers that might otherwise go unnoticed.

- Critical safety equipment (e.g., eye wash stations in laboratories) are accessible for people who use wheelchairs or have other common mobility and agility impairments and associated assistive devices.

- Personal protective equipment (e.g., facemasks, safety harnesses, and gloves) fit and operate properly when used alongside assistive devices or by people with unconventional body movement patterns.

- All employees have access to refrigeration for needed medications, and there are boxes for the safe disposal of used needles in bathrooms. This is relevant for several conditions, such as diabetes.

- Workplace social events are not unduly focused on alcohol consumption. This creates broad risk but also heightens risk levels for specific disabilities, such as alcoholism, and for people taking medications that do not mix well with alcohol.

- Signalers of an imminent hazard (such as a fire or an active shooter) can be perceived by people with hearing or sight impairments.

- In the event of an evacuation (e.g., a fire), safety officers are aware of people who may need extra help evacuating. This may include people with mobility and sight impairments and people with sensory and psychiatric disorders that may render them more likely to panic and hide rather than try to escape. There should be a specific plan with designated individuals assigned to help those people.

- There is a plan for what to do in the event an elevator cannot be used for evacuation and someone is unable to use stairs. (Tip: Effective preplanning would ensure such people have offices at ground level whenever possible.)

- People with disabilities are included on the health and safety committee to provide another perspective.

- Bullying and harassing behaviors between coworkers are effectively identified, addressed, and eliminated. People with disabilities are especially vulnerable to such bullying, with profound negative health implications. Unchecked bullying and harassment also increase the risk of more extreme forms of workplace violence.

Disability Management and Return to Work

Some workers acquire disabilities after they begin their employment relationship. They may, for example, be injured on the job, be involved in an offsite accident, or acquire a new illness such as cancer or long-haul COVID. Others may have temporarily worsened symptoms from pre-existing disabilities such as rheumatoid arthritis or MS. These sorts of situations are often addressed using a formal disability management or return-to-work plan, which enhances communication and provides clarity. These plans make sure everyone has a shared understanding of the path forward and their respective roles and responsibilities.

Disability management is an approach that seeks to maximize productivity and inclusion through a careful assessment of individual needs, workplace conditions, expected performance outcomes, and legal responsibilities. Return-to-work plans are formal documents used to support a person's return to the workplace as quickly as possible while respecting their health needs. These plans outline objectives, actions required by the worker and the employer to fulfill those objectives, and an estimated timeframe. The objectives need to be realistic and informed by expert medical opinions rather than a supervisor's gut feel. Return to work plans may include some of or all the following:

- A plan for a staged return in which the person slowly progresses from working very short hours to full days as their condition improves

- A plan for a return to modified duties or a new job role, either temporarily or permanently, according to the individual's medical prognosis

- A list of specific supports the employer will provide and barrier removal strategies they will use

- Conditions the employee must satisfy to maintain good standing (This is often used with people suffering from addictions and usually takes the form of agreeing not to use alcohol or drugs on the job.)

It is in everyone's best interest to have an employee return to work as soon as they are able, even if they return to modified duties or on a part-time basis. This can have a direct financial benefit to the organization as well as for the worker. The worker goes back to earning pay sooner, which is often helpful because disability benefits (if they have them) are usually less than their regular earnings. From the employer's perspective, if the injury or illness was acquired on the job, a return-to-work plan can minimize worker's compensation insurance claim amounts, helping keep employer premiums lower. In addition, there are both direct and indirect costs associated with absenteeism. A temporary replacement may have to be hired or trained, or other employees may be paid overtime or exposed to heightened stress due to excessive workloads. Heightened stress, if prolonged, may even lead to newly emerging health issues and more disability leaves! Many severely short-staffed organizations experienced this issue during the COVID-19 pandemic in 2020 and 2021, with remaining employees taking a disproportionate number of stress-related medical leaves of absence due to issues coping with the workload and lack of support.

In addition to financial benefits, return-to-work plans also have other positive aspects. For some types of disability, most notably addictions, these plans provide a fair opportunity for the employee while also respecting the employer's need to maintain a safe and functional working environment. The plans help balance the (sometimes conflicting) needs to maintain a safe workplace while also accommodating addiction-based disability. In addition, mental health, well-being, and self-esteem are considerably improved when people are able to maintain employment that is within their capacities. Disability management plans help clarify expectations and supports, and as a result, people stay employed. Usage of such plans by a coworker even sends a strong cultural signal to other workers that their employer cares about them and will support them in times of need. This increases job satisfaction and organizational commitment and reduces turnover rates. (For a closer look at how to prepare a disability management strategy and return-to-work plan, consult Chapter 7 and the Appendix.)

Developing Comprehensively Inclusive Organizations: The EY Experience

Let's explore a real-world example of a comprehensive approach to inclusion. Ernst and Young (EY) is one of the globally recognized "Big 4" firms delivering a range of accounting, audit, and consulting services.

Its approach to inclusion attempts to minimize the need for formal accommodations by creating a workplace that is inherently welcoming to people with a range of neurotypes, physiques, and abilities. (This method, which is termed *inclusive design*, is covered in more detail in Chapter 8.) Tammy Morris, network leader at EY's Canadian Neurodiversity Center of Excellence, emphasizes the importance of this mindset, stating,

> When there is a request for a formal accommodation we need to step in and ask, why did someone need an accommodation? Is there something in the workplace we need to change that could benefit a wider group of people as well? (personal communication)

EY supports inclusiveness for people with a wide range of abilities and conditions, including providing tools, technologies, and other resources for sight, hearing, and mobility impairments. Most of these supports do not require formal accommodation requests because they are already readily available. For example, the company makes available resources such as voice-to-text software without requiring a special approval process, and desks that accommodate a variety of body types, including standing desks and desks optimized for wheelchair users, are always onsite. Furthermore, if there is a needed accommodation that is not available and is relatively low cost, supervisors are empowered to provide it without a formal approval process, enabling a much faster response to emerging or unexpected needs. While their program is comprehensive, EY's inclusion initiatives centered around neurodiversity (employees with diagnoses such as autism and ADHD) are especially robust.

Recruitment and Selection

Inclusive design begins right at the recruitment and selection stage. Most companies use behavioral interviews when hiring, which tests the applicants' social and political skills as much as their job-related competence. This approach systematically disadvantages candidates with autism and ADHD who could perform the job but simply do not interview well due to differences in communication style and social perceptions. Instead of using behavioral interviews, EY begins with an *informational chat*, which is an informal conversation in which they share information with candidates and carefully explain all the steps in the recruitment and selection process, including timelines. This eliminates anxiety related to uncertainty. They then use virtual competency assessments that candidates can complete online from home. These assessments objectively test a range of technical skills such as coding and ability to interpret financial data. These assessments are complimented with a very brief interview consisting of a limited number (usually four) questions that are very concrete, asking about prior workplace experiences. Abstract and vague questions are avoided, as are questions that require the candidate to reflect on hypothetical rather than real-world scenarios. The applicants are provided the questions in advance and can write or video record their answers. They can edit their answers as often as they like before submitting them. All this allows neurodiverse candidates (especially those who experience high levels of social anxiety) to perform at their best, while also benefitting neurotypical candidates, who generally also appreciate the process-related clarity, objectivity and fairness of the skills assessment, and lack of need to engage in onerous political impression management behaviors during selection processes.

Onboarding and Training

Once hired, the training and onboarding process also represents best practices in inclusion. New team members participate in virtual "Super Days." These days offer what Tammy Morris describes as "overt, slow socialization that sends cultural signals of supportiveness." The first day is largely a "listening day," in which new hires find out more about the company, expectations, and the many resources available to support them. Later days focus on meeting other new hires, learning more about amenities, and hearing from guest speakers with long experience in the firm. This gentle, virtual introduction allows people who are socially anxious or who have sensory sensitivities to get to know their coworkers and the organization in a manner that is comfortable, allowing maximum retention of information and an emerging sense of belonging.

In addition to Super Days, new hires are also supported by being assigned an "EY Buddy," a formal mentor and support person at the same rank or one rank above who can help them navigate their first year at EY. Any special hardware or software needs are addressed before their first day so they can hit the ground running rather than having to wait for appropriate tools. Finally, continual feedback is provided as they start their work, enabling any misunderstandings about expectations to be corrected immediately. This also lessens uncertainty and anxiety—for *all* employees, not just the neurodiverse!

The Workplace

Physical space is a big part of inclusion, and Ernst and Young has this covered too. There is a great deal of flexibility regarding the worksite. Remote work options are readily available, which is appreciated by many employees for many reasons but specifically helps those with sensory sensitivities since they can have more control over their immediate environment.

For those who do choose to work in the office, they use a hoteling approach without formally assigned workspaces. Instead, a wide variety of desk types and workspaces are provided, and people can select what they find most suitable on a given day. Pod seating creates visual barriers between workstations to minimize distractions and sensory overload. Senior managers and executives who have designated, permanent offices are on the inside of the building, giving hoteling employees priority access to quieter corners and spaces with windows. (Being able to see outside is known to help with anxiety and depression.) In addition, there are nonreservable *just-in-time* rooms, which are quiet spaces for people to de-stress when feeling overwhelmed. Since they cannot be reserved for formal meetings and other company events, they are always available to those who need them. Furthermore, common accommodations such as sound dampening headphones are available in all workspaces without the need to make a special request; this equipment is perceived as normal, standard office equipment like staples and pens.

Promotion paths and supervisory practices are also heavily influenced by inclusion-related priorities. Recognizing that not all employees want to move into managerial roles, EY offers nonmanagement, technical career paths that allow people to evolve into valued subject matter experts in needed areas. Supervisors, along with all other employees, receive training on neurodiverse communication patterns and are encouraged to be flexible and aware of employees' cognitive differences. For instance, they may provide some employees with written instructions while others prefer to receive verbal instructions. Efforts are made to avoid anxiety-inducing surprises by doing small things such as providing meeting agendas in advance. Positive supervisory practices and regular feedback round out their approach.

Performance evaluation is also done with an eye to inclusion and fairness. Performance metrics are generally objective and measurable to avoid nonconscious biases based on irrelevant social skills. 360-degree feedback mechanisms (which consist of gathering performance feedback from subordinates, peers, and sometimes clients as well as managers) are used quarterly, and employees also self-rate themselves. Managers are attentive to discrepancies between self-evaluations and peer and managerial evaluations. Such discrepancies often indicate either a lack of self-confidence or an unrealistic self-perception, and in either case the manager would address the issue through reassurance or realistic identification of areas that need further work. This approach helps avoid bias in performance assessment. Furthermore, if an employee's social behaviors are misunderstood (a common occurrence for people with autism), then support circles exist to help mediate those difficulties. All employees are encouraged to seek clarification and understanding, even for things that may seem obvious to others, without being socially penalized for doing so. This is an enormous relief for neurodiverse workers, who are often mocked for not understanding neurotypical communication patterns and unstated social rules in the broader world.

Regarding employee benefits, EY once again exceeds the norm to offer true inclusion. In addition to in-house mental health supports such as mindfulness training, every employee is given up to $5,000 per year for formal therapy or similar professional mental health support. Each large EY facility is equipped with a gym and fitness area that offers programming and equipment for varied bodies and needs. Workers receive a $1,000 annual allowance for fitness-related purchases such as gym memberships, sport participation fees, sports equipment, and home fitness equipment. As such, even those working from smaller offices without onsite gyms receive fitness benefits. The company also offers a highly unique peer support service called "We Listen," which operates as follows: Volunteers (who are not on the same team as those participating) are available to hear people out when they feel something is not working well, they are struggling, or they just need to vent. The volunteers are trained to support, direct, and coach those participating to access the many EY mental health and well-being resources that are available, including the annual $5,000 mental health benefit. Just being heard often makes people feel better. This helps create a sense of connection and belonging within EY, mitigating some of the social tensions and burnout symptoms that can arise during the stressful busy season. It lessens the potential for small interpersonal conflicts to grow into large team-destroying battles based on situations or personality or neurotype differences.

With this truly comprehensive approach to inclusion, EY shows that one-off accommodations are not what it's all about. There is a great deal companies can do to make their overall environment more inclusive and attractive to highly skilled workers with disabilities and varied neurotypes. And these initiatives generally benefit all workers, not just those with unique needs. In fact, with approaches such as positive supervision, they often represent known evidence-based best practices for everyone!

FURTHER READINGS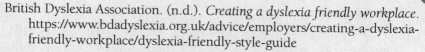

British Dyslexia Association. (n.d.). *Creating a dyslexia friendly workplace.* https://www.bdadyslexia.org.uk/advice/employers/creating-a-dyslexia-friendly-workplace/dyslexia-friendly-style-guide

Curtis, J., & Scott, L. R. (2004). Integrating disability management into strategic plans. *AAOHN Journal, 52*(7), 298–301. https://doi.org/ 10.1177/ 216507990405200

Public Service Commission of Canada. (2009). *Structured interviewing: How to design and conduct structured interviews for an appointment process.* https://www.canada.ca/content/dam/canada/public-service-commission/migration/plcy-pltq/guides/structured-structuree/rpt-eng.pdf

Smith, A. (2018, October 22). *Can people with disabilities use your careers website?* A Life Worth Living. https://alifeworthliving.ca/can-people-with-disabilities-use-your-careers-website/

REFERENCES

Bates, M. (n.d.). *Dyslexia font and style guide.* Reading Well. https://www.dyslexia-reading-well.com/dyslexia-font.html

Bono, J. E., & Yoon, D. J. (2012). Positive supervisory relationships. In L. Eby & T. Allen (Eds.), *Personal relationships: The effect on employee attitudes, behavior, and well-being* (pp. 43–66). Routledge.

Blaker, N., Rompa, I., Dessing, I., Vriend, A., Herschberg, C., & Vugt, M. (2013). The height leadership advantage in men and women: Testing evolutionary psychology predictions about the perceptions of tall leaders. *Group Processes & Intergroup Relations, 16*(1), 17–27. https://doi.org/10.1177/1368430212437211

Brecher, E., Bragger, J., & Kutcher, E. (2006). The structured interview: Reducing biases toward job applicants with physical disabilities.

Employee Responsibilities and Rights Journal, 18(3), 155–170. https://doi.org/10.1007/s10672-006-9014-y

Breward, K. (2010). Disability accommodations and promotions at Bunco. *Case Research Journal, 30*(1), 65–72.

Canadian Human Rights Commission. (2022). *2021 CHRC Annual Report*. https://2021.chrcreport.ca/by-the-numbers.html

Campion, M. A., Outtz, J. L., Zedeck, S., Schmidt, F. L., Kehoe, J. F., Murphy, K. R., & Guion, R. M. (2001). The controversy over score banding in personnel selection: Answers to 10 key questions. *Personnel Psychology, 54*(1), 149–185. https://doi.org/10.1111/j.1744-6570.2001.tb00090.x

Dewa, C. S., Trojanowski, L., Joosen, M. C., & Bonato, S. (2016). Employer best practice guidelines for the return to work of workers on mental disorder–related disability leave: A systematic review. *Canadian Journal of Psychiatry, 61*(3), 176–185. https://doi.org/10.1177/0706743716632515

Dong, S., Hespe, P., & Monagas, K. (2022). Requesting workplace accommodation among individuals with mobility disabilities: A qualitative investigation on barriers and facilitators. *Journal of Applied Rehabilitation Counseling, 53*(3), 193–209. https://doi.org/10.1891/JARC-D-21-00005

Dong, S., Hoeflich, C., & Sirota, P. V. (2022). An examination of the psychosocial factors impacting workplace accommodation requests in individuals with mental disabilities. *Work, 72*(3), 865–874. https://doi.org/10.3233/WOR-210518

Equal Employment Opportunity Commission. (2022a). *Charge statistics (charges filed with EEOC) FY 1997 through FY 2021*. https://www.eeoc.gov/data/charge-statistics-charges-filed-eeoc-fy-1997-through-fy-2021

Equal Employment Opportunity Commission. (2022b, May 19). *EEOC report analyzes situation of workers with disabilities in the federal workforce*. https://www.eeoc.gov/newsroom/eeoc-report-analyzes-situation-workers-disabilities-federal-workforce

Elmers, D. (n.d.). *The job-search statistics all job seekers should know*. TopResume. https://ca.topresume.com/career-advice/7-top-job-search-statistics

Favaro, A., Neustaeter, B., & St. Philip, E. (2021, September 13). Stress, staffing shortages brought on by COVID-19 causing nurses to leave the front lines. *CTV News*. https://www.ctvnews.ca/health/coronavirus/stress-staffing-shortages-brought-on-by-covid-19-causing-nurses-to-leave-the-front-lines-1.5582781

Gilliland, S. W., & Hale, J. M. (2013). How can justice be used to improve employee selection practices? In J. Greenberg & J. A. Colquitt (Eds.), *Handbook of organizational justice* (pp. 411–438). Routledge.

Government of Canada. (2011, September 21). *How to build a disability management program: The steps.* https://www.canada.ca/en/government/publicservice/wellness-inclusion-diversity-public-service/health-wellness-public-servants/disability-management/how-to-build-disability-management-program-steps.html

Henry, S. L. (2022, September 6). *WCAG 2 overview.* W3C Web Accessibility Initiative. https://www.w3.org/WAI/standards-guidelines/wcag/

Hunt, H. A. (2009). *The evolution of disability management in North American workers' compensation programs.* Report prepared for Victoria, British Columbia, Canada, NIDMAR. https://research.upjohn.org/reports/179

Jetha, A., LaMontagne, A. D., Lilley, R., Hogg-Johnson, S., Sim, M., & Smith, P. (2018). Workplace social system and sustained return-to-work: A study of supervisor and co-worker supportiveness and injury reaction. *Journal of Occupational Rehabilitation, 28*(3), 486–494. https://doi.org/10.1007/s10926-017-9724-z

Johanson, M. (2021, October 12). Why service workers are so burned out. *BBC.* https://www.bbc.com/worklife/article/20211007-the-service-roles-that-lead-to-burnout

McKinney, E. L., & Swartz, L. (2021). Employment integration barriers: Experiences of people with disabilities. *International Journal of Human Resource Management, 32*(10), 2298–2320. https://doi.org/10.1080/09585192.2019.1579749

Nugent, S. E., & Scott-Parker, S. (2022). Recruitment AI has a disability problem: Anticipating and mitigating unfair automated hiring decisions. In M. Ferreira & M. Tokhi (Eds.), *Towards trustworthy artificial intelligent systems* (pp. 85–96). Springer. https://doi.org/10.1007/978-3-031-09823-9_6

Prince, M. J. (2017). Persons with invisible disabilities and workplace accommodation: Findings from a scoping literature review. *Journal of Vocational Rehabilitation, 46*(1), 75–86. https://doi.org/10.3233/JVR-160844

Sainato, M. (2020, September 23). "I cry before work": US essential workers burned out amid pandemic. *The Guardian.* https://www.theguardian.com/us-news/2020/sep/23/us-essential-workers-coronavirus-burnout-stress

Sousa, C., Esperança, J., & Gonçalves, G. (2022). Pets at work: Effects on social responsibility perception and organizational commitment.

Psychology of Leaders and Leadership, 25(2), 144–163. https://doi
.org/10.1037/mgr0000128

Spirito Dalgin, R., & Bellini, J. (2008). Invisible disability disclosure in
an employment interview: Impact on employers' hiring decisions and
views of employability. *Rehabilitation Counseling Bulletin, 52*(1), 6–15.
https://doi.org/10.1177/003435520731131

Von Schrader, S., Malzer, V., & Bruyère, S. (2014). Perspectives on disability disclosure: The importance of employer practices and workplace
climate. *Employee Responsibilities and Rights Journal, 26*(4), 237–255.
https://doi.org/10.1007/s10672-013-9227-9

Wimmer, R. (n.d.). 8 job-search statistics every job seeker should know.
TopCV. https://www.topcv.com/career-advice/job-search-statistics

Young, J., Pritchard, R., Nottle, C., & Banwell, H. (2020). Pets, touch, and
COVID-19: Health benefits from non-human touch through times of
stress. *Journal of Behavioral Economics for Policy, 4* (COVID-19 Special
Issue 2), 25–33.

CHAPTER 3

Peer Attitudes and Psychological Aspects of Inclusion

While some workers with disabilities are embraced as full members of the team and treated with respect and dignity, many people with disabilities report that peer attitudes negatively impact their work lives. A meta-analysis of 48 studies that was conducted by Katharina Vornholt, Sjir Uitdewilligen, and Frans J. N. Nijhuis in 2013 confirmed that negative, exclusionary, and even hostile peer attitudes exist in many workplaces. Common problems workers with disabilities experience include social exclusion, bullying and harassment, contribution undervaluation, condescending treatment, lack of cooperation in providing needed accommodations, avoidance by team members, and exclusion from skill enhancement and development opportunities. Social opportunities with coworkers outside work are also impacted, limiting the ability to develop more positive relationships. For example, one office worker whom the author interviewed in 2021 used a wheelchair. She reported that most of her department would go together for a drink after work on Thursdays, but the bar they habitually selected was not wheelchair accessible. Making matters worse, she was told when she first started, "Well, this is everyone's favorite bar, but if we really need to change just for you, tell us so." Understandably, she did not perceive that comment as a genuine attempt to include her, rather it was perceived as an effort to highlight how inconvenient others found it to address her most basic needs. This noninclusive attitude prevented her from participating in casual offsite workplace social events, but also subsequently inhibited her from requested necessary workplace accommodations due to anxiety about being seen as a burden. Workers with disabilities are often told, "It's not personal," even as they are unfairly excluded, yet this empty phrase provides no comfort in the face of experienced exclusion and discrimination.

In addition to the obvious issue of legal liability, this prejudice is a problem because experiencing discrimination leads to a host of negative impacts on work performance, job satisfaction, organizational commitment, self-esteem, mental health, and well-being. Workers, whether they have disabilities or not, perform at their best when they feel supported, respected, valued, and included in their workplaces. They also perform best when they have the resources and tools they need. Yet fear of stigma and discrimination inhibits many workers with disabilities from revealing their disability (if invisible) and from requesting needed accommodations, even when those accommodations are free or simple to provide. This negatively impacts their performance potential. Making matters worse, many workers with disabilities face negative social consequences when their peers incorrectly perceive their needed accommodations (such as extra breaks or working from home) as unearned perks, triggering peer resentment and frustration.

In addition to diminished task performance, the failure to provide proper resources and a safe and respectful working environment can also increase counterproductive work behaviors such as unwarranted absenteeism, *quiet quitting* (a phenomenon in which people still go to work but only do the bare minimum required), petty theft, and unhelpful interpersonal behaviors. (Note that this is true for all workers, not just workers with disabilities.) Negative emotions in an organization can also be contagious, infecting a broad swath of the workplace. And without formal interventions, bullying and harassment tend to escalate into even more problematic forms, up to and including workplace violence. To avoid all these negative outcomes, understanding the root causes of exclusion and prejudicial and discriminatory behaviors is important. This knowledge helps plan effective interventions and ways to proactively avoid the problem from emerging in the first place.

The Underlying Psychology of Nonconscious Prejudice

Some discriminatory actions are done on purpose, with the explicit, conscious endorsement of the parties engaging in the behavior. Correction of deliberate prejudice relies on formal behavioral controls that create consequences for discrimination. Examples of behavioral controls include legislation, formal anti-harassment policies, and well-defined behavioral expectations within the workplace that are actively enforced. When retraining people prone to deliberate discrimination, focusing on their day-to-day behaviors is best rather than attempting to change underlying attitudes because attitudinal change of this nature is extremely difficult to achieve in a workplace training context. Happily, research suggests that a process called cognitive dissonance can lead to changes in attitudes over time if people are forced to behave in respectful and equitable ways. Cognitive dissonance theory, put simply, suggests that having a mismatch between attitudes and behaviors is psychologically uncomfortable, and therefore when there is a lack of alignment, one or the other will change, albeit very slowly and only with consistent reinforcement of the desired behaviors and attitudes. One important reinforcer during this process is the leader of the organization. Leaders set tone and should model equity-focused behaviors.

Inadvertent and nonconscious forms of prejudice, however, are much more pervasive than deliberate discrimination and due to their sometimes-subtle nature can be more difficult to identify and address. Our brains process an overwhelming amount of data every minute of every day. Even doing something as simple as traveling down the street exposes us to a wide variety of visual, auditory, tactile, olfactory, and other sensory stimuli that must be processed. If we were to be overtly attentive to everything in our environment it would be difficult, if not impossible, to function through the crush of data input and analysis. So, our brains take shortcuts to keep us functional. On a nonconscious level, we are continuously identifying the elements in the environment that we need to overtly pay attention to, and we are disregarding or automatically sorting other stimuli into categories. This automatic processing tends to lead to perceptual errors and stereotyping—and, ultimately, prejudice. People being unaware that their thought process is being influenced by stereotyping is common.

The Implicit Association Test

This automatic mental processing phenomena is famously demonstrated by the extremely well-validated Harvard implicit association test (IAT). On Harvard's active IAT page they describe the test as follows:

> The IAT measures the strength of associations between concepts (e.g., black people, [people with disabilities, immigrants]) [, evaluations (e.g., good, bad)] or stereotypes (e.g., athletic, clumsy [, capable, incapable]). The main idea is that making a response is easier when closely related items share the same response key[—meaning people nonconsciously associate the concept (i.e., people with disabilities) with the stereotypical evaluation (i.e., incapable).]

> When doing an IAT you are asked to quickly sort words into categories that are on the left and right hand side of the computer screen . . .

> In the first part of the IAT you sort words relating to the concepts (e.g., fat people, thin people [, people with disabilities, people without disabilities]) into categories . . .

In the second part of the IAT you sort words relating to the evaluation (e.g., good, bad [, capable, incapable]) . . .

In the third part of the IAT the categories are combined and you are asked to sort both concept and evaluation words. So the categories on the left hand side would be [people with disabilities and capable] and the categories on the right hand side would be [people without disabilities and incapable.] It is important to note that the order in which the blocks are presented varies across participants, so some people will do the [people with disabilities and capable, people without disabilities and incapable] part first and other people will do the [people with disabilities and incapable, people without disabilities and capable part first].

In the fourth part of the IAT the placement of the concepts switches. If the category . . . was previously on the left, now it would be on the right. Importantly, the number of trials in this part of the IAT is increased in order to minimize the effects of practice.

In the final part of the IAT the categories are combined in a way that is opposite what they were before. If the category on the left was previously [people with disabilities and capable], it would now be [people with disabilities and incapable.]

The IAT score is based on how long it takes a person, on average, to sort the words in the third part of the IAT versus the fifth part of the IAT. We would say that one has an implicit preference for [people without disabilities relative to people with disabilities] if respondents are faster to categorize words when ["people with disabilities" and "incapable"] share a response key and ["people without disabilities" and "capable"] share a response key, relative to the reverse.

IAT tests have been in use for quite a few years (give it a try here: https://implicit.harvard.edu/implicit/iatdetails.html) and have demonstrated that almost everyone has nonconscious prejudices. This can have tragic results. For example, it is one of the contributing factors impacting how different ethnic groups are treated by police, with Black and Indigenous men being especially likely to be perceived as threatening due to persistent negative stereotypes regarding these groups. This results in much higher incidence of inappropriate use of force among these populations when interacting with police, up to and including fatal interactions in which innocent people doing innocuous things end up being shot by officers. This occurs in part because of the speed with which police officers (and other people) make nonconscious stereotypical mental associations and then react based on those erroneous associations before thinking through the situation properly, as demonstrated in IAT tests.

Social Identity Theory

The negative impacts of automatic information processing and attendant stereotyping are magnified by social identity effects. Social identity effects were first highlighted by researchers John Turner and Henri Tajfel in the 1970s. Since then, their theory has been widely supported in both lab and field experiments. In essence, social identity theory is about how people perceive others. We, as humans, tend to sort other people into two broad categories: in-group members (people who we feel are similar to us) and out-group members (people who we feel are not similar to us). These in-group and out-group social categorizations can be based on almost anything: ethnicity, religious or political affiliation, occupation, hobbies and interests, liking the same sports team, and even being a "dog person" or a "cat person." The definition of an in-group or out-group member is situational. One might feel that someone is an in-group member when they meet that person at a political rally, when the same person may be perceived as an out-group member in a professional work setting due to some triggering characteristic.

This perception of being in the in-group or out-group is important because we tend to, without even being aware of it, attribute positive characteristics, motivations, and actions to in-group members and negative characteristics, motivations, and actions to out-group members. This preference for perceived in-group members has been demonstrated throughout the lifecycle, from preverbal infants to seniors. For example, gaze studies done with infants have demonstrated that they prefer faces that appear to be from the racial group or groups that they are already familiar with seeing among their primary caregivers and family.

Social identity effects contribute to stereotyping because it predisposes us to make negative associations about people who we feel are different from ourselves. Among other things, we are more likely to attribute poor performance to their supposed inherent failings as opposed to considering the broader situation. For example, if a perceived in-group member made a mistake in an important report, we would be more inclined to believe that they are generally a good, conscientious worker, but they were given incomplete instructions, poor training, or insufficient time. A perceived out-group member making the same mistake, by contrast, would more likely be perceived as incompetent or careless. These perceptions have broad social and professional consequences, with the potential to influence everything from hiring decisions and task assignments to performance assessments and compensation.

Importantly, recognize that social identity effects in the workplace not only create disadvantages for out-group members, but they also create active advantages for in-group members. Since White men of European ancestry still dominate as decision makers and executives in industry, their disproportionate influence tends to result in the perpetuation of historical patterns of privilege for those who are White, male, heterosexual, and do not have disabilities. For example, in North America in 2021, women held only 24% of C-suite jobs (e.g., chief executive officer, chief financial officer, and chief operations officer), and within that group women of color held only 4%. In the same year, globally, among the top Fortune 500 companies, only 23 (4.6%) had female chief executive officers, and among them only six (1.2%) were women of color (Catalyst, 2022). Since social identity effects often operate on a subconscious or nonconscious basis, they can unfairly impact outcomes even when people have the explicit intention to treat others equitably and avoid bias. This is one reason objective measurement of skills, knowledge, performance, and contribution are valuable and generally preferable to relying on the subjective impressions of recruiters, supervisors, and managers.

Social identity effects can be triggered when people without disabilities perceive people with disabilities as out-group members. These effects can also be demonstrated within and between disability communities. For example, workers with physical disabilities may believe themselves to be in a different social category than workers with psychiatric disabilities. Social identity–related biases are best mitigated through personal mindfulness and conscious questioning of our own attitudes while actively looking for evidence that our perceptions might be wrong. In an organizational context, social identity effects can be manipulated for positive impact. Since the definition of an in-group member is situational, positive in-group effects can be triggered by convincing employees that they are all part of one team and by giving them an outside rival to compete against. For instance, a marketing team may perceive themselves as in competition with another company selling similar products, or a not-for-profit agency may sponsor a friendly competition with a related not-for-profit to see who can raise the most funds for a given project. The immediate focus on the team goal and the rivalry with the competitor has potential to switch in-group perceptions away from demographic variables toward task-oriented ones, increasing the probability that workers perceive all teammates as part of the in-group.

Stereotyping

Thus far we have reviewed how our brains automatically process data below the level of our conscious awareness. We have also seen that this phenomenon extends to people, who are automatically sorted into perceived in-group and out-group members based on nonconscious associations. Stereotyping is another consequence of this dynamic. Stereotypes may be triggered on a conscious or nonconscious basis, and they represent fixed, over-simplified, and often inaccurate generalizations about how certain types of people or groups think, feel, and behave. Stereotypes can heavily influence whether we perceive potential in another person, what skills and abilities we think they have, and the attributions we make about their behavior. For example, decision-makers who believe the common stereotype that people with moderate depression are just lazy and need to snap out of it are going to respond very differently to a subordinate asking for extra time to complete a project due to struggles with depression as compared to a decision maker who understands that the illness is caused by a correctable chemical imbalance in the brain.

To better understand how stereotypes impact workers with disabilities, we need to understand the nature of the stereotypes associated with disability. Acknowledging that different types of disability are perceived in different ways is important. For example, people with psychiatric disabilities are frequently stereotyped as being highly prone to violence (an impression that is not supported by statistical evidence), and women with invisible pain disorders are often portrayed as *drama queens* looking for attention. The latter example highlights how other aspects of identity can also impact which specific stereotypes are triggered. A White man wearing a yarmulke with the same disability as a dark-skinned woman wearing a hijab may be perceived—and stereotyped—very differently. This is referred to as *intersectionality*, which acknowledges the interconnected nature of social categorization and the complexity inherent in these interdependencies. Intersectional stereotypes are not necessarily additive. People with a disability cannot assume, for example, that stereotypes about their disability will trump stereotypes related to ethnicity; instead, people who have multiple stigmatized identities tend to be stereotyped in complex ways that are influenced by which aspect of their identity seems most relevant to the perceiver in the current situation.

Broadly speaking, disability in general has historically been stereotypically associated with being dependent, passive, incapable, unreliable, and even infantile. People with invisible impairments are often stereotyped as being overly sensitive—or even fakers. People with psychiatric disabilities are frequently stereotyped as lacking control and being aggressive or violent. None of these traits are associated with being an effective employee, creating a nonconscious, false association between disability and poor work performance that can be hard to overcome without deliberate awareness and effort.

The Stereotype Content Model, originally developed by researchers Susan T. Fiske, Amy J. C. Cuddy, Peter Glick, and Jun Xu in 2002, divides stereotypes along two dimensions: perceptions of social warmth and perceptions of competence. Subsequent research using this model has shown that people with disabilities are generally stereotyped as high in social warmth but low in competence, triggering paternalistic forms of prejudice (meaning that the prejudice is typified by not only feelings of pity and sympathy but also passive harm through isolation and neglect). Some categories of disability that are erroneously perceived as the individual's fault (e.g., addictions) lead to perceptions of low social warmth and low competence, resulting in contemptuous prejudice typified by contempt, hostility, and active harm. To date, no studies on stereotypes have shown workers with disabilities placed into the *high social warmth, high competence* category, in which people are treated with admiration and have their efforts actively facilitated. The fact that nondisabled people often get placed in this category (unless other identity variables prevent it) creates not just disadvantage for workers with disabilities but active advantage and privilege for those without.

In 2000, researchers Walter S. Stephan and Cookie White Stephan developed the Integrated Threat Model of Prejudice to predict attitudes toward a given group (e.g., immigrants and people with disabilities). This model integrated decades of research on the topic. According to the model, in addition to stereotyping, attitudes are also influenced by the level of anxiety people feel when interacting with someone from the relevant group and their perceptions (often inaccurate) of the threat posed by members of the group. Their level of anxiety and perception of threat are in turn informed by their level of knowledge and familiarity with the given group, the amount and nature of previous contact with members of the group, the degree to which the group in question is perceived as an out-group, their relative group status, and their relevance to the day-to-day lives of the perceiver, including any history of prior conflict between the perceiver's identity group and the target group. For example, if the perceiver is from an ethnic group that has a history of armed conflict with the ethnic group represented by the person being evaluated, the perceiver is much more likely to experience perceptions of threat and anxiety. Regarding positive contact, knowledge, and familiarity, more is better since getting to know people individually reduces stereotyping and anxiety considerably.

This model is informative when considering perceptions of workers with disabilities. Social awkwardness causes anxiety, and many people without disabilities report fearing social awkwardness when interacting with members of the disability community, particularly those with hearing, psychiatric, and communication-related impairments. This anxiety actively inhibits the type of positive social contact that can reduce stereotyping. Lack of social contact and exposure, in turn, impairs the development of familiarity and knowledge, significantly diminishing opportunities to develop perceptions free from stereotypes and to start to view people with disabilities as fully rounded individuals.

Regarding perceived threat (when applying the Stephan and Stephan model), some people may question how workers with disabilities could be perceived as threatening given stereotypes about dependence and passivity. People with psychiatric disabilities are often stereotyped as violent even though there is considerable group-level statistical evidence to the contrary. (People with psychiatric impairments are, in fact, much more likely to be victims of violence rather than the perpetrators of violence.) And workers with autism are also stereotyped as lacking empathy and concern for others, although there is evidence to the contrary, including emerging evidence that the exact opposite may be true: Some people with autism are hyper-empathetic but may express that empathy in unconventional ways that go unrecognized by neurotypical people. Perceptions of threat in the workplace may include alleged threats to team performance, potentially impacting compensation and career progression. Seen through this lens, stereotypes about workers with disabilities being incapable increase perceptions of threat and make people resistant to inclusion, either overtly or on a nonconscious level.

Addressing Anxiety

Happily, the Integrated Threat Model also points toward effective interventions and solutions for these perceptual issues. Colleagues and coworkers are more likely to perceive workers with disabilities fairly if their anxiety is reduced, stereotypes are disconfirmed through lived experience, and erroneous perceptions of threat are corrected. These can all be achieved through increased positive contact, knowledge, and familiarity, and by fostering the sense that all workers and team members are in-group members. Contact, knowledge, and familiarity can be encouraged through formal diversity training initiatives that are focused on perspective sharing and storytelling rather than legislative compliance. This means that the training should allow workers to talk to each other and understand each other's lived experiences rather than just telling people that discrimination is against the law, obey the law.

The well-known Invisible Knapsack exercise developed by Peggy MacIntosh is an example of the effectiveness of this type of training. Her program helps workers recognize differentials in levels of privilege and the diversity of their lived experiences through guided shared storytelling. First, workers go through a pen and paper exercise in which they identify their privileges. For example, they are asked about whether their employer allows them time off for holidays that are important to them, whether they can go into emergency rooms and anticipate being treated with dignity and respect, whether colleagues listen to their ideas in meetings, and whether they can walk through a parking garage alone and feel safe. Responses are then shared, compared, and used as a launching point to foster small group discussions and storytelling about the day-to-day consequences and hassles associated with a lack of privilege. This exercise tends to be very eye-opening for all participants, particularly those who have not recognized their own privileges due to lack of awareness about the experiences of others. It has been demonstrated to increase empathy among participants, resulting in concrete behavioral changes in the workplace. For example, it has been successfully used in American hospitals to help address systemic biases related to the triage and treatment of non-White populations (Holm et al., 2017).

Contact, knowledge, and familiarity can also be fostered through team building initiatives, although care must be taken to ensure they are disability-inclusive, and through the use of self-managed work teams, job rotation, and temporary project assignments. Even something as simple as encouraging (but not requiring) people to eat together in a pleasant lunchroom in lieu of eating alone at their desks may help.

Incentive and compensation plans can also be designed in a way that minimizes perceived threat by lessening the impact one worker's performance has on another worker's performance evaluation. While team-based incentives can create a sense that everyone is working together on a shared goal, they can also create undue blame and shame. When one member is perceived as unable to fulfil their role, then group-based incentives may magnify existing problems related to discounting, bullying, and harassment. However, employing individual performance measures instead avoids this issue and can also provide confirmatory evidence of the individual competence of workers with a disability, which should lessen discounting over time. For that to work, of course, the successes of the workers with a disability need to be visible to other workers. Formal recognition programs for all employees with notable achievements can help in that regard.

Any interventions that lessen anxiety generally within the workplace can be helpful since that can lessen the severity and frequency with which stereotyping occurs. Reasonable workloads and deadlines, supportive supervisory behaviors, fair treatment, and benefits that help employees balance work and life responsibilities can all help serve this goal.

Of course, these organizational interventions assume that any occurring marginalization and stereotyping is inadvertent, and coworkers are well intentioned and benevolent. Unfortunately, that is not true in all instances. There are people who are consciously, overtly biased and engage in discriminatory actions with full knowledge of their harm. For those individuals, progressive disciplinary actions consisting of remedial education about anti-harassment policies, warnings for inappropriate behavior, and, if such behavior continues, termination may be required. It is worth noting that if an employee needs to be relocated to physically separate a harasser from their victim during a progressive discipline process, the burden of relocation should be placed on the perpetuator, not the victim.

How to Mitigate Personal Biases and Be an Effective Ally

Thus far, we have explored sources of prejudice and organizational interventions that can help lessen stereotyping. Individual workers also have a role to pay in mitigating their personal biases. The first step is acknowledging one's own potential for bias. This is often a significant mental barrier for people who want to believe they are good, prosocial citizens who are innocent of wrongdoing. Their perception of their own innocence creates a barrier to acknowledgment of the issue, with that denial preventing any attempts at improvement or remediation. To address this barrier to learning, educating people about how human cognition works enables them to accept that they can engage in discrimination without being an inherently bad, hateful, or evil person.

Some people with privilege are resistant to the idea of subtle perceptual barriers for equity-seeking groups because they believe that acknowledging another group's disadvantages invalidates all their personal achievements as members of a privileged group. They might believe that they are being accused of not earning what they have or having easy lives with success handed to them. Since even people with privilege have often worked very hard through significant challenges to earn their current workplace status, they respond very defensively, sometimes even in hostile ways. This barrier to attitudinal change can be lessened by pointing out that having privilege does confer unacceptable and unfair advantages, but those advantages do not invalidate personal achievements. Rather, they can provide an entryway to empathy creation when privileged people reflect sincerely and honestly about how much more difficult their path would have been without their privileges.

Some members of minority communities falsely believe that they, as members of a marginalized group, are themselves immune to stereotyping involving racism, sexism, or ableism. This is simply not true. In fact, every human being engages in stereotyping and can behave in discriminatory ways. In addition, negative stereotypes about one's own community can be internalized and result in discriminatory attitudes toward other members of the same community. There is also the issue of personal compliance with stereotypes due to *stereotype threat*, a psychological phenomenon in which stereotypes, once activated, impact the performance of people subject to them. The classic example of stereotype threat is that women and girls, when primed with stereotypes that females do poorly in math, actually perform worse on objective math tests. This *self-stereotyping* is nonconscious and can also impact disability communities who are seen as less competent and capable.

Once an individual has acknowledged their potential to engage in stereotyping and discrimination without their own conscious endorsement, they are better able to take steps to be an effective ally. The following practices can help:

☐ Combat stereotyping by taking time to critically evaluate your own attributions and perceptions in real time. This requires the practice of mindfulness, and there are many learning resources available to enhance mindfulness.

☐ Actively look for evidence that might disconfirm your understanding of events or your impression of a person and their actions.

☐ Be aware of patterns of privilege in your community and how historical relationships have impacted and created barriers for different communities. For example, you might educate yourself about Canadian colonial practices used to suppress Indigenous peoples and how that intergenerational trauma impacts First Nations communities today.

☐ Connect with and listen to people who are different from yourself. You can take steps to increase your contact, knowledge, and familiarity with other groups including personal conversations, formal classes, reading books and memoirs, or viewing YouTube videos created by members of another community. Personal connections are optimal.

☐ Speak up in your own social circles when prejudicial and discriminatory attitudes are expressed. Challenge those attitudes to help create and reinforce social norms of inclusion.

☐ Amplify the voices of members of marginalized communities. Share their stories in social media, create time and space for them at conferences and training events, and do anything else that is within your power to enable them to be heard.

☐ Show up. Attend relevant events and protests, vote, sign petitions, and be engaged.

☐ Avoid performative allyship. This means avoid making shallow, empty token gestures as your primary form of being an ally. Examples include merely forwarding social media posts or wearing a visible symbol of support (such as a shirt or ribbon) with no other actions whatsoever. Performative allyship is about being perceived as a good person rather than being a good person. Focus on being the good person instead.

☐ Get more comfortable with being uncomfortable. Learn formal techniques to control your anxiety response in interpersonal situations, such as deep breathing.

☐ You will not be perfect. Nobody is. Learn from your mistakes, apologize sincerely when you do make errors, and try to do better next time.

Organizational Culture and Belonging

Organizational culture is a descriptive term that highlights how employees and others, such as clients, vendors, and the community at large, perceive a firm. Culture helps create a sense of identity. It defines acceptable and unacceptable behaviors. Culture provides a lens through which people perceive their actions, creating shared meanings and expectations. As a result, organizational culture can influence the degree to which people perceive themselves as in-group members; the degree to which norms of supportiveness, inclusion, and respectful communication are encouraged; and whether diverse perspectives, viewpoints, and abilities are valued or shunned.

Researcher Sandra Spataro (2005) defined three different broad types of organization culture, each with different implications for diversity-related inclusion: differentiation cultures, unity cultures, and integration cultures.

Differentiation cultures focus on specific characteristics that are valued by the organization, and those without those narrowly defined sets of characteristics tend to be shunned. Power and status distinctions are derived from the degree to which an individual fits the ideal corporate model, and conflicts tend to focus on interpersonal disputes related to achieving and keeping power and status. In these types of cultures, people who are perceived as different, including workers with disabilities, tend to have their contributions discounted and have limited opportunities.

In unity cultures, demographic-, personality-, and perspective-related differences are ignored in favor of a *one team, one approach, one vision* mentality that emphasizes unified goals and suppression of individual differences. While this does lessen conflict, it also eliminates the inherent value of diverse perspectives for fostering creativity, innovation, and continuous improvement. These cultures do not tend to thrive in contexts in which environmental conditions shift, requiring ongoing change. They also tend to make individuals feel less visible and valued on a personal level, with potential to negatively impact work attitudes and performance. For workers with disabilities the emphasis on everyone being the same may negatively impact willingness to do things differently to accommodate one individual, negatively impacting performance potential.

In integration cultures, by contrast, different viewpoints are perceived as highly valuable and worthy of being fostered. Differences between team members are highlighted as potential sources of strength, and most conflict is of the easier-to-resolve task-related variety as opposed to interpersonal conflict. In these cultures, diversity in all forms, including demographic, attitudinal, and personality-based, is explicitly valued. Not surprisingly, integration cultures tend to result in the best outcomes for workers with disabilities. Notably, they encourage people with disabilities to proactively identify their needs and formally request accommodations since differences are respected and valued, reducing commonly held and all-too-frequently realized fears of negative social consequences associated with making requests and appearing needy or demanding.

Going into more granular detail, categorization of organizational culture considers the following variables:

- The degree to which activities are focused around teams or individual achievement

- Control orientation, meaning the degree to which rules, policies, and direct oversight are used to control employee behavior

- Tolerance of conflict, or the degree to which open criticism and disagreement is welcome
- Permissibility of interpersonal aggressiveness and competitiveness
- Focus on means versus ends
- Support for innovation and risk-taking
- Humane orientation, or the degree to which the well-being of employees is considered in business decisions
- Stability versus openness, meaning the degree to which the organization emphasizes growth and change versus maintaining the status quo
- Attention to detail and the degree to which people focus primarily on the big picture or are attentive to precision and data analysis
- Reward orientation, meaning the degree to which rewards are based on outcomes versus effort, and the degree to which they are assigned based on factors such as seniority or favoritism rather than objective performance

Organizational cultures are complex and multifaceted. Some larger organizations have numerous subcultures based on geographic area, department, level in the hierarchy, or occupational specialization. Yet within all that complexity some clear patterns do emerge. Some cultural orientations are much more likely to result in positive equity outcomes than others.

The aspects of culture previously listed influence the nature and type of barriers experienced by workers with disabilities. Specifically, having work activities focused on teams is initially more likely to result in coworker hostility or hesitancy to work with individuals with disabilities due to false stereotypes about reduced competence. This is especially true if rewards are also team-based rather than focused on individual contributions. That said, contact and familiarity reduce stereotyping. Over the long-term, team-focused organizations may end up having a reduced level of discounting and stereotyping overall as employees work together and get to know each other as individuals rather than stereotypes. This reality is supported by the results of research conducted by Frank Dobbin and Alexandra Kalev (2016), which looked at equity outcomes in 829 mid-size and large firms in the United States. They found that practices that brought people together and required them to interact as teams, such as cross-training and the creation of self-managed teams, improved equity outcomes to a greater degree than conventional diversity initiatives such as diversity training and targeted hiring (although voluntary training and targeting recruitment also had positive effects).

In addition, heavy emphasis on rules and policies may result in excessively legalistic approaches to accommodation that focus on what the employer *has* to do rather than what they *should* do. This can lead to less optimal outcomes since the focus is legal compliance rather than genuine, individual accommodation of a unique person with unique needs. Tolerance of open conflict can help resolve problems more quickly; however, it can also take a toxic direction when combined with an environment in which interpersonal aggressiveness and competitiveness are supported. That can lead to increased bullying and harassment when accommodation needs are perceived as problems, special treatment, or perks.

Moving on to other elements of culture, a focus on results can be positive when it means there is support for achieving aims in unconventional ways, but negative when it means that performance barriers will not be seriously considered when assessing outcomes. Excessive focus on quantitative results (such as sales quota attainment) without any regard for other performance criteria can also result in inappropriate tolerance for bullying and harassing behaviors when those behaviors are exhibited by high-performing members of the team. This can disadvantage any employees who are vulnerable to such harassment, including workers with disabilities. Meanwhile, support for innovation and risk-taking often extends to making less conventional hires and accepting some degree of failure as learning processes occur. This is generally positive for people with unique needs that may take some trial and error to accommodate properly.

Along with tolerance of (temporary) failure to innovate and learn, organizations with humane orientations value human dignity and well-being as much or more than profits. This is a positive trait for supporting diversity of all types. It results in better mental health and well-being for all employees. These organizations also tend to be subject to higher levels of scrutiny by both employees and the public since they often make their humane orientation part of their brand. Employees who feel there is hypocrisy or who find themselves unsupported will generally have a more intensely negative reaction than those working in organizations in which they never expected support in the first place.

Finally, reward orientations that focus on objective performance offer the best supports for workers with disabilities since they lessen the impact of nonconscious stereotyping and discounting. That said, systems that consider effort and not just outcomes can benefit workers who are still optimizing their accommodation strategy and finding out what works best for them.

The Special Problem of Hypermasculine Cultures

Many organizations are hampered by a hypermasculine ethos that encourages a toxic *masculinity contest culture*. Jennifer L. Berdahl, Peter Glick, and Marianne Cooper (2018) researched these cultures using data from a survey conducted with thousands of U.S. workers. They found that these cultures shared the following traits: (1) a heavy emphasis on not showing weakness of any kind, including doubt or vulnerable emotions; (2) an emphasis on strength and stamina, such as overtime expectations, even when they confer no clear advantage in the job role; (3) an expectation that work will be prioritized over all other aspects of life, such as medical or family leave; and (4) a dog-eat-dog ethos characterized by extreme competition in which the winner takes all. Traits such as emotional toughness and ruthlessness are valued. In these cultural settings image and status are perceived as zero-sum games, workers gain status by taking it from others.

Masculinity contest cultures are highly problematic because they cause workers to focus on repeatedly proving their dominance and toughness rather than focusing on organizational goals. Harassment, including sexual harassment, and bullying are widespread and may even be indirectly rewarded in these cultures. Average stress levels and workloads tend to be very high, with negative physical and psychological consequences. Some of these negative consequences, such as the depersonalization and lack of empathy that are created by stress-related burnout, magnify the problem. Anyone who does not comply with the manhood ideal is perceived as having less value and seen as a suitable target for scorn. This seriously disadvantages women, men perceived as having feminine qualities, people who are transgender, and people with disabilities. Workers with disabilities experience extreme discounting since their disability is incorrectly perceived as weakness, medical needs are perceived as unacceptable distractions from work, and the competitive atmosphere does not encourage the personal supportiveness that fosters positive accommodation outcomes.

These masculinity contest cultures are not only common in the military and policing but also prevalent in high tech; finance; resource extraction, such as mining, fishing, and forestry; firefighting; and field sales. Recent examples of organizations who have experienced significant backlash as a result of the negative consequences of their hypermasculine cultures include Uber, gaming company Activision Blizzard, numerous police forces in major U.S. cities, Canada's Royal Canadian Mounted Police, and Hockey Canada.

Creating and Maintaining Inclusive Cultures

Now that we have explored the types of cultures that are more or less supportive, let's delve into how to go about transforming an organizational culture into a more supportive version of itself. Organizational culture often emerges organically from the ideals of the founder because they hire like-minded individuals, socialize and train those employees, and role model acceptable behaviors. As such, it is relatively straight forward, if starting from scratch, to model the respectful and inclusive practices and attitudes that are expected and ensure hiring decisions support those priorities. Unfortunately, that is not the circumstance many companies find themselves in. Rather, organizations, after recognizing toxic and nonfunctional aspects of their culture, are in the difficult position of changing an established culture to make it more inclusive.

Culture change is difficult but possible. While a full exploration of best practices in this area is beyond the scope of this book, some basic guidelines are a useful place to start. Formally explaining the reasons that change is needed is important to minimizing resistance. Change is painful. But explaining why *not* changing will create more pain than changing is motivating, especially when presented in terms relevant to individual employees. Put another way, explain how cultural change will make their lives easier. Leaders set the tone for an organization, so any change initiatives must have the full, visible support from leaders. Leaders should also model the desired attitudes and behaviors. Remember to consider the informal leaders as well as formal ones, since both influence employee behavior, then monitor progress. Performance metrics and reward systems need to be realigned to support the desired culture and associated behaviors. Management by objective and balanced scorecard processes are especially useful as monitoring tools. Communicate often and celebrate the wins, such as unique contributions by diverse workers, to keep momentum going. Finally, make efforts to document and institutionalize new approaches to ensure changes persist over time.

Peer Attitudes and Inclusion in Action: An Example of a Very Subtle Barrier

Many organizational events, both work-related and social, are centered around dining. Whether it be the pizzas delivered for a lunchtime meeting, the homemade cookies brought in by a colleague, the elegant celebration dinner after a successful year end, or anything in between, group dining can be one of the subtlest forms of exclusion and judgment for people with disabilities. There are many disabilities that impact dining and restrict food choices including severe allergies, celiac disease, irritable bowel syndrome, Crohn's disease, and autism. With the exception of upper limb agility impairments (which may limit the types of foods that are manageable independently or may require the individual to have direct personal support to enable eating), disabilities that impact diet are generally invisible. That invisibility can lead to attribution errors that magnify negative social judgments and trigger out-group effects. That is especially true when dining needs associated with legitimate disabilities become dietary trends, such as the recent gluten-free craze, which has led to large numbers of people who do not have allergies requesting gluten-free foods. As a result, some people with allergies have found that requesting gluten-free items leads to social sanctions for being "trendy," "bandwagon jumpers," or "high maintenance." This situation predisposes others to perceive dining requirements as mere preferences rather than medical needs, leading to scorn for the individual who is causing what is erroneously perceived as needless effort.

Eating together is a fundamental way that humans bond and connect with each other. Historically, in almost every human culture from paleolithic times to the present, shared hospitality has been a strong sign of acceptance and willingness to work together. A refusal to eat together or to eat the foods offered by one's host signals distrust and even outright rejection. These nonconscious associations still exist today, such that people who appear unwilling to partake in specific food rituals are often perceived as standoffish or not wanting to be part of the team.

These nonconscious associations are not necessarily eliminated when someone becomes aware of a dining limitation or allergy. In addition, many people without food restrictions are unaware of the potential severity of ignoring those restrictions. To provide a personal example, I, the author, am celiac, meaning, among other things, that I have a severe gluten allergy. I have frequently experienced skepticism and been told I am "too high maintenance" when informing people that my dining limitations include avoidance of foods with small trace amounts of gluten such as soy sauce. Likewise, people with autism are particularly prone to such judgments since many people erroneously believe that sensory sensitivities related to food are something that can be overcome by force of will alone. Even for coworkers who are willing and eager to embrace unique dietary needs, trying to find appropriate foods can create anxiety, which can lead to avoidant and negative attitudes toward the source of the problem: the person with an allergy or other dining limitation.

The most common solution for group dining events is to have a separate meal delivered in a separate container for those with allergies and other dining restrictions. While this is a helpful practice that shows concern and care, it also separates that diner from the others in a clearly visible way. It sends a subtle signal that this person is an out-group member. It can also be perceived as special treatment or a perk by some, especially if the alternate food is perceived as higher quality or more desirable than the primary offering. That can trigger resentment. On the flip side, when the alternate food is lower quality, it can leave the diner feeling like they are less valued than the rest of the team. As a result, whenever practical, ordering a meal that meets the required dietary guidelines for everyone without drawing attention to it is preferable. It is also recommended that employees, especially senior leaders, avoid selling things like Girl Scout cookies in the workplace because it creates pressure to participate and be a good team player, which is problematic for those who are not able to consume the items in question. No amount of reassurance can guarantee that employees will not fear negative social consequences for failing to buy things they do not want and cannot even eat.

Consequences of not partaking in meals with others or not buying fundraising food items may seem inconsequential and merely social, but the out-group effects, awkwardness, and anxieties generated can have reverberations in other areas. For example, performance assessments, work team assignments, access to training opportunities, and day-to-day treatment by peers can all be heavily influenced by perceived social warmth and in-group effects. Eating differently and not participating in fundraising initiatives negatively impact perceptions of social warmth and being an in-group member, heightening the potential for nonconscious negative attitudes toward members of a group—people with disabilities—who are already socially disadvantaged due to widespread discounting and stereotyping.

FURTHER READINGS

Canton, E., Hedley, D., & Spoor, J. R. (2022). The stereotype content model and disabilities. *Journal of Social Psychology, 163*(4), 480–500. https://doi.org/10.1080/00224545.2021.2017253

Kniffin, K. M., Wansink, B., Devine, C. M., & Sobal, J. (2015). Eating together at the firehouse: How workplace commensality relates to the performance of firefighters. *Human Performance, 28*(4), 281–306. https://doi.org/10.1080/08959285.2015.1021049

Salter, N. P., & Migliaccio, L. (2019). Allyship as a diversity and inclusion tool in the workplace. In A. Georgiadou (Ed.), *Diversity within diversity management* (pp. 131–152). Emerald.

Shaw, L. R., Chan, F., & McMahon, B. T. (2012). Intersectionality and disability harassment: The interactive effects of disability, race, age, and gender. *Rehabilitation Counseling Bulletin, 55*(2), 82–91. https://doi .org/10.1177/0034355211431167

REFERENCES

Abben, D. R., Brown, S. G., Graupmann, V., Mockler, S. A., & Fernandes, G. F. (2013). Drawing on social psychology literature to understand and reduce workplace discrimination. *Industrial and Organizational Psychology, 6*(4), 476–479. https://doi.org/10.1111/iops.12088

Aysola, J., Barg, F. K., Martinez, A. B., Kearney, M., Agesa, K., Carmona, C., & Higginbotham, E. (2018). Perceptions of factors associated with inclusive work and learning environments in health care organizations: A qualitative narrative analysis. *JAMA Network Open, 1*(4), e181003. https://doi.org/10.1001/jamanetworkopen.2018.1003

Baldridge, D. C., & Veiga, J. F. (2006). The impact of anticipated social consequences on recurring disability accommodation requests. *Journal of Management, 32*(1), 158–179. https://doi.org/10.1177 /0149206305277800

Barsade, S. G., Coutifaris, C. G., & Pillemer, J. (2018). Emotional contagion in organizational life. *Research in Organizational Behavior, 38*, 137–151. https://doi.org/10.1016/j.riob.2018.11.005

Berdahl, J. L., Glick, P., & Cooper, M. (2018, November 2). How masculinity contests undermine organizations, and what to do about it. *Harvard Business Review*. https://hbr.org/2018/11/how-masculinity-contests-undermine-organizations-and-what-to-do-about-it

Breward, K. (2016). Predictors of employer-sponsored disability accommodation requesting in the workplace. *Canadian Journal of Disability Studies, 5*(1), 1–41. https://doi.org/10.15353/cjds.v5i1.248

Catalyst. (2022). *Women in management quick take.* https://www.catalyst .org/research/women-in-management/

Colella, A. (2001). Coworker distributive fairness judgments of the workplace accommodation of employees with disabilities. *Academy of*

Management Review, 26(1), 100–116. https://doi.org/10.5465/amr.2001.4011984

Dirth, T. P., & Branscombe, N. R. (2018). The social identity approach to disability: Bridging disability studies and psychological science. *Psychological Bulletin, 144*(12), 1300–1324. https://doi.org/10.1037/bul0000156

Dobbin, F., & Kalev, A. (2016). Why diversity programs fail and what works better. *Harvard Business Review, 94*(7), 52. https://hbr.org/2016/07/why-diversity-programs-fail

Fiske, S. T., Cuddy, A. J., Glick, P., & Xu, J. (2018). A model of (often mixed) stereotype content: Competence and warmth respectively follow from perceived status and competition. In S. Fiske (Ed.), *Social cognition* (pp. 162–214). Routledge.

Higgs, S. (2015). Social norms and their influence on eating behaviours. *Appetite, 86*, 38–44. https://doi.org/10.1016/j.appet.2014.10.021

Høgh, A., Clausen, T., Bickmann, L., Hansen, Å. M., Conway, P. M., & Baernholdt, M. (2021). Consequences of workplace bullying for individuals, organizations and society. In P. D'Cruz, E. Noronha, E. Baillien, B. Catley, K. Harlos, A. Høgh, & E. Gemzøe Mikkelsen (Eds.), *Pathways of job-related negative behaviour. Handbooks of workplace bullying, emotional abuse and harassment series* (Vol. 2, pp. 177–200). Springer.

Holm, A., Gorosh, R., Brady, M., White-Perkins, D. (2017). Recognizing privilege and bias: An interactive exercise to expand healthcare providers' personal awareness. *Academic Medicine, 92*(3), 360–364. https://doi.org/10.1097/ACM.0000000000001290

Huntsinger, J. R., Sinclair, S., & Clore, G. L. (2009). Affective regulation of implicitly measured stereotypes and attitudes: Automatic and controlled processes. *Journal of Experimental Social Psychology, 45*(3), 560–566. https://doi.org/10.1016/j.jesp.2009.01.007

Lindsay, S., Cagliostro, E., Leck, J., Shen, W., & Stinson, J. (2019). Disability disclosure and workplace accommodations among youth with disabilities. *Disability and Rehabilitation, 41*(16), 1914–1924. https://doi.org/10.1080/09638288.2018.1451926

Neubaum, G., Sobieraj, S., Raasch, J., & Riese, J. (2020). Digital destigmatization: How exposure to networking profiles can reduce social stereotypes. *Computers in Human Behavior, 112*, 106461. https://doi.org/10.1016/j.chb.2020.106461

Paetzold, R. L., García, M. F., Colella, A., Ren, L. R., Triana, M. D. C., & Ziebro, M. (2008). Perceptions of people with disabilities: When is accommodation fair? *Basic and Applied Social Psychology, 30*(1), 27–35. https://doi.org/10.1080/01973530701665280

Pavalko, E. K., Mossakowski, K. N., & Hamilton, V. J. (2003). Does perceived discrimination affect health? Longitudinal relationships between work discrimination and women's physical and emotional health. *Journal of Health and Social Behavior, 34,* 18–33. https://doi.org/10.2307/1519813

Payne, B. K. (2005). Conceptualizing control in social cognition: How executive functioning modulates the expression of automatic stereotyping. *Journal of Personality and Social Psychology, 89*(4), 488–503. https://doi.org/10.1037/0022-3514.89.4.488

Sawyer, P. J., Major, B., Casad, B. J., Townsend, S. S., & Mendes, W. B. (2012). Discrimination and the stress response: Psychological and physiological consequences of anticipating prejudice in interethnic interactions. *American Journal of Public Health, 102*(5), 1020–1026. https://doi.org/10.2105/AJPH.2011.300620

Sethi, B., Vito, R., & Ongbanouekeni, V. (2021). Organizational culture, diversity, and employees' health in social/human services: A systematic review. *International Health Trends and Perspectives, 1*(1), 74–95. https://doi.org/10.32920/ihtp.v1i1.1418

Spataro, S. E. (2005). Diversity in context: How organizational culture shapes reactions to workers with disabilities and others who are demographically different. *Behavioral Sciences & the Law, 23*(1), 21–38. https://doi.org/10.1002/bsl.623

Stephan, W. S., & Stephan, C. W. (2013). An integrated threat theory of prejudice. In S. Oskamp (Ed.), *Reducing prejudice and discrimination* (pp. 33–56). Lawrence Erlbaum.

Vornholt, K., Uitdewilligen, S., & Nijhuis, F. J. (2013). Factors affecting the acceptance of people with disabilities at work: A literature review. *Journal of Occupational Rehabilitation, 23*(4), 463–475. https://doi.org/10.1007/s10926-013-9426-0

4

Sensory, Mobility, and Agility Impairments

S ensory, mobility, and agility impairments include disabilities related to sight, hearing, and both upper- and lower-limb strength, agility, and functioning. While human resource (HR) representatives tend to have a better grasp of needs related to these disabilities (compared to, for example, psychiatric disabilities), there are still nuances that tend to be overlooked. People on the more severe end of the continuum related to these disabilities also tend to experience high levels of stereotype-driven discounting, when in fact the people with even the most profound support needs can make important and valuable contributions in the workplace. Haben Girma provides a concrete example of the capabilities of people with more extensive functional limitations. Her contributions remind us that stereotypes are exactly that, and employers and coworkers should be openminded about the abilities and strengths that stereotypes tend to mask.

Haben Girma's Story

Haben Girma is an accomplished lawyer who works in the United States. She is also a public speaker, disability rights advocate, surfer, rock-climber, author, and kayaker. She was the first deafblind person to graduate from Harvard Law School. In 2013, her legal work and advocacy efforts led her to be honored as an official "Champion of Change" by President Barack Obama. In 2016, she was named to the Forbes "30 Under 30" list of accomplished individuals whose careers bore watching. One of her notable professional wins involved accessibility rights.

In July 2014, while working as a staff attorney for Disability Rights Advocates (DRA), she successfully represented the National Federation for the Blind in a suit against e-book company Scribd for violating the Americans with Disabilities Act (ADA). It had failed, despite numerous requests, to provide access to their digital library for blind readers. Scribd moved to dismiss the case, arguing that the ADA only applied to physical locations. In March 2015, the U.S. District Court of Vermont ruled that the ADA covered online businesses as well. A settlement agreement was reached, with Scribd agreeing to provide content accessible to blind readers by the end of 2017. This decision had far-reaching implications because it clarified for the first time that ADA accessibility requirements applied in the digital as well as physical world.

Ms. Girma has since continued to use her voice and her lived example to advocate for disability rights and inclusion, inspiring others with a 2019 memoir that was named a *New York Times* "New and Noteworthy" title. However, she rejects the "inspiring" label, saying, "Some people use it as a disguise for pity. They'll say, 'You're so inspiring,' but in their minds they're thinking, 'Thank God I don't have your problems.'" She then adds her own perspective: "I hope people can move away from seeing those with disabilities as incompetent. If we remove barriers, we can have great inclusion" (Nahas, 2019).

Roles and Responsibilities: A Review of Basic Approaches to Accommodations

Disability-related impairments and associated accommodation needs will vary significantly from person to person based on the details of their conditions, the tasks they are required to perform, and the broader working environment they find themselves in. People with similar types of disability may require different accommodations, or no accommodations at all, based on these variables; one size does not fit all. Before developing any accommodation strategies, meet with the individual who is impacted and discuss the limitations they experience, if any, and the impact of those limitations on job performance. No assumptions should be made without consulting the worker directly.

Managers and HR personnel should work together with the individual employee to identify specific job tasks that require support and then identify available accommodations that reduce or eliminate the barrier(s). In these consultations, the manager serves as a subject matter expert on the job itself. They need to help outline requirements related to relevant job tasks, such as where, when, and how often tasks need to be performed; learn about the employee's needs; and ensure recommended accommodations are workable in real-world conditions. In most jurisdictions with Western democratic social norms and laws, the manager is not entitled to any specific medical information, such as diagnostic reports. Instead, they are only entitled to know task-based limitations and accommodations.

HR personnel participate as subject matter experts on the accommodation process itself. They ensure processes are followed properly in a manner compliant with the law, make specific accommodation suggestions, and monitor and enforce supervisory compliance with accommodation plans. When needed, HR also receives, verifies, and stores paperwork from healthcare practitioners in support of disability claims. The worker participates as a subject matter expert in their own needs. They may identify limitations and make accommodation suggestions but are not ultimately responsible for finding solutions. HR is most responsible for the final accommodation plan and would be the party charged with researching innovative solutions should the need arise. Small organizations that lack dedicated HR staff may wish to outsource this role to appropriate experts to ensure the process is implemented soundly.

Some forms of accommodation require the cooperation of supervisors and peers. When that is the case, training needs to take place promptly. Supervisor and peer training needs to focus on the accommodation itself without revealing the private medical information of the affected worker. While employers are not required to provide a worker with their preferred accommodation, but merely a functional accommodation, every reasonable effort should be made to empower the worker to choose their optimal solution. When a less preferred accommodation is provided, the rationale for that decision should be explained to the worker. This helps maintain trust within the relationship. And importantly, follow up regularly and ensure that accommodations are functioning as anticipated and that no other accommodation-related needs have emerged over time. Workers, especially those new to the job, may take some time to identify the full range of needed accommodations. In addition, both medical needs and job tasks change over time, so this is a dynamic and ongoing process.

Approaches for Sensory Impairments

Sensory impairments are disabilities related to vision, hearing, and other senses such as taste or smell. For practical purposes, a lack of taste and smell are seldom relevant to fulfilling job roles, so this book focuses on vision and hearing. Sight impairments are relatively common. In the United States, they affect 6% of people between the ages of 18 and 44 and 11% of people between 45 and 65. (These numbers do not include people who simply need corrective lenses to achieve full vision.) Hearing impairments are also common. The American-based National Institute for Deafness and

Other Communication Disorders reports that two to three children out of 1,000 are born with impaired hearing. Many more people acquire hearing impairments through illness, disease, accident, or excessive ongoing exposure to loud noise. Among those 12 and older, 13% have some degree of hearing loss. For adults aged 45–54, 2% have disabling hearing loss, and this number increases to 8.5% among those aged 55–65. Given the relatively high prevalence of these disabilities, human resource managers will likely encounter employees who need accommodations.

Accommodations for People With Vision Impairments

There are a wide variety of vision impairments that can impact workers. Some people may not be able to see at all, while others may see light or shapes to varying degrees. Some workers may have only their peripheral vision negatively impacted, resulting in tunnel vision, or only their core vision impacted while peripheral vision remains intact. Certain conditions are congenital (i.e., present at birth), while others develop over time, leading to a slow deterioration of vision. Vision loss can also occur quite abruptly, due to either disease or accidents.

Other sight-related disabilities are less well recognized among the general population. Extreme sensitivity to light is a problem often related to other medical conditions, such as albinism, or might be a side effect of certain commonly prescribed medications. People with numerous chronic conditions, such as diabetes and glaucoma, can experience vision issues at night or in dark settings. Color-blind workers may confuse green and red—a problem for safety labeling, which traditionally uses green to mean *safe* or *go* and red to mean *danger* or *stop*—or they may not perceive color at all, seeing the world in monochrome grays. People with vision in one eye only may experience difficulties with depth perception and peripheral vision that are relevant in safety-sensitive contexts. This wide range of vision impairments means that needs and accommodations also vary significantly from one person to the next. As with any accommodation scenario, engaging in detailed consultation with the affected worker to determine the best supports is important rather than making assumptions about needs.

There are many technical devices designed to assist workers with vision impairments and include tools commonly thought of as *technology*, such as software programs and computerized smart devices, as well as more basic assistive tools such as walking canes. Screen readers, that is, software that reads text aloud to the user, are now available not only for desktop and laptop computers but also a wide range of mobile devices.

These tools assist with reading emails, documents, and any other digital written communications. Although, reading speed is limited to the pace of the spoken word, which often slows down information processing. Websites also need to conform to WCAG standards for the tools to work well with their content, and not all sites meet these standards. Screen magnifiers, which magnify the entire screen to present text in a larger font, are also widely available, as is voice-to-text software that enables independent creation of written work. Voice-to-text software differs from screen readers because it enables generation of new text, not simply the reading of existing text. As such, people with sight impairments can use it to dictate emails and other communications. These tools are helpful but imperfect. They are most convenient for office jobs, although there are versions of these tools available for cell phones. Some people may find that voice-to-text software either does not understand their speech patterns due to speech impairments or an accent, while other, more sophisticated types that use machine learning take a while to perceive their speech accurately. More specialized devices also exist. For example, refreshable braille display devices can be connected to a computer or SD memory card, enabling the text to be translated into braille for the reader. High contrast fonts and large fonts can also assist those with partial vision to read more easily.

Physical navigation through the workspace can be rendered easier with signage that is clear and unobstructed, with high degrees of contrast between background colors and the sign content. (This strategy helps people with impaired vision but not people who are completely blind.) Do not over-rely on color in signs and alarms to signal hazards in production settings; there should be other cues for those who are color-blind. Use of contrasting texture strips on stairs and main thoroughfares can also create tactile clues about location. Texture strips are thin strips, often made of rubber, with bumps or other clearly perceptible textural contrasts on one side that are permanently stuck to floors and walkways. They are similar to the rumble strips used on highways that produce a distinct rumble and a felt vibration when a car moves outside its lane. For example, different texture strips can signal that a hallway intersection is coming in which vehicles, such as forklifts, may be traveling. Texture strips should include textures prominent enough to be felt through shoes. On stairs, high contrast color strips can assist with visual depth processing, reducing incidents of slips and falls. Given the rate of technological development and change, it can be hard to keep up with all new technology offerings. Most developed Western nations, as well as many other countries, have agencies that are involved with research and advocacy for visual impairments, such as the American Institute for the Blind (AFB) and Canada's National Institute for the Blind (CNIB), and they are excellent sources of information about the latest developments in technical assistive devices. They provide comprehensive, searchable lists of available devices with links to vendors, as well as access to reviews and recommendations from actual users. (Explore the AFB website about assistive devices in the Further Readings section at the end of this chapter.)

Beyond technology, there are also many other policy-related accommodations that can enhance equity, productivity, and well-being for workers with vision impairments. It begins at the recruitment phase. Professionally certified HR professionals, when available, should always assist line managers to develop disability-friendly recruitment and selection strategies, since certified HR professionals are generally more aware of equity-related barriers, mitigation strategies, and evidence-based best practices than nonexperts. Small organizations that lack a formal HR department or who have hired uncertified personnel into the role should consider hiring temporary talent or using professional recruitment firms to support their hiring processes until they develop reasonable equity-related competence in-house.

Online job ads are extremely common these days. A survey conducted in the United States in 2019 looked at 507 people who had found work in the previous 6 months. They found that 44% of the women and 33% of the men had found their jobs using online job boards, while an additional 14% found their jobs on social media (Bayern, 2019). The latter statistic was not divided by gender. Online job boards are a significant resource for job seekers, yet not all job posting sites are equally accessible for the vision impaired. Formal hiring policies should include requirements to ensure that the recruitment method used, whether it be online or not, is fully accessible. Selection tests and onboarding materials also need to be available in accessible formats, and, most importantly, recruiters need to be open to the idea that people with vision impairments can perform a wide variety of jobs. Anti-bias training can help with the latter because it can reduce stereotyping, make recruiters more aware of the abilities and potential of employees with vision impairments (including highlighting examples of successful placements), and provide knowledge about concrete accommodation strategies, which can in turn help reduce recruiter anxiety. Anxiety may be triggered by uncertainty related to ability to accommodate and has been demonstrated to result in avoidant behaviors, so anxiety reduction is an important goal of training.

Company policies that encourage active outreach recruiting through ad placement within disability community publications and the routine use of not-for-profit agencies that help place workers with disabilities are especially useful for maximizing the likelihood of meeting equity and inclusion goals. Most large urban centers have not-for-profit organizations whose sole mission is matching talented workers with disabilities with employers. Advocacy organizations such as the AFB and CNIB can assist in locating agencies within one's region. Worth noting is that advocacy organizations for a wide range of other disability types, such as autism and developmental disabilities, offer similar employment matching services. (A quick internet search will generally reveal relevant organizations within a given area.)

Some other accommodation policies that can be helpful include adjusting work schedules to be compatible with public transit availability or to enable someone with night-vision issues to drive to and from work during daylight hours. For the latter, work from home could also be supported during those times of year when days are especially short. Communication practices may also require tweaking, regardless of whether people work from home or in the office. Employers can encourage increased use of voicemail and audio clips for formal communications, ask formal note-takers to take meeting minutes or record meetings in full in video format, and mandate the routine placement of tactile dots on equipment and tools.

Health and safety policies should also be formalized, and resources allocated for supporting those policies. For example, any safety or warning devices that rely on visual input, including color perception, such as a flashing red light on a piece of equipment to signal a mechanical problem, need to have auditory or tactile warnings as appropriate. The material safety data sheets and warning labels that inform workers about chemical hazards under legislation such as the Occupational Safety and Health Administration (OSHA) in the United States and the Workplace Hazardous Materials Information System (WHMIS) in Canada may need to be available in braille. A formal *buddy* could be assigned to help people with severe vision impairments if an evacuation is needed, such as during a fire. As mentioned previously, tactile floor strips may be required in production facilities to provide warnings about where vehicles, such as forklifts, may travel. Forklift operators may need to be trained to honk before going around corners since the mirrors often used to mitigate the risk of a pedestrian and forklift collision are not helpful for the vision impaired.

Formal policies and guidelines about the physical workspace are also essential to ensure behavioral compliance. For example, deliberate, mindful efforts to keep hallways and common areas free of clutter and maintaining predictable and consistent placement of furnishings are important to ensure easy navigation of the physical workspace. Entrance paths into the workplace need to be clear and unobstructed, too, and are often overlooked in accommodation planning. Make entrance paths an explicit, formal part of health and safety committee responsibilities to avoid the problem of cluttered or otherwise unsafe entrance ways. Additionally, as previously mentioned, emergency evacuation policies should include designated personnel assigned to assist those with serious vision impairments to exit the location.

Travel also can be particularly onerous for some people with severe vision impairments. Many jobs that do not otherwise require travel might require it on occasion, often for training and developmental opportunities or special company events. Consideration should be given to the needs of staff with visual impairments (and staff with other forms of disability) when planning such events. Nonessential travel should be avoided if the employee with the impairment communicates this need. Alternative options, such as remote participation, can be offered as a choice. Developmental training that is equally accessible to all is especially important, so companies with centralized headquarters for training may need to consider more distributed approaches to avoid indirect discrimination.

Employers and employees may need reminding that, under law, service animals are welcomed in public spaces in which animals such as dogs are not normally permitted. For many employers accommodating a dog at work is a fairly simple process that requires little more than providing a water bowl and allowing the owner to take the animal outside for bathroom breaks. Accommodating a service animal, while still legally and morally necessary, is not without its challenges. It may require physical distancing between an employee with a severe allergy or phobia and the employee with the service animal, ideally on different floors or sections of the building, if feasible. Virtual meetings can help ensure there is no conflict between the accommodation needs of allergy sufferers and people using service animals. There are a small number of industrial settings, such as a food manufacturing or meat processing plants, in which service animals cannot access certain areas for food safety reasons. This may necessitate workstation relocation or redesign. In a very small number of cases, an ability to work without a service dog present may be a legitimate bona fide occupational requirement if working at the location in question is required to fulfill the primary responsibilities of the job and the dog's presence would introduce contaminants that compromise consumer safety.

As with any disability group, peer and supervisory attitudes are especially important to ensure a healthy and productive working environment. A willingness to use alternate communications methods (e.g., voicemail instead of a written note) is an important first step, as is a general willingness to be helpful, just as one would be for any colleague. That said, one common mistake that well-intended sighted people make is being overly helpful when assistance is not really required. This (often nonconscious stereotype-driven) solicitousness may be perceived as condescending and inappropriate by the individual with the vision impairment, so supervisors and peers should be encouraged to ask before assuming someone needs help with a given task. One form of help that is often (but not always) welcome by those completely lacking vision is to be led by another party when moving around an unfamiliar space. Coworkers should be aware of the basics of how to lead someone appropriately, which is something that brief formal training can assist with, or, in a pinch, they should simply ask the affected person what is appropriate rather than making assumptions. For example, abruptly grabbing their hand, arm, shoulder, or cane is not appropriate. Nor should a colleague try to steer the individual. Instead, let them take an arm and lead them at a steady pace, with them positioned slightly behind and to the side of their guide, generally about a half step back. Conventionally, one would stop briefly when encountering curbs or stairs while providing a verbal warning about whether the step is up or down, then allowing the person who is blind a moment to locate the edge of the step before proceeding. Moving the guiding arm slightly behind the body may be required in narrow areas in which people are only able to pass single file. When in doubt about how to lead someone effectively, openly asking is best. Employees may also need to be reminded that taking advantage of vision impairments to talk behind someone's back using visual cues, such as quietly passing a written note during a meeting or otherwise excluding them from communications and interactions is inappropriate.

Accommodations for People With Hearing Impairments and Sensitivities

There are many workers with hearing impairments, but not all hearing impairments are alike. People who are hard of hearing (HoH) have varying degrees of hearing loss but can generally use hearing to communicate, although they often require assistive devices such as hearing aids. Those who are deaf are not able to hear enough to rely on it as a way to process information. A distinction is made between being Deaf and being deaf. When capitalized, it refers to people who were born without hearing or lost their hearing in infancy, before verbal language development could occur. These individuals generally rely on sign language. People who are deaf lost their hearing later, after linguistic development had occurred. There is considerable controversy within the Deaf community about the classification of Deafness as a disability, with many instead viewing it as a normal human variation. The Deaf community is also a culture in its own right, which, like all cultures, evolved over time based on a shared language (sign language) and a host of unique values, traditions, and norms. Much like spoken languages, sign language is not universal, and many different variations exist, such as American Sign Language (ASL), Japanese Sign Language (JSL), and Arabic Sign Language. Each would be considered a subculture within the Deaf community.

Hearing impairments impact not only communication and information processing but also safety plans because many safety devices, such as fire alarms, use sirens or other forms of audible alarm. A wide range of technical devices have been devised to assist with these challenges. Hearing aids focus on amplifying sound for one individual. They are seldom provided by employers as a formal accommodation, although many benefits plans do cover the cost, because they are viewed as something that an individual is expected to provide themselves for daily life, much like prescription glasses. In call centers or for roles that involve a lot of time on the phone, the specialized headsets required for some types of hearing aids would, however, be an employer responsibility.

Other devices focus on translating auditory information into something that can be interpreted visually. Employers are expected to provide these devices or software. Examples include closed captioning, live captioning, and other technologies that transcribe audio input, as well as vibrating watches and alarms and visual (light-based) emergency notification systems. Teletypewriters (TTY) are an older technology that enable use of traditional telephones by those with hearing impairments. TTY is now available for many mobile devices, too. New and improved options emerge regularly. National associations for the Deaf and HoH exist in most countries and are an excellent source of information about emerging technologies.

Human intervention to assist with communication is another common accommodation in the workplace. Sign language interpreters and notetakers are the most obvious examples, but there are also hybrid technology and human solutions such as video relay calls, which is a videoconferencing technology that enables a sign language interpreter to assist on a call translating audio to sign language, and Communication Access Realtime Translation (CART) tools that provide near real-time translation by a professional stenographer. Many companies also use a formal buddy system for emergencies, with a designated person assigned to alert and assist the person with a hearing impairment in the event of an evacuation or other crisis. This is especially common in organizations that lack visual emergency signalers.

Of course, managers, supervisors, and peers can also choose from the many communication technologies that are not audio-based, which avoids the issue of barrier creation altogether and is therefore a better solution. Texting, email, instant messaging, and other forms of written communication should be used preferentially. The relatively recent emergence of cheap and effective video conferencing tools such as Zoom can also help because they enable lipreading and text-based chat, and many of them have add-ons for live captioning. Options are quickly increasing in both quantity and quality. For example, on November 17, 2022, Microsoft announced the introduction of a specialized sign language view in the popular MS Teams remote meeting software.

Many of the accommodations required by Deaf, deaf, and HoH individuals are social and require nothing more than thoughtful consideration from colleagues. For people who read lips, one should get their attention before speaking, face the person directly, and not cover one's mouth. (Transparent masks are available should conditions required it, such as during a pandemic.) This often gets overlooked in group meetings and other contexts that involve many people taking turns to speak. In those settings, colleagues should be encouraged to take extra care to only speak one at a time, and a visual signal should be devised to indicate who will speak next. Quiet, well-lit spaces with favorable acoustics also should be used for such gatherings. Settings such as restaurants and cafeterias generally have excessive background noise, creating difficulties for the HoH. Soundfield systems, which are wearable wireless devices that amplify sound and use speakers to spread it evenly throughout the room, can help. Colleagues should also be prepared to spend more time making clarifications because lipreading is a challenging and imperfect art. Talking louder, a common response to not being heard, will not enable better lipreading. In fact, it impairs it because increased volume exaggerates lip movements in a manner that makes reading them more difficult. When difficulties do occur, dismissing someone by saying "Never mind" or "I'll tell you later" is not acceptable. This practice can make people with hearing impairments seem and feel less valued than other workers. Instead, take the time to ensure that people who are Deaf and HoH can fully participate. Furthermore, when someone is using a sign language interpreter, one should direct their speech to them, not to their interpreter.

Company sensitivity training can also help colleagues recognize behaviors that tend to isolate or inadvertently demean Deaf and HoH colleagues. While many Deaf and deaf people are capable of speech, they should not be expected to use it if they prefer written or other forms of communication. Coworkers and the individual themselves can instead be encouraged to always have pens and paper in ready reach. Coworkers should also be sensitive to and avoid making personal comments to others about Deaf and deaf colleagues in their presence, knowing they cannot be heard. For instance, many Deaf people who have learned to speak have a distinctive accent, and sometimes coworkers might comment on that accent behind their backs when coworkers would not do so for other colleagues who have accents based on their country or community of origin. Sensitivity training can educate employees to recognize that not only is this rude and disrespectful, but also Deaf people are as capable as any others of telling when those around them are bullying them, even without auditory cues. Another common behavior that sensitivity training can help hearing people avoid is leaving a deaf or Deaf person waiting while those with hearing talk for an extended time. This can make the deaf or Deaf person feel isolated, even when that is not the intent of the parties engaging in the practice. Also, reading the screens of people with hearing impairments without their express permission is also highly problematic. Since screens and text are often their primary communication mode, this represents unacceptable eavesdropping.

In warehouse and industrial settings, there are a few issues that require special attention. Heavy equipment, such as forklifts, should have established routes of travel that are clearly marked, such as lanes that are clearly painted on the floor. This will help avoid accidents caused by not hearing an approaching vehicle. Mirrors that permit seeing around corners should be installed for much the same reason. When the person with the hearing impairment is the driver, a rear-view system may also help prevent accidents caused by not hearing someone behind you.

Not all hearing-related disabilities relate to hearing loss. Some people have very sensitive hearing and experience discomfort and even physical pain due to sounds that a person with average levels of hearing would find tolerable. (Chapter 5 discusses guidance on assisting these individuals, as well as managing sensory sensitivities in the context of autism.) Other people suffer from a medical condition called tinnitus, which is a persistent ringing, buzzing, or tinny sound coming from inside the ear or head. This ongoing, inescapable noise can cause significant physical and psychological distress over time and can impair focus and concentration.

Helpful interventions include reducing external noise, which can otherwise magnify the tinnitus. This can be done using a range of methods, including physical shielding, hearing protection, noise-canceling headphones, and adjustments to building structure and materials, such as fewer workspaces in close proximity, and cubicle walls or specialized ceiling panels that dampen sound. Some people also find white noise machines helpful.

As with all disabilities, these interventions should be available at all stages of employment. That means that job interviews and initial orientation and training also should be designed in an inclusive manner, using the tools and best practices discussed.

Accommodations for People Who Are Deafblind

People who are deafblind have both vision and hearing impairments to varying degrees. Some of these people are fully deafblind, meaning they have no sight or hearing and communicate primarily by touch. Other people who are deafblind have partial sight, partial hearing, or both. The accommodation strategies recommended for vision and hearing issues that were reviewed earlier in this chapter can be tailored to the unique needs of each individual who is deafblind based on their level of impairment for each sense.

In addition to the wide variety of strategies already explored, there are some unique accommodations for this group. Tactile dots that identify tools and equipment and vibrational alarms are among those accommodations. Having a personal support worker to help move around is not uncommon, especially early on when a new employee is still familiarizing themselves with the workspace. Supervisors and coworkers may need to learn some basic sign-based communication, meaning communication using direct touch on the person's palm, with the shape outlined representing words or letters. This method of communication might be recognizable to many people familiar with Helen Keller, a deafblind author and disability rights advocate who famously used it. Workplaces should plan to have a trained, designated worker assigned to help with evacuations in the event of an emergency, and having a shared, commonly understood emergency signaler is important. In many workplaces the agreed on emergency alert is to use a finger to lightly draw an X on the back of the person who is deafblind, letting them know there is an active concern. Coworkers also should be trained on simple matters related to communication and courtesy, such as lightly touching a shoulder to gain a deafblind person's attention. A person who is deafblind may, in consultation with coworkers, develop a tactile sign for each individual (analogous to a name) so people can readily identify themselves when they meet. Willingness to participate in these processes is important since enabling communication not only helps accomplish work tasks more effectively but also sends a signal of inclusion and acceptance, enhancing the well-being and psychological safety of workers.

Approaches for Mobility and Agility Impairments

Mobility impairments refer to a broad range of disabilities involving functional limitations in the limbs (arms, legs, or both). It also includes people with gross and fine motor skill limitations. Agility impairments refer to a wide range of conditions involving issues with mobility, coordination, dexterity, and fatigue. This section focuses primarily on upper- and lower-limb impairments that are permanent, with consistent symptoms and accommodation needs. Examples include people with paraplegia, quadriplegia, amputations, and congenital limb differences. Some other types of conditions lead to similar accommodation needs. For example, arthritis, multiple sclerosis, and cerebral palsy can all lead to mobility and agility impairments. They differ in that their symptoms are not necessarily consistent day to day. People can experience changes over time, remissions, or increases or reductions in symptom severity at unpredictable intervals, so these conditions are referred to collectively as intermittent disabilities. And some are more intermittent than others. For example, levels of impairment related to arthritis can shift rapidly day to day, or even hour to hour, while changes in functioning for people with cerebral palsy tend to occur less frequently and evolve more slowly. Many of the recommendations in this section are also suitable for people with intermittent conditions. Wheelchair users, for example, require similar accommodations regardless of the reason the wheelchair is in use. (Readers are encouraged to also explore the issues that arise with intermittent disabilities described in Chapter 7 to develop a more complete picture of types of impairment and associated accommodation-related needs.)

Accommodations for People With Upper Limb Differences, Amputations, and Agility Impairments

There are a wide variety of upper limb differences that can impact the way workers perform tasks. Differences may include missing or fused fingers, paddle-like limbs (a condition most often associated with prenatal thalidomide usage, and therefore more prevalent in workers over 55), amputation of one or both hands or arms, and weakness, shaking, or inability to coordinate finger usage due to a broad spectrum of medical conditions ranging from ulnar nerve palsy to essential tremor.

An array of specialized technical devices exists that enable the completion of tasks with only one hand. These include one-handed keyboards, tool balancers (i.e., devices that provide a counterweight so tools can be used one-handed), book holders, and winches and chain hoists for lifting—there are even one-handed syringes available to healthcare workers. Since most of these devices are task-specific, listing them all is impossible, and so employers should be prepared to research available options. In some instances, specialized products are not required; instead, creativity is needed. For example, removing staples is almost impossible one-handed, but using paper clips instead eliminates the problem completely. Similarly, automatic transmissions on vehicles, while not conventionally considered a disability aid per se, can also make it much easier and safer for people with only one hand to drive. In addition, if the worker only has use of their left hand, there are tools such as scissors, circular saws, and lathes that are designed for left-handed use. Using tools designed for right-handed use can be a hazard to left-handed people because safety guards and cut-out switches are positioned assuming use by a right-handed user.

For workers who have no hands or have both hands but are unable to grip or coordinate finger usage, there are also specialized tools available. Some of these tools are more appropriate for people with no hands, some better for those who have finger dexterity issues, and some are used by both groups. These tools include, but are not limited to, grip aids, hands-free phones, vacuum pick-up tools, carrying carts, touchless faucets, auto-dialers, patient lifts and other lift devices, head- or eye-tracking-based data input, foot controls on vehicles, remote control window blinds, automatic filing systems, and automatic door openers. With the wide variety of specialist tools and ongoing innovation in this area, employers should regularly research accommodation options.

In addition to technical devices, social consideration is also helpful. Something as simple as a colleague helping carry books and coffee to a meeting can make the workplace more functional for an employee with upper limb impairments. However, creation of unnecessary dependence should be avoided such that the individual does not feel chagrined or inconvenienced by a need to impose on others, which is a common source of social anxiety for workers with disabilities. For example, a carrying cart can enable independence even when colleagues are willing to carry things for their coworker. And if an employee has a dual amputation, then in meetings there should be a way to indicate that one wishes to speak that does not require raising one's hand.

There are also security and safety planning and policy development needs that should be considered. For instance, fingerprint or handprint biometrics may be problematic or impossible to provide, so if the organization uses biometrics for building or device access, then an alternate solution will be needed. Ideally that solution should not unduly inconvenience the worker by, for example, requiring them to go through an onerous manual check-in process that is not required of other employees. Practical solutions may involve having designated security personnel capable of recognizing the employee on sight who can allow them to pass without requiring a daily inspection of paperwork, or the addition of an iris scanner in addition to fingerprint-based biometrics. Similarly, many standard safety devices, such as eye rinse stations and pull-activated fire alarms, are difficult or impossible to use for someone without hands or with significant limb differences. Alternate devices are often available, and employers should locate and install them.

Care should also be taken when planning employee team building and recreational events. These events should involve activities that those with limb differences are able to fully participate in. Buffet-style meals can create social awkwardness for those with limb differences, who may require someone else to collect food for them, so alternates, such as table service, should be considered. Inquiries should be made prior to the meeting regarding styles of food that can be better managed independently. For example, pizza may be easier to eat than a meal requiring utensils. In some cases, people with limb differences may need a support person to assist with eating.

Accommodations for People Who Have Lower Limb Differences or Amputations or Are Wheelchair Users

There is considerable variation in disabilities related to lower limbs and mobility, with causes including accidental injuries, diseases, wear and tear on joints, and congenital conditions. While some people use highly visible wheelchairs, scooters, walkers, canes, or prosthetic legs, not all lower limb mobility impairments are readily visible. Some people appear to walk unaided but have issues with pain, balance, coordination, ability to walk on rough or uneven surfaces, or ability to walk significant distances.

Physical accessibility for wheelchairs and scooters is among the more obvious accommodations. When constructing new buildings, there are many ways to make the physical space more wheelchair friendly. (Chapter 8 also discusses inclusive design.) In existing structures, automatic door openers and ramps must be at an appropriate angle for safe navigation, that is, five degrees of incline, or one inch of rise for every 12 inches of length. In places with cold winters, prompt snow removal and de-icing in parking lots, entrances, and on ramps are also key components of accessibility and should be scheduled for completion before the main workday begins. People with mobility impairments should also be given preferential access to the closest parking spaces. In harsh climates many workplaces have a double set of doors with an air lock in between for energy efficiency purposes. Having sufficient space between the two sets of doors for a wheelchair or scooter is imperative, while also allowing ready access to the automated button to open the second door. This detail can be overlooked when accessibility is modified post-construction, creating a trap in which people in scooters can get through one door only to find themselves unable to reach the opener for the second one, leaving them stuck until a passerby assists. Bathrooms and bathroom stalls also should be accessible and have grab bars. Ideally at least one sink and mirror in the bathroom should be placed lower, at the height of a typical wheelchair user.

Workstations will often need ergonomic adjustments for wheelchair and scooter users. Adjustable desks with variable heights are widely available, as are desks specifically designed for wheelchair users. There should also be wheelchair-accessible or height-adjustable tables in team meeting rooms and common areas such as lounges and cafeterias. Coworkers should be strongly encouraged to keep hallways and common thoroughfares free of clutter and to avoid moving furniture in ways that creates obstacles. Another helpful accommodation is placing filing cabinets, printers, and copiers at lower heights that can be reached by all. When this is not possible—some types of industrial copiers, for example, are simply not available at accessible heights—then other solutions can include use of a digital interface in lieu of loading the machine manually with originals on paper, human assistance, or provision of special height-adjustable chairs. Jobs that require operating a vehicle or tools may require hand controls and other modifications.

From a policy perspective, there are several steps companies can undertake to make life easier and safer. For one, emergency evacuation plans should take mobility impairments into consideration. Offer people with such conditions preferential access to first floor offices and offices close to exits, as well as a designated and trained evacuation buddy to assist them if needed. In other instances, some people with mobility impairments who use public transportation are more limited in their transportation options. For example, buses typically have a very limited number of spaces for wheelchairs and some people may have to wait for several buses to pass if the spots are all taken. In other communities, people using wheelchairs need to schedule specialized HandiTransit services with limited operating hours. Policies that allow for flexible scheduling and tolerance of unexpected lateness may be required. Work-from-home options can help, too. Furthermore, people with mobility impairments often need longer bathroom breaks because getting to the washroom and into a stall is more physically onerous. Uniform expectations may need to be revisited if uniforms are not styled in a manner that is appropriate for wheelchair users. Custom tailoring may be necessary.

The need for work-related travel in general, and particularly air travel, should be considered carefully. As of 2022, airlines still treat mobility aids as luggage. There is significant evidence that damage to wheelchairs and scooters is widespread and common. The *Washington Post* reported that the United States' largest airlines collectively lost or damaged 10,548 wheelchairs in 2019 alone, or 29 chairs per day. Since these devices are generally instrumental in maintaining personal independence, highly customized, expensive, and difficult to replace, the fear of this happening is a significant personal stressor. Potential for mobility problems, and even personal humiliation (some users of lost chairs reported having to crawl through airports), is higher than for other employees, and alternatives to travel, such as online meetings, should be considered whenever possible.

Socially, there are several common courtesies employers, supervisors, and coworkers should be aware of and trained on when working with people who use wheelchairs. First and foremost, a wheelchair should be considered an extension of the person using it and should not be touched, leaned on, or otherwise handled without express permission. One also should not assume someone wants to be pushed in their wheelchair; one ought to wait for an invitation to do so. When speaking for more than a moment or two with someone in a wheelchair, sitting is the politest thing to do so that the conversation can continue at eye level. Also avoid terms that imply that their wheelchair is somehow a prison; for example, terms such as "confined to a wheelchair" or "wheelchair bound" imply confinement when wheelchairs in fact offer the opposite, they offer mobility. As with all disability types, if a person who is a wheelchair user has an attendant helping with personal needs, make sure to speak directly to the person not their attendant.

When planning offsite work events and after-work social events, ensuring locations are accessible is important. Sometimes people believe that only a few stairs are not a problem if coworkers can lift the individual in a wheelchair, so they book inaccessible venues. This is a bad idea! Being lifted by inexperienced people is both dangerous and potentially humiliating and can be frightening for some individuals. Nor is it fair to put pressure on workers in wheelchairs by openly complaining that some favorite venues cannot be used due to lack of accessibility. Finally, as a small token of consideration, keeping wet wipes readily available in common areas and offices that are often frequented by wheelchair users is useful. Pushing a wheelchair tends to result in dirty hands, which can create momentary awkwardness that is quickly resolved when cleaning products are readily at hand.

There are also a wide variety of accommodations that enable more productive work for people with lower limb mobility impairments or amputations who do not require the use of a wheelchair. Note that many of the accommodations recommended for wheelchair users, such as elevators, prompt snow removal, clutter-free walking paths, extra time for bathroom breaks, and appropriately tailored uniforms, are also relevant and helpful for this population. In addition, anti-slip surfaces, anti-fatigue matting (which enables standing for a long time with less discomfort), rest breaks from tasks that require standing and walking, and rest stops after climbing stairs are all helpful. People with prosthetic limbs who use tools may require some sort of balancing aid (external or part of the tool itself) for safe operation. Socially, people with prosthetics are often excluded from physical activities, such as recreational sporting teams, associated with an employer due to assumptions about their abilities. Coworkers should be prepared to ask rather than assume and should endeavor to plan social activities that are more inclusive.

Accommodations for People Who Are Quadriplegic

People with quadriplegia are paralyzed in all four limbs. While some may have mobility in their arms, they are unable to grasp things using their hands. The ability to speak may or may not be impacted depending on the condition or injury that initially caused the quadriplegia. People with quadriplegia use tools to help them communicate and interact with the world. These tools range from relatively low-tech mouth-held typing sticks to highly sophisticated tongue- or eye-movement-controlled computing devices that enable data entry and even a mind reading exoskeleton controlled by thought. These thoughts are automatically interpreted by brain implants linked to the exoskeleton suit, permitting movement such as walking. While the latter technology is not yet widely available or particularly affordable, advances are being made regularly that could make the use of such devices more widespread in the future.

Data collected from Equal Employment Opportunity Commission hearings in the United States suggest that workers with quadriplegia are among the most discriminated against in the workforce due to heavy stereotyping and general lack of awareness about how to accommodate such individuals in the workplace (McMahon et al., 2005). Yet when appropriate accommodations are provided, people with quadriplegia can make valuable professional contributions. Stephen Hawking may be the most famous example. As one of the greatest minds of the 20th century, he made invaluable contributions to physics over a long and distinguished career as a university professor, researcher, author, and community educator. Other examples of accomplished professionals with quadriplegia include Charles Krauthammer, a Pulitzer Prize-winning *Washington Post* reporter; Teddy Pendergrass, a well-known and award-winning musician and performer; Steven Fletcher, a Canadian member of Parliament who held Federal Cabinet posts for 5 years; Jill Kinmont, a respected teacher and painter; and Hilary Lister, an adventurer well known for her solo sailing trips around Britain and the Kingdom of Bahrain.

In addition to the self-evident challenges associated with paralysis, such as moving and manipulating objects, people with quadriplegia may also have decreased stamina or overall body weakness, and they will need specialized supports to address toileting needs. Transportation to and from the workplace can also be difficult. Accommodations, as with all disability types, need to be tailored to the individual and decided on in consultation with them.

Technical devices and workstation customization are major components of any accommodation strategy for a worker with quadriplegia. Common requirements include specialized desks that can be elevated to accommodate a wheelchair user, other forms of customized desks, and keyboards and computers that can be controlled with puffs of breath, eye movements, tongue movements, or mouth-held sticks. Telephones should have goosenecks or other holder devices tailored to the individual's needs. There are also a wide variety of highly specialized technical devices that are designed to help achieve unique tasks, and exploration of options should occur in consultation with the affected worker. Bathrooms would need appropriate grab bars and a stall large enough to accommodate wheelchairs. Transfer aids, which are devices to help move from sitting to standing positions, may be required elsewhere, too. Other accommodations previously discussed for wheelchair users, such as automatic door openers, are relevant for this population, too.

In addition to technical devices, many people with quadriplegia require an aide to assist with certain tasks, including personal hygiene and eating. Permission for their pre-existing aide, someone from whom they have been receiving personal support services prior to the employment relationship, to accompany them to the workplace, and occasionally provision of a new aide, may be required as an accommodation. In addition, flexible scheduling, task rotation, and the ability to work from home as needed can lessen fatigue. The flexible scheduling and work-from-home options also help address transportation-related challenges. Also helpful is for employers to understand that most forms of public transportation are not suitable for quadriplegic people, who may have to use specialized services (generally government-operated paratransit services) that operate on limited hours or that limit the number of trips per week. Employers who have the means to offer direct transportation assistance are appreciated.

Supervisors and peers may need additional guidance on how to communicate respectfully with workers who are quadriplegic, especially those who use communication technologies that result in a brief time delay. Common, offensive mistakes people make include directing their conversation to the worker's aide rather than the worker themselves, failing to make the usual level of eye contact or otherwise engaging in physical avoidance behaviors, getting visibly impatient with slower forms of communication, and interrupting or assuming they know what the person is going to say, such as finishing their sentences before they can do so themselves. Following these guidelines and putting sensitive company policies in place can help make the workplace more welcoming, respectful, and inclusive for those with any of these impairments.

FURTHER READINGS

American Institute for the Blind's *Access World*. Newsletter. https://www.afb.org/aw

Dong, S., Hespe, P., & Monagas, K. (2022). Requesting workplace accommodation among individuals with mobility disabilities: A qualitative investigation on barriers and facilitators. *Journal of Applied Rehabilitation Counseling*, 53(3), 193–209. https://doi.org/10.1891/JARC-D-21-00005

Dong, S., Warner, A., Mamboleo, G., Guerette, A., & Zegarra Zalles, M. (2017). Barriers in accommodation process among individuals with visual impairments. *Journal of Rehabilitation*, *83*(2), 27–35.

Haynes, S., & Linden, M. (2012). Workplace accommodations and unmet needs specific to individuals who are deaf or hard of hearing. *Disability and Rehabilitation: Assistive Technology*, *7*(5), 408–415. https://doi.org/10.3109/17483107.2012.665977

National Employment Resource Center for the Deaf and Hard of Hearing. https://www.nad.org/nerc/

REFERENCES

Adwar, C. (2014, August 20). 26-year-old deaf-blind lawyer sues Scribd for alleged discrimination. *Business Insider*. https://www.businessinsider.com/haben-girma-sues-scribd-2014-8

Attanasio, J. (2022, November 18). Turned away from flights, crawling down aisles and rejected loo breaks: Australians with disabilities say they are being 'dehumanised and humiliated.' *9News*. https://www.9news.com.au/national/australians-with-disabilities-suffer-dehumanising-treatment-at-airports-travel-news/b7de6139-258a-4e86-a615-031eb0e89074

Bayern, M. (2019, January 9). 15% of job seekers now land a job through social media. *Tech Republic*. https://www.techrepublic.com/article/15-of-job-seekers-now-land-a-job-through-social-media/

Bell, J. (2019, December 16). Five of the most innovative assistive devices for people living with quadriplegia. *NS Medical Devices*. https://www.nsmedicaldevices.com/analysis/assistive-devices-quadriplegia/

Bobrow, E. (2019, August 2). Haben Girma is a trailblazer for the deaf and blind. *Wall Street Journal*. https://www.wsj.com/articles/deafblind-trailblazer-haben-girma-has-a-vision-of-inclusion-11564761224

BraunAbility. (n.d.). *What is the proper wheelchair ramp slope measurement?* https://www.braunability.com/us/en/blog/disability-rights/wheelchair-ramp-slope.html

Burton, A. (2018). Expecting exoskeletons for more than spinal cord injury. *Lancet Neurology, 17*(4), 302–303. https://doi.org/10.1016/S1474-4422(18)30074-7

Canadian Hearing Services. (2022). *Deaf culture*. https://www.chs.ca/deaf-culture#:~:text=Deaf%20culture%20is%20the%20culture,point%20of%20view%20of%20deafness

Canadian National Institute for the Blind. (2022a). *What is blindness?* https://www.cnib.ca/en/sight-loss-info/blindness/what-blindness?region=mb

Canadian National Institute for the Blind. (2022b). *Workplace accommodations.* https://www.cnib.ca/en/sight-loss-info/blindness-work/workplace-accommodations?region=mb

Colour Blind Awareness. (2022). *Types of colour blindness.* https://www.colourblindawareness.org/colour-blindness/types-of-colour-blindness/

The Deaf Health Charity, SignHealth. (n.d.). *What is the difference between deaf and Deaf?* https://signhealth.org.uk/resources/learn-about-deafness/deaf-or-deaf/

Girdhar, A., Mital, A., Kephart, A., & Young, A. (2001). Design guidelines for accommodating amputees in the workplace. *Journal of Occupational Rehabilitation, 11*(2), 99–118. https://doi.org/10.1023/a:1016655302305

Health Policy Institute, Georgetown University. (n.d.). *Visual impairments.* https://hpi.georgetown.edu/visual/

Job Accommodation Network. (n.d.a). *Amputation.* https://askjan.org/disabilities/Amputation.cfm?csSearch=2472617_1

Job Accommodation Network. (n.d.b). *Hand amputation.* https://askjan.org/disabilities/Hand-Amputation.cfm?csSearch=2472617_1

Job Accommodation Network. (n.d.c). *Quadriplegia.* https://askjan.org/disabilities/Quadriplegia.cfm

Kovac, L. (2018, November 30). Accommodating workers with physical or mobility disabilities. *Accessibility for Ontarians with Disabilities Act.* https://aoda.ca/accommodating-workers-with-physical-or-mobility-disabilities/

Mastin, L. (2012). Other handedness issues - Handedness and tools. https://www.rightleftrightwrong.com/issues_tools.html

McMahon, B., Shaw, L., West, S., & Waid-Ebbs, J. (2005). Workplace discrimination and spinal cord injury: The national EEOC ADA research project. *Journal of Vocational Rehabilitation, 23*(3), 155–162.

Nahas, A. (2019, August 9). Why the first deafblind person to graduate from Harvard Law doesn't want to be called 'inspiring.' *People Magazine.* https://people.com/human-interest/haben-girma-first-deafblind-person-to-graduate-from-harvard-law/

National Institute on Deafness and Other Communication Disorders. (2021, March 25). *Quick statistics about hearing.* National Institutes of Health. https://www.nidcd.nih.gov/health/statistics/quick-statistics-hearing

Sampson, H. (2021, June 7). Airlines have lost or damaged more than 15,000 wheelchairs since late 2018. *Washington Post*. https://www.washingtonpost.com/travel/2021/06/07/wheelchair-scooter-damage-airplane-flights/

Sano, C. (2022, November 17). Introducing sign language view for teams meetings. *Microsoft*. https://techcommunity.microsoft.com/t5/micro-soft-teams-blog/introducing-sign-language-view-for-teams-meetings/ba-p/3671257

Spinal Cord Injury BC. (n.d.). *Accommodating employees who use wheelchairs*. https://sci-bc.ca/wp-content/uploads/2019/11/Accommodating-Employees-Who-Use-Wheelchairs-Job-Accommodation-Network.pdf

World Health Organization. (2021, April 1). *Deafness and hearing loss*. https://www.who.int/news-room/fact-sheets/detail/deafness-and-hearing-loss

Neurodiversity

Autism, ADHD, and Learning Impairments

N eurodiversity is an umbrella term used for a variety of conditions in which people think differently, meaning that their cognitive (brain) functions, sensory processing, and associated behavioral traits vary from what is most often observed in the general population. Examples include autism, attention deficit hyperactivity disorder (ADHD), dyslexia, and other learning disabilities. People without such conditions are termed *neurotypical*, and those with such conditions are called *neurodiverse*. There is considerable debate both within and outside of the neurodiverse community about whether these conditions represent disabilities or merely normal human variations that are poorly accommodated in modern society. This debate is complicated by the reality that different individuals experience different levels of symptom severity and ability to meet neurotypical expectations. For example, some people with autism and ADHD can integrate into workplaces, with coworkers scarcely noticing their differences. Others experience a combination of symptoms and structural barriers that make employment a significant struggle. There is a common saying in the neurodiverse community: When you know one neurodiverse person, you know one neurodiverse person. This saying highlights the fact that one cannot make assumptions and must engage with each neurodiverse employee as an individual, accepting that people with the same diagnosis may experience enormously different barriers, limitations, and support needs.

Neurodiverse workers' ability to think differently also has significant benefits for employers, making them sought-after employees in industries that value what they can offer. This is one reason that human resource (HR) programs focused on recruiting the neurodiverse, especially people with autism, have blossomed in industries such as computer science, accountancy, insurance, and risk management. For example, people with dyslexia might struggle with reading but often excel at three-dimensional thinking and associated problem solving. While research results are mixed, many studies suggest that dyslexia is also associated with higher levels of creativity. And autism is often associated with intense focus, development of deep expertise in areas of interest, logic and evidence-driven decision making, and an attention to detail that is beneficial in many occupations. ADHD is associated with spontaneity, high energy levels, and, under the right circumstances, hyper focus that allows for rapid task completion. While the caution that all neurodiverse people are individuals remains true, those individuals can offer a range of valuable skills, abilities, and inherent predispositions that can benefit employers and provide a competitive edge.

Understanding Workers With Autism

Let's begin with a discussion about vocabulary. There is a passionate ongoing debate in the autistic community over preferences for identity-first language (i.e., an autistic person) and person-first language (i.e., a person with autism). Both perspectives have merit. Proponents of identity-first language argue that autism is central to who they are, a defining trait worthy of acknowledgment and celebration. Proponents of person-first language believe in always emphasizing personhood over all other traits. For the discussion in this chapter, person-first language has been used to maintain consistency with other chapters in the book; however, all HR personnel, managers, and supervisors are encouraged to inquire about the preferred choice of individual workers with autism and respect their preferences.

Autism is a term used to describe a complex, multifaceted, genetic developmental difference (termed a disorder in medical literature) that presents in highly variable ways. While all disabilities differently impact the individuals who have them, this is especially true of people with autism. As such, the presenting symptoms and behaviors, functional limitations, and required accommodations vary enormously between individuals. Members of the autism community often comment that managers and coworkers cannot assume that one worker's experiences or needs are like that of another. Since symptoms are multifaceted and there are considerable differences in severity levels, even opinions about the nature of autism vary within the community. Some experts and people with autism consider themselves disabled, while others reject that label and view autistic differences as a natural and normal expression of human variation that ultimately benefits the species by providing society with people who think and problem-solve a little differently. As such, any discussion about cures for autism can be considered highly offensive by members of the community, some of whom perceive such comments as genocidal. But legally speaking, and regardless of the debate, autism is recognized as a disability in the United States, Canada, the United

Kingdom, Europe, Australia, Japan, India, China, Brazil, Chile, Morocco, South Africa, and many other jurisdictions. The presenting symptoms can be classified into different types based on whether impacts are cognitive, emotional, sensory, behavioral, or physical—although there can be some overlap in those categories.

Cognitive aspects of autism often include issues with executive functioning, intense devotion to special interests, extreme detail orientation, heightened ability to recognize patterns and visually process complex data, and, in some cases, increased levels of creativity. *Executive function* refers to a set of processes required to generate and carry out plans, particularly mid- and long-term plans. It is a complex concept that includes working memory, cognitive flexibility, the ability to maintain attention, impulse control, and the ability to tune out irrelevant stimuli. Some of the cognitive aspects of autism can present a challenge in workplaces. For example, problems with executive functioning can create issues with remembering assigned tasks, knowing how to prioritize those tasks, or independently planning how to achieve long-term goals. Problems with cognitive flexibility can lead to difficulties changing gears quickly when task priorities shift, as well as resistance to broader organizational changes, especially when the reasons for the change are not explicitly justified and explained. People with autism may experience mental distress when rules are illogical and nonfunctional, others do not follow rules, or rules are haphazardly enforced. Extreme detail orientation can be positive or negative depending on the context and the organization's needs. Other cognitive aspects of autism, such as heightened pattern recognition and creativity, are highly valued in the workplace—especially in industries such as risk mitigation, institutional analysis, graphic design, and software development—and are actively sought out and fostered. Despite stereotypes to the contrary, there is as wide a variation in intelligence among people with autism as in the neurotypical community. In fact, autism is associated with both high intelligence (giftedness) and intellectual disability, with a higher percentage of people at the extreme ends of the continuum in both directions than in neurotypical populations. This means that proportionately, among people with autism, there are more highly intelligent people than in the neurotypical community; however, there are also proportionately more with significant cognitive delays or impairments.

Verbal language skills vary considerably within the autistic community. Some people have advanced skills beyond most peers, while others are completely nonverbal, relying on other forms of communication such as writing or hand signals. Some people with autism have selective mutism, meaning they can communicate verbally sometimes but cannot do so when unduly stressed, uncertain, or anxious. Despite the term *selective*, people with this condition generally do not have control over when they are able to speak and when they are not. Increased pressure to speak only magnifies the problem. Recognizing that, despite stereotypes to the contrary, verbal language skills and intelligence are not the same is important for managers, peers, and employers. There are both nonverbal and verbal people everywhere along the intelligence continuum.

Many people with autism have difficulty interpreting social and emotional cues and responding to those cues in the manner expected by neurotypical people. Informal social norms can be difficult for people with autism to perceive and respond to. The unspoken rules of the workplace that everyone is expected to simply know may be a complete mystery to them: Do you need to greet coworkers each time you see them in the hallway or only the first time you see them that day? When is it appropriate to go over someone's head and take an issue, such as a process-related problem, to a more senior manager, and when will that same behavior be interpreted as toxic insubordination? When do managers truly want authentic feedback on a process, program, or their leadership style? When will such feedback, regardless of how gently expressed, be perceived as a challenge to their authority? What are you supposed to do when you have finished one task but not yet been given another? Is it okay to refuse to go for drinks after work if you are tired or is that social time somehow mandatory for career advancement?

This confusion can negatively impact not just social inclusion but also job performance when task expectations and work standards are not clearly communicated. They may fail to notice, or incorrectly interpret, the emotional reactions of others, leading to socially inappropriate responses. Specific challenges may include reading facial expressions and body language, understanding vocal tone cues, such as those that indicate sarcasm, and taking comments overly literally. In addition, workers with autism may speak in a monotone with limited emotional expression or have unconventional facial expressions that do not necessarily reflect their internal feelings. They may dominate conversations, focusing on narrow topics of interest to them while not picking up on cues that others would like to speak or change the topic. Eye contact is an especial problem. Many people with autism find eye contact difficult, uncomfortable, and distracting. For some, thinking and communicating clearly while also maintaining eye contact is difficult, so they avoid it and look elsewhere when speaking to others.

All these differences taken together mean that people with autism frequently come across as awkward, cold, uncaring, or arrogant when interacting with neurotypical people. These attributions are often a poor reflection of the intent and internal emotional state of the individual. The frequency with which people with autism experience confusion and social rejection because of these mistaken attributions leads to social withdrawal, which in turn magnifies and reinforces the faulty assumption that people with autism are unconcerned with those around them. While lack of empathy is regularly cited as an autistic trait, this characterization is hotly disputed by many members of the autistic community and by emerging evidence from cognitive psychology. Both suggest that some people with autism may in fact experience excessive levels of empathy that overwhelm them, but that the way they express and communicate that empathy is not well understood or recognized by others. For example, when listening to another person tell a story about something negative that happened to them (e.g., a health scare or relationship problem), many people with autism attempt to display empathy by relating a story about something similar that happened to them. This is done to demonstrate that they can relate to the underlying emotional response since they have experienced something similar; yet neurotypical people frequently misinterpret this behavior as dismissive, accusing the person with autism of selfishly ignoring another's pain to make the conversation all about themselves.

Another common aspect of autism is heightened sensitivity to stimuli such as noise, smell, and touch. Sensory input that seems reasonable for neurotypical people can overwhelm the senses of a person with autism, leading to difficulties with focus, concentration, and even physical pain. For example, many people with autism have problems with fluorescent lights, which flicker at a rate of 120 cycles per second. This flickering is perceptible to many of those with autism, resulting in eyestrain or even a disorienting feeling that the room itself is pulsating. Furthermore, fluorescent lights make a humming sound that is audible, and highly annoying, to many people with autism. These sensory sensitivities can create problems working effectively in open-concept, noisy workspaces and working around strong scents; and can trigger an inability to wear certain fabrics or styles of uniform. Tactile objects that are imperceptible to others, such as tags on the back of clothing or seams in socks, can be unbearable for those with sensory sensitivities. This heightened sensitivity to stimuli can lead to reactions that seem extreme to neurotypical people. A lack of understanding of those reactions often leads to people with autism being labeled weird or difficult, with the attendant social problems those negative labels create.

When people with autism experience sensory overload or are otherwise overwhelmed, they often fight back against anxiety and panic by engaging in repetitive behaviors known as *stimming*. Stimming activities may include anything from arm or hand flapping, rocking, pacing, bouncing one's legs, repeating certain words or phrases many times, or using devices such as fidget spinners, or chew jewelry. Stimming is a way of retaking control of the situation and calming oneself by focusing on something specific to tone down the *noise* created by other stimuli. Many workers with autism report finding stimming socially embarrassing because it is perceived as weird, yet it is critical to their ability to cope with overwhelming situations. As such, the lack of understanding and social acceptability of stimming can be a much greater disruption in the workplace than the activity itself, although in some cases coworkers may find specific stimming behaviors distracting or noisy.

Physical limitations are among the least well-known aspects of autism, and not all people with autism are impacted. Common problems include digestive issues, hypermobile joints, and extreme muscle tightness and tension. Some people with autism experience motor planning difficulties combined with poor coordination and balance, leading to increased incidents of tripping, falling, and bumping into things. Gross and fine motor skills may also be impacted, although this particular symptom occurs more often among children rather than adults with autism. (For a discussion on accommodating physical issues with agility and mobility, consult Chapter 4.)

Importantly, many of the traits that are associated with autism are highly valued in many workplaces, making them sought-out employees in industries requiring those abilities. These strengths may include the ability to focus intensively on tasks, even monotonous ones, for a long period of time, as well as persistence, being detail-oriented, and having heightened pattern recognition skills. Workers with these traits often become recognized technical experts in their field of choice. For example, Temple Grandin, an openly autistic professor at Colorado State University, is a world-renowned expert in animal science who has been named to *Time* magazine's 100 Most Influential People list. She has almost single-handedly improved standards for animal care and transport through her research. Vernon Smith, a professor at Chapman University, won a Nobel prize in 2002 for his work in experimental economics. He is also openly autistic. And Satoshi Tajiri, the world-renowned creator of Pokémon, demonstrates the artistic creativity that sometimes accompanies autism.

People with autism tend to be highly focused on justice and find unfairness extremely distressing and difficult to move on from. As a result, they are less likely to engage in toxic interpersonal workplace politics, which tends to bewilder them, and they are often honest and forthright to a fault. That means they provide excellent, if perhaps overly frank, feedback and are less tempted to hide problems due to the desire to manage impressions. These traits, while not always appreciated by those receiving the constructive criticism, can help organizations recognize and correct problems before they escalate in severity.

There are many, many potential accommodations for autism. There is also significant overlap in the types of accommodations that are helpful for those with autism and the types of accommodations that are helpful to those with ADHD. Before moving into specific workplace accommodation strategies, let's explore ADHD in more depth.

Understanding Workers With ADHD

ADHD is considered a neurodevelopmental disorder, although, much like autism, many people consider it a natural human variation rather than a disorder. People with ADHD generally have issues with focus and concentration, are easily distracted, and demonstrate lower than average levels of patience and impulse control. Executive functioning skills are impacted, so planning can be a struggle, and they may be easily frustrated and experience mood swings, especially when under stress. Losing things, sometimes almost immediately after putting them down, is a common source of aggravation for people with ADHD, one that they struggle to control even with significant effort. This can lead to chronic anxiety about where important items are located and repeated checking that can seem somewhat excessive to an outside observer. There are three subtypes of ADHD: predominantly inattentive, predominantly hyperactive, and a combined presentation. People with the predominantly inattentive type may struggle to organize, prioritize, and finish tasks. They are easily distracted and often, despite their best intentions, have difficulty paying attention to detail, including conversations and verbal instructions. They may forget details of work routines quickly. People with the predominantly hyperactive variation of ADHD may fidget a lot, struggle to sit still, talk to an excessive degree, be especially restless and impulsive, and have issues with turn-taking. People with the combined variation of ADHD exhibit symptoms associated with both groups. As with autism, individual symptoms and impacts vary tremendously from one person to another.

There are several strengths commonly associated with ADHD that are valued in many workplaces. People with ADHD tend to be more creative, and often thrive in the arts. Actors Emma Watson, Michelle Rodriguez, Will Smith, and Woody Harrelson have all been identified as having ADHD, as have many musicians such as Adam Levine and Zayn Malik. This creativity can generate innovative ideas for new products, processes, and service offerings. For example, famous entrepreneurs with ADHD include Bill Gates and Richard Branson. They often have abundant energy and a spontaneous approach that can help them effectively address unexpected emerging problems. Since day-to-day life, especially during the school years, is often challenging for people with ADHD, many have developed a resiliency and problem-solving mentality that serves them well during stressful times. Counterintuitively, under certain conditions, some people with ADHD are capable of hyper-focus, a state in which they can tune out all other stimuli and focus intensively on a task until it is completed.

Neurodiversity and Gender

There are numerous differences in the way autism and ADHD present based on gender that have been recognized and studied only in the last decade. For example, when overstimulated as children, boys are more likely to act out physically in highly visible ways, whereas girls are more likely to retreat within, going into shut-down mode. This means, practically speaking, that only the boys' behavior is likely to draw attention and be perceived as problematic, leading to help-seeking by parents and, more likely, a diagnosis. In the past, these unrecognized differences meant that the diagnostic criteria for autism and ADHD were systematically gender biased such that female neurodiversity was routinely overlooked. Females with these conditions who grew up in the 1950s through to the mid-2000s were much less likely to be formally diagnosed and supported than their male counterparts. It is very common for these women to not realize they are neurodiverse until they are well into their 30s and 40s, or even later. (I, the author, was formally diagnosed as autistic at age 50, and only after decades of self-recrimination for unexplained struggles in the social domain.) The diagnosis of their children is often a trigger for the realization that they themselves are neurodiverse. Psychologists refer to these women collectively as the Lost Girls due to the lack of supports they experienced in childhood.

For the Lost Girls there are two struggles: They have autistic or ADHD traits that may need accommodation, but they also go through a major realigning of their identity, personal narrative, and history when they do finally receive a diagnosis. This is often a positive and hopeful process because these women realize that traits and behaviors they have been blamed and shamed for are not due to them being a bad, thoughtless, cold, or lazy person but are the result of disability-related limitations. While the journey of realization is often productive, the path there can be very painful. Recently diagnosed women may find they are unusually emotionally volatile or extremely distracted as their minds involuntarily go through their entire life history, experiencing a series of revelations along the lines of "Oh, *that's* why that happened" and "Oh, *that's* why people found my response odd." It can be exhausting.

Temporary workplace accommodations may be required to support these Lost Girls, such as permitting flexible scheduling to attend therapeutic appointments or simply allowing quiet time away to process such a drastic new understanding of oneself. In addition, people who are newly diagnosed as neurodiverse often attempt to *unmask*, meaning they try to act in a manner that feels more natural for their personality rather than attempting to play the role other people expect. Unmasking after a lifetime of masking is difficult, and it may take some time for recently diagnosed people to adjust and start to understand how to interact effectively while unmasked. In the meantime, some extra understanding, social consideration, and gentle coaching may be needed.

Accommodations for Workers With Autism and ADHD

Accommodation needs will vary considerably from one individual to another when workers have autism, ADHD, or both. (Comorbidities are common, and experts estimate that between 50% and 70% of individuals with autism also have ADHD.) Listing every accommodation isn't possible because the options are limited only by the creativity of the parties involved. But general guidance can still help point managers in the right direction. Since functional limitations and severity levels are highly individual and their impacts are context-specific, there is a heightened need to make customized plans in consultation with the affected party and to engage in ongoing evaluation and tweaking as necessary. Accommodations for people with autism and ADHD tend to fall into four very broad categories: reduction of unnecessary or unwelcome stimuli, support for executive functioning-related needs, support for direct and clear communication, and assistance with social-emotional elements of work.

Unnecessary stimuli, such as excess noise, visual distractions, and strong scents, negatively impact people with ADHD primarily because such stimuli are intrusive, further impairing focus and concentration. They negatively impact people with autism primarily due to sensory sensitivities. There are many ways to reduce unnecessary stimuli at work. Several examples are provided here but this should not be considered an exhaustive list of options. Physical blocking of personal workspaces can reduce auditory and visual distractions. Examples include providing private offices with doors or cubicles that face a corner and have sound dampening walls. Whenever possible, fluorescent lights should be avoided; LED lights are a much better option. Noise-canceling headphones can also be used, although some people with autism will not be able to tolerate the sensation of the headphones on their head. Similarly, standard uniforms can be a problem if the fabric is stiff or itchy, cuffs and collars are tight, or there are nonremovable tags that irritate the skin. Some flexibility in wardrobe choice may be needed.

Other options for reducing unwanted stimuli include permitting work from home, when home is in fact a quieter environment, and offering flexible scheduling when possible. Flexible scheduling means that workers can come in for their preferred hours if they work the required number of hours per day. For example, they may choose to work from 7:00 a.m. to 3:00 p.m. rather than 9:00 a.m. to 5:00 p.m., or they may choose to work from noon to 8:00 p.m. Some companies require work to be done within specific hours, such as between 7:00 a.m. and 8:00 p.m., while others offer truly open scheduling, including the option of working nights. Flexible scheduling allows people with autism and ADHD to select working hours that are less busy, lessening over-stimulation, distractions, and social demands. It also allows them to modify their schedules in response to events that fatigue them, such as choosing to come in later after a particularly busy prior day, and it permits easier scheduling of medical appointments and other important life tasks. In fact, flexible scheduling offers similar benefits to all employees and is demonstrated to have positive impacts on work attitudes and performance while lessening turnover intentions and work-life conflict. As such, offering it to all employees when practical is ideal rather than making individual exceptions as an accommodation. This approach lessens the potential for resentment from coworkers, which may occur if only neurodiverse workers are permitted to use flexible scheduling.

Beyond the physical workspace, encouraging social norms that minimize interruptions can also help reduce excessive stimuli and distractions. For example, encourage the use of email instead of phone calls between coworkers, and ask employees to use meeting rooms instead of hallways for conversations lasting more than a couple of minutes. This has the side benefit of preventing workers with ADHD from impulsively jumping into conversations that do not involve them, potentially creating political friction. Coworkers could be asked to schedule time to chat with a given employee instead of dropping in with questions at random intervals. Although, recognize that some workers with ADHD may struggle to follow the latter rule given their spontaneous nature, so appropriate consideration should be given, and such breaches of the rule should not be treated punitively. Positive behavior modification strategies that focus on praise for rule compliance are a more effective strategy.

Regardless of efforts to reduce stimuli, workplaces may still overwhelm someone with autism on occasion. That is, when a *quiet room* can be very beneficial to help someone calm themselves and return to a productive mindset. Quiet rooms are generally darkened rooms in a noise-free section of the workplace that contain comfortable furniture; perhaps soft, calming music; and minimal other sources of stimulation. Spending several minutes in a quiet room helps people with autism cope when they become overwhelmed; non-autistic workers also report psychological benefits from such a space, including reductions in stress and anxiety (Beaver, 2011). Permitting occasional work from home is another excellent way to address becoming overwhelmed since it provides a break from both the troublesome sensory input and from the need to engage in casual socializing, which is often a significant strain for people with autism.

Some workers with ADHD may find a quiet room especially helpful when processing their emotional responses to workplace events. Others with the same diagnosis would fare better with the opposite of a quiet room—an area in which they can be loud, physical, and burn off excess energy without experiencing negative social sanctions. Allowing more frequent breaks can help address this need. Areas, such as hallways or large rooms, in which people can pace without bothering others are a good start. Access to outdoor spaces, when available and weather permitting, is also an excellent choice. Larger organizations may even invest in an onsite gym, which will help workers with ADHD when they need to burn off physical energy, with all the attendant physical and mental health benefits—and other employees can enjoy the gym as well. Another consideration is purchasing group seating, such as tables for meeting rooms, with designs selected that permit more fidgeting without negatively impacting others. For example, some designs will cause vibrations to the entire table if one person sitting around it is bouncing their legs. Furniture design can assist here. Even better, many organizations now permit people to stand up and walk around the back of the room unobtrusively during meetings. This is a great strategy to help workers with ADHD maintain focus without distracting others with their restlessness.

As discussed, executive functioning can be problematic for both workers with autism and workers with ADHD. Simple and free changes to supervisory practices can help immensely. Task lists, processes and procedures, meeting agendas and minutes, and other workplace instructions should be provided in writing, not just verbally, so that the worker can review them as needed. Color coding of such lists is especially helpful for workers with ADHD because it helps them locate the relevant information without getting distracted by other text. Changes to those tasks, policies, or instructions should also be documented in writing, preferably with plenty of advance warning and an explanation for the rationale behind the change. Managers and supervisors should be prepared to break complex tasks into smaller, more manageable parts; explicitly explain priorities; and help with planning related to achieving long-term goals. Keeping objects, tools, files, and instructions that are needed to complete day-to-day tasks in the same place is helpful, and a written list of those places posted as a reminder is also beneficial.

Perception of time and time management can both be a significant challenge, and calendar applications that include alarms are enormously helpful to ensure meetings and other important time-sensitive events are remembered. That said, some people with ADHD may struggle to maintain their calendar, so having formal email meeting requests that automatically populate the calendar when accepted is helpful. When planning a meeting, let the employee or employees with autism or ADHD know in advance if they will be required to speak and on what topic so they can prepare appropriately concise notes for themselves to keep their comments on track. Finally, workers with ADHD should be permitted extra time to complete tests related to training and development because any distractions make test-taking more challenging than it is for neurotypical people.

The communication and social difficulties experienced by people with autism and, to a lesser extent, ADHD are heavily intertwined. As such, resolving communication issues will also help with social difficulties. People with autism do not excel at reading between the lines or picking up on the unspoken rules of the workplace, so making unspoken norms explicit is helpful. Managers and supervisors should be trained to avoid ambiguity in task assignments, expected outputs, and the chain of command. Things that may seem obvious to a manager, such as how to prioritize multiple assignments or what someone is expected to do when they finish a given task, should be explicitly explained. Performance criteria should be clearly outlined, and employees should be capable of monitoring their progress against performance goals. It is worth noting that taking these steps helps neurotypical workers, too, and represents well-documented general best practices in management. Workers with autism also report that their ability to communicate effectively is increased when they can see questions and prepare responses in advance, when people avoid jumping around between multiple topics in one conversation, and when their communication intent is not judged by vocal tone or conventional body language–related criteria such as degree of eye contact or having the corresponding facial expression.

Workers with ADHD do not have the same difficulties interpreting social cues, but they may struggle to communicate with the appropriate emotional tone, especially when excited or agitated, and they may be perceived as dominating conversations or interrupting others to an excessive degree. Supervisors should encourage workers who are impacted to take a 15-minute break before attempting to communicate when they are very emotional (recognizing that due to poor impulse control this may prove difficult). They can also use a concrete, held object in meetings to designate who has the right to speak at that moment, or use other formal turn-taking strategies, such as roundtable discussions, to discourage unintentional interrupting. Individual coaching, when done gently and mixed with praise, can also help employees with both ADHD and autism better understand how and when their communications have been ineffective. After all, behavior modification is impossible when you cannot perceive the problem—unless someone is willing to tell you!

Since social events, even positive and fun ones, can be a considerable strain for people with autism, they should be permitted to avoid workplace events that are purely social without being sanctioned. This can, however, alienate the individual from other coworkers, resulting in isolation. While the social events should remain optional, people on the autism continuum will often feel more encouraged to participate if the event has the following characteristics:

- Expectations provided in advance

- Brief in duration, lasting only an hour or two

- Structured and predictable social interactions, such as an organized game rather than a networking cocktail party

- Held in a space that is not excessively busy, noisy, or with multiple competing distractions

- Does not require additional focus on the complexities of dining etiquette, such as how to eat unfamiliar foods with unfamiliar utensils

Even with the described supports, workers with autism may find the social and emotional behaviors of others mystifying and may struggle to project a socially acceptable persona. This is generally not due to antisocial tendencies but difficulty reading cues and understanding how their own social cues are interpreted by others. A coach or mentor can be very helpful in this regard. That mentor could be an appropriately trained senior level coworker or an outside expert. Being able to call on someone to help interpret social and emotional cues can not only improve communication and social outcomes, but it can significantly lessen stress and anxiety levels as well. Employees with ADHD may similarly benefit from a coach who helps with task planning and time management. The people who work most often with the individual(s) with autism or ADHD may also benefit from receiving formal information about autism and ADHD and their impacts on communication to increase understanding and empathy. While such training should be comprehensive, one particularly helpful tip is not to socially sanction workers with autism for harmless stimming behaviors, which are a common trigger for workplace bullying. That said, such education efforts can only be undertaken with the express permission of the individual with autism or ADHD or in the context of broader generic diversity training initiatives due to privacy considerations.

Workers with autism and, to a lesser extent, ADHD are often targets of bullying in workplaces in which their neurotypes are poorly understood or heavily stereotyped (Cooper & Kennady, 2021; Yokell, 2023). Their tendency to inadvertently cause offense without being aware of it magnifies this problem and causes some employers to inappropriately blame them for the bullying they experience (Cooper & Kennady, 2021). Receiving accommodations that are perceived as desirable privileges, such as extra breaks or working from home, can also heighten the abuse from peers. Managers and supervisors need to take special care to prevent bullying and mitigate it when it occurs. The aforementioned training can be a good start in that direction, as are respectful, anti-bullying, and anti-harassment workplace policies that are enforced. Importantly, ensure the respectful workplace policies are not weaponized to punish people for overly direct or blunt styles of communication that are being directly influenced by their disability. For example, a message that points out a flaw in a process without softening it to save another's ego, but that does not include name calling, accusations, or clearly inappropriate language, should not be considered a violation of a respectful workplace communication policy merely because it hurts the feelings of the person who developed the flawed process. Punishing neurodiverse workers for such direct and forthright social behaviors when they are incapable of predicting that it will cause offense for reasons that are directly related to their disability would constitute discrimination under law.

Thus far we have addressed accommodations to help employees with autism and ADHD in the workplace. To even get to that step, however, these individuals must acquire jobs in the first place. Interviews, by their very nature, tend to be excessively challenging for people with autism and ADHD. The interview process presents a huge barrier to employment, even for workers who would excel in the jobs they are applying for. People with autism struggle with interviews because they tend to speak very honestly and openly without engaging in political impression management behaviors. This violates behavioral expectations, leading to lower interview scores. They may also be confused by vague or irrelevant questions, or take questions overly literally, leading to surprising and unconventional answers. In addition, people with autism are often sanctioned for lack of eye contact, which is erroneously assumed to indicate either shiftiness or lack of confidence. This is especially a problem when artificial intelligence (AI) is used for screening interviews because most AI interviewer applications monitor and judge facial expressions. And interviews held with multiple people at once or in highly distracting environments may cause issues with focus and attention. For job candidates with ADHD, distractibility can become a challenge, especially when interviews are held in busier areas such as cafeterias or offices with glass walls adjacent to hallways. In addition, if questions are overly long or contain multiple parts, they may struggle to remember all components of the question long enough to provide a full answer.

There are many strategies to make interviews more valid for neurodiverse people. The location of the interview should be quiet, distraction-free, and preferably should not include fluorescent lights. Questions should be brief, clear, and job related. Avoid people-pleasing questions that are not directly tied to work tasks because these questions mostly test political skill (unless political skill is a bona fide occupational requirement, in which case such questions would be valid). Some companies provide questions in advance, either a day before or immediately before the interview. When longer questions are inevitable, for example when using situational interview questions, offer written copies in addition to stating them verbally. Avoid panel interviews, which require focusing on multiple people at once, but maintain multiple reviewers to avoid bias. This can be achieved through use of sequential interviews, which are one-on-one interviews conducted with multiple interviewers in sequence, with each interviewer asking a different subset of questions. Some companies are even replacing components of the interview entirely, using objective skill, knowledge, and competency testing instead. However, if testing is used, then previous comments about making tests accessible (e.g., by providing extra time accommodations or ensuring online tests are WAG compliant) are important to keep in mind. See Chapter 2 for more details about accessible tests. Employers should encourage job candidates to identify any accommodation needs by directly asking them (but *not* about specific disabilities) early during the application process and providing concrete examples of available accommodations. If online tests, such as personality or knowledge tests, are part of the automated prescreening process, it is especially important to provide clear information about how to receive accommodations because candidates must take these tests before having direct contact with the organization's recruiters.

Other innovative hiring strategies are available. In fact, employment agencies that cater exclusively to neurodiverse job seekers are becoming increasingly common as more and more employers embrace the benefits of having workers with autism and ADHD. Integrate Employment Advisors, operating out of San Francisco, New York, and Cincinnati, is one such agency. It places workers with autism in well-known companies, many of whom are on the Fortune 500 list. These organizations not only offer conventional employment matching services but also offer extra support to both the employer and the employee to ensure a successful placement. (Chapter 2 also discusses some of the specific strategies used by Ernst and Young in their efforts to hire members of the neurodiverse community.)

Understanding Workers With Dyslexia

The Yale Center for Dyslexia and Creativity defines dyslexia as "an unexpected difficulty in learning to read. Dyslexia takes away an individual's ability to read quickly and automatically, and to retrieve spoken words easily, but it does not dampen their creativity and ingenuity." The International

Dyslexia Association provides a similar but more nuanced definition, which states that

> dyslexia is a specific learning disability that is neurobiological in origin. It is characterized by difficulties with accurate or fluent word recognition and by poor spelling and decoding abilities. These difficulties typically result from a deficit in the phonological component of language that is often unexpected in relation to other cognitive abilities and the provision of effective classroom instruction. Secondary consequences may include problems in reading comprehension and reduced reading experience that can impede growth of vocabulary and background knowledge.

Clarifying several elements of the latter definition is beneficial. People with dyslexia have trouble accurately perceiving letters on a written page and aligning them with phonetic sounds. This makes reading much more difficult. They may also have difficulties identifying separate sounds in speech, including sounds within words. This can lead to either subtle or overt issues understanding and using spoken language. Dyslexia is defined as an unexpected difficulty because people with dyslexia do not have delayed cognitive development, and their difficulties don't reflect their underlying intelligence. In fact, dyslexia is often associated with quick thinking, above-average reasoning skills, and creativity. It is also quite common. Well-regarded expert Sally Shaywitz reports in her book *Overcoming Dyslexia* that it impacts roughly 20% of the population, many of whom are never diagnosed, and represents between 80% and 90% of all learning disabilities. Brain imaging work indicates that there are underlying differences in brain connectivity that lead to dyslexia, and as such it represents a normal human variation and cannot be cured through medication or treatment.

Common workplace difficulties experienced by people with dyslexia include the following:

- Difficulties reading and understanding written material at the pace expected by others

- Extreme fatigue after completing reading intensive tasks

- Poor spelling

- Difficulty remembering names, a tendency to confuse similar sounding names, and a tendency to pronounce place names and personal names incorrectly

- Anxiety when asked to speak to groups, aversion and avoidance of public speaking, and extreme anxiety when asked to read aloud to others

- Needing more time to structure verbal responses, and increased tendency to use filler words such as "ums" and "ahs"

- Greater than average difficulties in learning new languages

These difficulties, if not addressed, can negatively impact self-esteem, leading to undesirable personal and professional consequences, such as under-performance, lowered job satisfaction, feelings of frustration, and heightened stress.

Common workplace strengths of people with dyslexia include a tendency to be nonlinear, creative thinkers. In fact, Albert Einstein (who famously did not learn to speak fluently until age 6) is one of the best known of the paradigm-changing scientists who are believed to have been dyslexic! In addition, many people with dyslexia have above average conceptualization skills, meaning the ability to identify, assess, and find solutions for intricate, complex, and abstract problems. Enhanced ability to see the big picture is also common. For example, entrepreneur Onyinye Udokporo, who has dyslexia, was able to see the big picture and launch a highly successful, specialized remote tutoring and learning service called Enrich Learning at the start of the pandemic. By tailoring to a niche market, that is, students with learning disabilities, with the right product at the right time, she created a highly successful company and has even been profiled in *Forbes Magazine*! Some people with dyslexia struggle with reading, writing, and spelling but not verbal communication. These individuals tend to be highly articulate. Celebrity chef and well-spoken TV personality Jamie Oliver is a good example.

Many of the accommodations for workers with dyslexia are self-evident, in addition to being either extremely low cost or no cost. As with all disabilities, the person impacted should always be consulted about their individual needs and accommodation preferences before developing a strategy. The most obvious accommodations are spellchecking software, text readers, voice-to-text (speech recognition) software, and colored screen overlays. Blue and yellow screen overlays, whether placed on monitors or written pages, help enhance readability for people with dyslexia. Smart pens that include voice recording, text scanners, or voice-to-text functions are especially convenient to carry around for jobs that do not involve sitting in one place at a desk, although similar applications are increasingly available for smartphones as well. These software tools are constantly being improved and updated. Dyslexia associations are excellent sources of information about the latest applications and offerings.

Managers, supervisors, and peers should avoid overloading a worker with dyslexia with too many written sources of information at once. Being given extra time to review written materials is a big help, but employers can also present material in alternate formats such as video or audio books. For some types of day-to-day communications that would usually go through email, an old-fashioned phone call or in-person chat may be more efficient. When use of written communication is absolutely required it should be kept brief and to the point. Having extra spacing between lines, increasing the spacing between words, and avoiding the use of underlining and italics is helpful. Use clean and uncluttered sans serif fonts that are monospaced such as Arial, Verdana, and Comic Sans to maximize readability. Consideration can also be given to using some of the emerging specialized fonts developed specifically for dyslexic readers, although the merits of such fonts are still controversial, with some studies citing improvements in reading with their usage and others not. While some specialized fonts must be licensed for use, both Open Dyslexic and Read Regular are available for free at time of printing.

Managers and supervisors should be aware that minor changes to job descriptions may need to be a component of their accommodation strategy. Since reading-intensive tasks are highly fatiguing for workers with dyslexia, secondary aspects of the job that are reading-intensive may be reassigned if that can be achieved without undue hardship. The definition of secondary aspects of the job must be derived from a properly completed job analysis rather than gut feel to ensure their legitimacy. In addition, managers should be sensitive to the need to provide written materials well in advance if they will be read or referred to in meetings. They should also provide agendas for meetings, and they should avoid putting a worker with dyslexia in a position that will require them to read material aloud to others.

Many organizations use formal testing as part of their hiring, training, and development programs. Thus, avoiding the indirect discrimination that can occur when tests are time limited is important. Workers with dyslexia should be provided extra time to complete written tests. Some may prefer an oral test, although that will not be suitable for everyone. In addition, organizations should try to avoid relying on multiple choice tests, which often offer very similarly worded answer choices that can unduly confuse readers who have dyslexia. This is especially important when test results inform hiring and promotion decisions. Given that many people with dyslexia have the creativity, conceptualization abilities, and big picture skills to excel as senior executives, employers do not want to miss out on that talent because of poorly considered testing! When using tests as a prehire selection tool, make it very explicit and obvious that accommodations, such as extra time, are available and explain how to go about requesting and accessing them.

Understanding Other Learning Disabilities: Dyscalculia and Dysgraphia

In addition to dyslexia, there are two less commonly occurring learning disabilities called dyscalculia and dysgraphia that employers should be aware of and aim to accommodate. Dyscalculia involves difficulty grasping mathematical concepts and processing numerical information. These difficulties are not related to overall intelligence, in fact many people with this condition have above average intelligence. People with dyscalculia will generally have unusual degrees of difficulty solving arithmetic problems, even simple ones, as well as issues tracking and managing time and processing numerical information, such as budgets and statistics. For example, they may unknowingly skip numbers when reading down a column.

Given the ease of accessing calculators and the automated nature of many cash registers and related billing programs, dyscalculia might be considered less of a day-to-day issue than it was in the past, especially by people unfamiliar with the condition. While that is true to a point, it can still make working life more difficult. For example, automated cash registers will tell a person how much change is due, but not how to make that change. Similarly, a software program can calculate a list of relevant numbers, such as the degree to which you are on budget for the quarter or your remaining inventory compared to outstanding orders, but human workers still need to understand and interpret those numbers. Numerical reasoning skills are required more often in day-to-day business processes than many people realize. Time management and accurate perception of time also tend to be a struggle for people with dyscalculia.

Common accommodations for dyscalculia include technical tools such as calculators, excel spreadsheets with preloaded formulas, and pre-measured guides for tools used to cut materials. Digital clocks with alarm systems are helpful for reminding workers when to transition between activities or as a warning that the time for a task will expire soon. Calendar and agenda tools also should have built-in alarms because merely documenting what time something should occur is not sufficient to address the primary issue: misperceived time and not forgotten meetings!

Adjustments to supervisory practices that can help workers with dyscalculia include providing more time for numerical tasks, limiting the number of numerical tasks per day, reassigning secondary aspects of jobs that involve intensive numerical tasks, and providing an *audit coworker* who can verify any calculations they have made. Not blaming or shaming workers with dyscalculia for their mathematical errors is important. People with this condition can find themselves the target of mockery and bullying, especially if they are seen counting on their fingers (a frequent occurrence). The manager is responsible for stopping any such bullying. A thoughtful manager may even offer extra support for the expense submission processes, since tracking and collating expenses that the employer should reimburse, such as conference travel, travel per diems, office supplies, or client meals bought with a personal credit card, is often a daunting task for those with dyscalculia.

Workers with dysgraphia have a neurological issue that causes them to have great difficulty with handwriting. This occurs without any other cognitive or language impairments. It does not mean they are not literate. In fact, the late Agatha Christie, one of the most famous and prolific mystery novelists in the world, struggled with dysgraphia. It is thought to be caused by a complex mix of issues with fine motor control, spatial perception, and language processing. Some people with dysgraphia find the act of writing physically painful, experiencing mild to severe cramping in the hands and fingers. Individual letters tend to be poorly formed, with missing letters or words, often to the point where even the person who wrote them cannot read them. Many people with dysgraphia report struggling to think and write at the same time, which interferes with note-taking during meetings and lectures.

Accommodations for dysgraphia include allowing workers to type instead of handwrite (a very easy accommodation in most workplaces) and allowing them to leave verbal, recorded messages. Forms and tests can be provided electronically. When unavoidable, tasks that require handwriting should be spread out over time, and the individual with dysgraphia should be given extra time to complete them. In some cases, human assistance, such as a scribe, might be required to ensure legibility. In addition, note-takers or recordings can be provided when important or voluminous information is presented verbally. People with dysgraphia should also be protected from mockery or bullying related to their handwriting.

FURTHER READINGS ●——————————————

Faraone, S. V., Banaschewski, T., Coghill, D., Zheng, Y., Biederman, J., Bellgrove, M. A., Newcorn, J. H., Gignac, M., Al Saud, N. M., Manor, I., Rohde, L. A., Yang, L., Cortese, S., Almagor, D., Stein, M. A., Albatti, T. H., Aljoudi, H. F., Alqahtani, M. M. J., Asherson, P., Atwoli, L., . . . Wang, Y. (2021). The World Federation of ADHD International Consensus Statement: 208 evidence-based conclusions about the disorder. *Neuroscience & Biobehavioral Reviews, 128*, 789–818. https://doi .org/10.1016/j.neubiorev.2021.01.022

Mandavilli, A. (2015, October 19). *The lost girls.* Spectrum. https://www .spectrumnews.org/features/deep-dive/the-lost-girls/

Milton, D. E. (2012). On the ontological status of autism: The 'double empathy problem.' *Disability & Society, 27*(6), 883–887. https://doi.org /10.1080/09687599.2012.710008

REFERENCES ——————————————

ADHD Centre. (2022). *Successful people with ADHD superpowers.* https:// www.adhdcentre.co.uk/successful-people-with-adhd-superpowers/

Arky, B. (2022, September 16). *Why many autistic girls are overlooked.* Child Mind Institute. https://childmind.org/article/autistic-girls-overlooked-undiagnosed-autism/

Attention Deficit Disorder Association. (2018). *ADHD accommodations guide.* ADHD @ Work. https://adhdatwork.add.org/adhd-accommodation-guide/

Beardon, L. (2017). Autism and Asperger syndrome in adults. *Disability & Society, 32*(8), 1280–1282. https://doi.org/10.1080/09687599.2017 .1362181

Beaver, C. (2011). Designing environments for children and adults on the autism spectrum. *Good Autism Practice (GAP), 12*(1), 7–11.

Bonnello, C. (2015, April 8). *"So . . . what's it like being autistic?"* autistic-notweird. https://autisticnotweird.com/so-whats-it-like-being-autistic/

Canadian Centre for Occupational Health and Safety. (2018, August 31). *Lighting ergonomics: Light flicker.* https://www.ccohs.ca/oshanswers/ ergonomics/lighting_flicker.html

Cooper, R., & Kennady, C. (2021). Autistic voices from the workplace. *Advances in Autism, 7*(1), 73–85. https://doi.org/10.1108/AIA-09-2019-0031

Crawford, N. S. (2003, February 1). ADHD: A women's issue. *Monitor on Psychology, 34*(2). https://www.apa.org/monitor/feb03/adhd

Doyle, N. (2022, December 16). Onyinye Udokporo: Early diagnosis builds exceptional resilience for dyslexics. *Forbes.* https://www.forbes.com/sites/drnancydoyle/2022/12/16/onyinye-udokporo-early-diagnosis-builds-exceptional-resilience-for-dyslexics/?sh=1522b53157f7

iansyst Ltd. (2011, April 19). *Workplace adaptions for employees with number blindness caused by dyscalculia.* Disabled World. www.disabled-world.com/disability/types/invisible/number-blindness.php

International Dyslexia Association. (2002, November 12). *Definition of dyslexia.* https://dyslexiaida.org/definition-of-dyslexia/

International Dyslexia Association. (2020). *Accommodations for students with dyslexia.* https://dyslexiaida.org/accommodations-for-students-with-dyslexia/

Mayo Clinic. (2022, December 14). *Adult attention-deficit/hyperactivity disorder (ADHD).* https://www.mayoclinic.org/diseases-conditions/adult-adhd/symptoms-causes/syc-20350878

Murray, F. (2018, November 30). Me and monotropism: A unified theory of autism. *Psychologist.* https://www.bps.org.uk/psychologist/me-and-monotropism-unified-theory-autism

Nall, R. (2021, January 19). *The benefits of ADHD.* healthline. https://www.healthline.com/health/adhd/benefits-of-adhd

Ozgen, H., Hellemann, G. S., Stellato, R. K., Lahuis, B., van Daalen, E., Staal, W. G., Rozendal, M., Hennekam, R. C., Beemer, F. A., & van Engeland, H. (2011). Morphological features in children with autism spectrum disorders: A matched case–control study. *Journal of Autism and Developmental Disorders, 41*(1), 23–31. https://doi.org/10.1007/s10803-010-1018-7

Psychology Today. (2021, September 10). *Dysgraphia.* https://www.psychologytoday.com/ca/conditions/dysgraphia

Roland, J. (2018, December 7). *What is dysgraphia?* healthline. https://www.healthline.com/health/what-is-dysgraphia

Rong, Y., Yang, C. J., Jin, Y., & Wang, Y. (2021). Prevalence of attention-deficit/hyperactivity disorder in individuals with autism spectrum disorder: A meta-analysis. *Research in Autism Spectrum Disorders, 83,* 101759. https://doi.org/10.1016/j.rasd.2021.101759

Shaywitz, S., & Shaywitz, J. (2020). *Overcoming dyslexia: Second edition, completely revised and updated.* Vintage Books.

Siegel, L. S. (1988). Agatha Christie's learning disability. *Canadian Psychology / Psychologie Canadienne, 29*(2), 213–216. https://doi.org/10.1037/h0084531

Singh, M. (2022, February 17). *Best and worst fonts for dyslexia.* Number Dyslexia. https://numberdyslexia.com/best-and-worst-fonts-for-dyslexia/

Yale Center for Dyslexia and Creativity. (2022a). *Signs of dyslexia.* https://dyslexia.yale.edu/dyslexia/signs-of-dyslexia

Yale Center for Dyslexia and Creativity. (2022b). *What is dyslexia?* https://www.dyslexia.yale.edu/

Yokell, C. (2023). *Attention deficit hyperactivity disorder: Lived experiences of adults diagnosed with ADHD* [Doctoral dissertation, Nova Southeastern University]. https://nsuworks.nova.edu/cgi/viewcontent.cgi?article=1426&context=fse_etd

6

Psychiatric, Mental, and Developmental Disabilities

Psychiatric and mental conditions that may require accommodation in the workplace include schizophrenia, mood disorders, schizoaffective disorder, anxiety, and obsessive-compulsive disorder (OCD). In addition, there are several developmental disabilities, such as Down syndrome and fetal alcohol spectrum disorders (FASDs), that have an impact on mental functioning. Memory impairments affect some workers. There are also traumatic brain injuries, which can alter cognitive and emotional functioning. (Addictions are also considered a psychiatric disability; however, addictions are addressed in Chapter 7, which focuses on episodic and intermittent disabilities.)

Recognizing that, except for developmental disabilities and some traumatic brain injuries, psychiatric conditions are treatable much (but not all) of the time is important. When controlled with medication, many people become asymptomatic or have significantly reduced symptoms such that functional limitations are minimized. Most psychiatric medications, however, have side effects. Accommodations may therefore be required for the medical conditions themselves or for side effects related to medication regimes.

Some of these disabilities, most notably schizophrenia and developmental disabilities, are ones for which sheltered workshop employment opportunities are sometimes created. These segregated employment settings can be controversial. Excellent, evidence-based programs that enhance independence and well-being, and provide meaningful skill acquisition, sometimes find their reputations blighted by poorly implemented programs or programs that offer substandard and exploitative wages and working conditions with little meaningful benefit for participants. Such programs are beyond the scope of this book, which focuses on inclusive, integrated workplaces that employ people with disabilities at market rates. Sheltered workshops should not be confused with supported employment, which places people with disabilities in integrated employment contexts with additional support structures. Readers interested in sheltered workshop programs and their outcomes are directed to the further readings list at the end of the chapter.

There are many myths and stereotypes about psychiatric conditions, which tend to be poorly understood and even feared by the general population. As a result, people with mental illnesses experience disproportionate employment challenges even when compared to other members of the disability community. For example, a 2011 study by S. An, Richard T. Roessler, and Brian T. McMahon found that the unemployment rate among persons with psychiatric disabilities was between 75% and 90% in the United States, 81% in the United Kingdom, 79%–84% in Australia, and 95% in Japan, which represents the highest rates of unemployment for people with any type of disability. A more recent government study conducted in 2017 in Canada found that the employment rate for people with mental impairments was only 46% compared to 80% for those without mental impairments. A 2021 government study out of the United Kingdom demonstrated that, among all disabilities, mental illness had the third strongest association with unemployment after severe learning difficulties and autism (Sparkles et al., 2022). It has been well documented in the academic literature that finding and maintaining employment can be a substantial challenge for people with psychiatric impairments due to a combination of discrimination, stereotyping, systemic skill discounting, lack of awareness of accommodation practices, and lack of access to accommodations. To have better outcomes, first gaining a greater understanding of the nature of these conditions is important.

Schizophrenia, Mood Disorders, and Schizoaffective Disorder

Schizophrenia, schizoaffective disorder, and mood disorders are all psychiatric conditions that tend to emerge in late adolescence and early adulthood. As such, younger employees may experience their initial symptoms while working, or they may come to the employer with a diagnosis established. In either case accommodations may be required. Providing managers with basic education about these conditions, their symptoms, and emergence patterns can be helpful. This might help them recognize when an employee's change in behavior could be a sign of a treatable medical condition that the employee can seek help for. While managers should never attempt to diagnose an employee, they may be able to recognize when a referral to appropriate medical personnel, medical benefits, and other employer-sponsored supports is warranted.

Schizophrenia

Schizophrenia is defined by the Mayo Clinic as "a serious mental disorder in which people interpret reality abnormally. Schizophrenia may result in some combination of hallucinations, delusions, and extremely disordered thinking and behavior that impairs daily functioning." This may include visual hallucinations, hearing voices in one's head, disorganized speech that seems nonsensical to outside observers, unpredictable agitation, behaving in a childlike manner, social withdrawal, and problems with personal hygiene and self-care. Difficulties in reading and responding appropriately to social cues and an inability to engage in social problem solving are common.

Heightened creativity is also common, and people with schizophrenia have contributed important scientific insights and works of art. For example, John Nash invented game theory, winning the Nobel Prize in Economics in 1994. Jack Kerouac authored several famous and well-loved books and poems and is remembered as a pioneer of the Beat Generation. Tom Harrell made many contributions to jazz, while Rufus May, who is both a clinical psychologist and person with schizophrenia, has contributed to improving institutional treatment for mental illness.

Schizophrenia typically emerges for the first time between the ages of 15–25 for men and 20–30 for women, meaning there may be people in the workforce who show early signs, such as odd behavior and unexplained declines in productivity, without realizing they have schizophrenia until their symptoms worsen. While these symptoms can be severe, recognizing that schizophrenia can often be controlled with medication is important. People who have regular access to appropriate medication may not experience any disabling symptoms, although the medication itself can have some side effects that require accommodation.

Schizophrenia is frequently portrayed in movies and television as being associated with extreme violence, and the degree to which this risk is exaggerated makes inclusion and acceptance much harder to achieve. In fact, an 18-monthlong study of 1,435 patients with schizophrenia that was conducted by Buchanan et al. (2019) found that only 5.4% engaged in "injurious violence" during that time (a number only slightly higher than what would be anticipated in the general population), and that the people engaging in such violence were not taking their needed medication. Furthermore, a meta-analysis of 20 studies involving 18,423 patients with schizophrenia that was conducted by Fazel et al. found that having an addiction as a comorbidity was much more predictive of violence than psychosis itself. The rates of violence were similar for substance abusers with and without schizophrenia, and many instances of violence were associated with drug seeking.

Mood Disorders

Mood disorders come in three main subtypes: depression, dysthymia, and bipolar disorder. Mood disorders have an underlying biological cause related to genetics and brain chemistry and cannot be controlled with willpower or strength of character. Medications are often but not always effective in treating mood disorders, although it can take some trial and error working with a physician to find the correct medication and the correct dose. Therapy and healthy lifestyle changes such as enhanced nutrition and getting regular exercise are generally also part of the treatment plan, and in some mild cases of depression and dysthymia, exercise alone has proven to have significant therapeutic value. Note that the term *depression* is used in the clinical rather than colloquial sense, as such one would have to meet the diagnostic criteria found in the *DSM-5*, the most recent version of the formal psychiatric diagnostic criteria that is approved by medical associations, to be diagnosed. It is not simply being *down* or *blue* for a few days. Being sad for a clear reason such as a recent death in the family would not qualify as clinical depression.

Depression is typified by symptoms such as the following, which occur for a period greater than 2 weeks:

- Persistent feelings of hopeless, emptiness, and sadness

- Loss of interest and pleasure in daily activities

- Unexplained weight loss or gain

- Insomnia or hypersomnia (sleeping all the time)

- Fatigue

- Difficulties with concentration

- Consistent physical restlessness or very slow movements

- Having thoughts of suicide, attempting suicide

Dysthymia is similar to depression, except that the symptoms are milder. It is often termed *depression light*, although this characterization significantly understates the day-to-day impact on individuals. Symptoms tend to be more consistent and persistent, sometimes lasting for years.

People with dysthymia often experience symptoms that impair their daily functioning without it reaching a severity threshold that leads to appropriate diagnosis and support. As such, it may negatively impact productivity to a greater degree than more evident cases of depression because the subtlety of the symptoms interferes with diagnosis and the associated realization required for self-care.

Bipolar disorder combines the symptoms of depression with manic phases. Individuals may experience either an elevated or depressed mood for long periods of time or they may cycle rapidly back and forth between the two. Both clinical depression and bipolar disorder tend to first emerge in the late teens and early twenties, so some people may experience symptoms and go through the diagnostic process for the first time while working. For some, it will require experimentation to find the best prescription for their particular symptoms and neurobiology, and taking many months to identify the best medication regime is not unusual. The manic phases of bipolar disorder are typified by the following:

- Elevated mood (this may present as being extremely excitable, happy, and expansive, or it may present as heightened irritation)

- Inflated self-esteem

- Reduced need for sleep

- Extreme talkativeness

- Racing thoughts

- Being easily distracted

- Physical restlessness

- Increased participation in risky or inappropriate behaviors such as reckless spending, hyper sexuality, driving at excessive speeds, or dangerous forms of thrill-seeking

Schizoaffective Disorder

Schizoaffective disorder is marked by a combination of schizophrenia symptoms, such as hallucinations or delusions, and mood disorder symptoms, such as depression or mania. Outcomes and the combination of symptoms experienced are highly individual; for example, some only experience depressive episodes while others experience mania as well.

Functional Limitations Associated With Schizophrenia, Mood Disorders, and Schizoaffective Disorder

The functional limitations associated with psychiatric disabilities are more multifaceted than those associated with most physical disabilities. Limitations can take many different forms, including emotional, social, cognitive, and physical. The limitations experienced will vary significantly from individual to individual, even when they have the same diagnosis. Symptoms may also come and go at unpredictable intervals when people are not being appropriately treated with medications, or during the therapeutic period in which medication effectiveness and appropriate dosing levels are being established. Many workers with these conditions are not fully aware of their accommodation needs until they begin working. Employer flexibility and a willingness to revisit accommodation strategies as necessary are therefore very important for long-term success.

Emotional limitations are part of the diagnostic criteria for psychiatric conditions such as schizophrenia, schizoaffective disorder, depression, and bipolar disorder. People with these disorders may sometimes have difficulty identifying and understanding their own emotions as well as the emotions of others. They may also have trouble regulating their emotional responses, especially workers who have been diagnosed with a mood disorder and have not yet had their medication(s) stabilized. These emotional limitations interact with other issues commonly associated with mental illness, such as poor self-esteem and low confidence. This combination of traits can impair social functioning. For example, problems interpreting social cues could lead to difficulties with conflict resolution, communication, and engaging in the types of impression management behaviors needed during job interviews to acquire a job in the first place. One of the difficulties associated with these emotional limitations is the degree to which other people interpret deliberate (and usually negative) intent to the worker's emotional presentation. For example, a worker with depression may be told to "just snap out of it" because they are "bringing everyone down," when they can neither control their own mood nor fully understand or control the impact that their expression of mood has on those around them. This is akin to asking a person who is a wheelchair user to "just snap out of it and walk up the stairs."

People experiencing severe depression or persistent dysthymia are often exhausted by the challenges of day-to-day life. These conditions exacerbate stress, leading to burnout. One of the key symptoms of burnout is depersonalization, which means treating people as objects and failing to empathize with them. As a result, the preexisting underlying difficulties in regulating emotional response may be magnified by burnout, resulting in workers who appear unconcerned with those around them but who are actually just so overwhelmed that it impairs their expressions of empathy. Blaming such workers for their burnout rather than providing support is common, which magnifies the problem.

Cognitive limitations are also frequently encountered among those with psychiatric conditions, including problems with focus, sequencing, memory, and decision-making. Cognitive impairments are more strongly associated with schizophrenia and schizoaffective disorder than with mood disorders, although any of these conditions can impair concentration and memory.

Some physical limitations experienced by people with these disorders are due to symptoms of the underlying illness, such as the fatigue that is often associated with depression and dysthymia or the inability to sit still associated with manic phases of bipolar disorder. More often, however, physical symptoms occur because of side effects associated with psychiatric medications. These side effects can include dry mouth, difficulty staying hydrated, frequent urination, lack of energy, difficulty getting up in the morning, restlessness, sensitivity to bright lights, and pseudoparkinson-ism, which causes tremors that can interfere with fine motor skills.

Accommodations for Workers With Schizophrenia, Mood Disorders, and Schizoaffective Disorder

Accommodations for workers with schizophrenia, mood disorders, and schizoaffective disorder are highly individual and may change over time as work tasks evolve or as medication regimes are stabilized. The broad categories of accommodation that should be considered include flexible scheduling, human support, cognitive support, supervisory style adjustments, policy and social environment interventions, and physical supports that address medication side effects.

Flexible scheduling helps address a variety of the functional limitations of workers with psychiatric disabilities by promoting better work-life balance and lessening overall stress levels. This is especially relevant because stress can exacerbate symptoms of psychiatric illness. Flexible scheduling also enables ongoing contact with healthcare professionals in case getting an appointment during standard working hours is easier. This increases the likelihood that any issues with medication or emerging symptoms can be quickly addressed. Because focus and concentration can be a challenge, some people with psychiatric conditions prefer to work at nontraditional times when fewer coworkers are present and commutes are less stressful.

One study about accommodation needs, conducted by Clifton M. Chow and Benjamin Cichocki (2015) involved 370 workers with psychiatric disabilities. They found that among 804 accommodations requested, fully 37.5% of them related to flexible scheduling, showing a clear need that can be easily addressed and be cost effective for employers. When flexible scheduling is combined with paid sick days that can be used for mental health days rather than only for physical illnesses, the benefits are magnified because the ability to engage in self-care and stress reduction as needed is heightened.

Social behavior can be bewildering for some people with psychiatric disabilities, yet the correct interpretation of social behavior is often critical to successful integration into the workplace. A professional workplace coach can provide advice on a range of behaviors that support success in the workplace, including communication, task prioritization, providing and receiving feedback, managing stress, and reading social cues. The study by Chow and Cichocki found that 35.6% of accommodation requests made to employers related to the need for direct human support. Job coaches provided the most benefits when employees were permitted to contact them on an as-needed basis, including during work hours. When workers with psychiatric disabilities did not have access to an outside coach, then providing an internal mentor was useful, although the degree to which that was true varied based on the training of the mentor.

Direct coaching is one form of human support. Another, more nebulous, form of support involves the social environment. Since psychiatric disabilities are invisible, coworkers underestimating or being unaware their impacts is common. For example, people with depression may be erroneously told that their mood disorder is a character flaw that they could control with sufficient willpower or moral fortitude. Alternately, people who have experienced mild negative moods on occasion may fail to grasp the difference between their experiences and clinical forms of depression and dysthymia, resulting in unhelpful and unsolicited advice that is perceived as both intrusive and dismissive. Training coworkers so they have a basic understanding of mental illness (without identifying any individual employees with such conditions) is therefore important in ensuring helpful and respectful peer attitudes.

Cognitive impairments related to decision making, memory, and prioritization occur in some workers with psychiatric disabilities, particularly schizophrenia and schizoaffective disorder. Many workers do not know this is a problem for them until after they arrive in the workplace, highlighting the need for accommodation to be an ongoing rather than a one-and-done process. The following practices are commonly requested as accommodations, and they are completely free:

- Providing written rather than verbal instructions

- Breaking down large work assignments into smaller tasks

- Assistance with prioritization of tasks

- Clear performance expectations

- The ability to self-monitor performance levels or receive clear and timely performance feedback

Negative affect is a common challenge for people with psychiatric diagnoses, especially those with mood disorders. Emotion can be contagious, and more positive emotions can be caught from others under the right circumstances. (Although, this will not always hold true for people who have depression.) Similarly, negative emotions or negative energy radiating from others may make existing levels of depression and anxiety worse. Supervisory practices that focus on creating a supportive and positive environment are helpful for maintaining a heightened level of affect (i.e., positive energy) in the workplace overall such that emotional contagion works for and not against the organization. For example, a survey conducted by Granger et al. (1997) found that among 194 job coaches who worked with psychiatric clients, the use of positive feedback-based supervision was identified as the third most frequently requested accommodation. Even more compelling, among workers with psychiatric impairments, positive supervision has been demonstrated to result in higher rates of job retention (Huff et al., 2008). Many people are unsure what is meant by *positive supervision*; however, it is remarkably easy to implement. Examples of behaviors that qualify include the following:

- Knowing individual workers by name and having some interest in what is going on in their lives beyond work

- Noticing and demonstrating concern for their personal well-being when individuals appear to be struggling or stressed

- Noticing, acknowledging, and celebrating strengths, accomplishments, and achievements of employees in addition to providing corrective feedback

- Willingness to adjust work pace and workspaces as needed and acknowledge individual needs.

In addition to positive supervision, support for healthy lifestyles and work-life balance can also help diminish symptoms, particularly those associated with mood disorders. Basics such as access to sunlight, good nutrition, exercise, and adequate sleep make a big difference. Employers have some control over these variables through office and workspace design, such as access to sunlight; flexible scheduling and attentiveness to shift implications, such as not scheduling someone for the late evening shift followed immediately by a morning shift the next day, or not changing shift schedules from day to night overly frequently; and providing sufficient breaks to ensure people are able to eat regularly, perhaps providing healthy snacks such as fruits and vegetables. In addition, employers can encourage regular exercise by providing onsite facilities or free gym and sport memberships, starting lunchtime walking or yoga clubs, offering direct financial support for fitness equipment and activities, and similar initiatives. While many of these things fall outside the expected and reasonable accommodations, they add value and can improve working conditions and lessen disability-related symptoms for employees with psychiatric disabilities, and all other employees as well.

The stigmatization that often accompanies psychiatric diagnoses can create attitudinal barriers between workers with these conditions and their coworkers. While maintaining appropriate privacy is important, there are circumstances under which a worker's medical condition could become known to colleagues, most notably voluntary disclosure. Providing anti-stigmatization information to all employees as part of standard diversity training efforts can be helpful. Some people with psychiatric disabilities, particularly those who have had bad experiences in the past, prefer to protect themselves from stereotyping by avoiding unnecessary contact with coworkers altogether. Empirical data suggests that permitting this sort of avoidance is negatively associated with job retention over the medium- and long-term. Support and understanding from coworkers, by contrast, is positively associated with job retention. Whenever possible, educating other employees to lessen bias and maximize inclusion, rather than solve and perpetuate the problem through avoidance, is more practical, ethical, and productive. But increased social contact should not be forced, merely encouraged and supported.

Physical side effects of psychiatric disorders, particularly mood disorders, can include fatigue or its opposite: excessive, distracting high energy levels and agitation. Flexible scheduling and work-from-home options can help with fatigue. Paid sick days that can be used for mental health reasons are also helpful. For those with high (manic) energy levels, access to physical outlets for their energy may be required. This can take many forms, from allowing someone to pace discretely at the back of a room during a meeting to offering more frequent breaks and access to a safe outdoor space.

Many commonly prescribed psychiatric medications have noticeable side effects that demand attention. Dry mouth and problems staying hydrated are among the most common, so allowing water at workstations when it is otherwise not permitted is important, barring any significant safety concerns. Policies that limit restroom breaks are not only intrusive for everyone but may be especially problematic for employees dealing with a medication-induced need for frequent urination. Extreme sensitivity to bright lights may necessitate a change in lighting, while hand tremors may require devices to assist with fine motor control. Chronic fatigue may require some concessions in the work pace in addition to flexible scheduling. Finally, some medications that need to be taken during the day are temperature sensitive, so a small private fridge can ensure that colleagues do not inadvertently see personal prescriptions.

Transportation to work can also be a challenge for workers with psychiatric impairments because some (though, not all) are not eligible for driver's licenses due to symptoms associated with their illness or side effects of their medications. Taking public transportation also presents unpredictable social and emotional challenges, so some workers may request transportation assistance. This request falls into a gray area, legally speaking, because transportation to work is not considered an employer responsibility in most jurisdictions. For example, in the United States, courts and tribunals have generally concluded that employers are not responsible for transportation, while in many Canadian communities, transportation for people with disabilities is considered a municipal responsibility, albeit with widely varying levels of service. While the responsibility for transportation may not legally fall to the employer, it would still be beneficial to provide solutions whenever possible, which may include direct (that is, incentivized) encouragement of employee carpooling or another creative solution.

Anxiety and Obsessive-Compulsive Disorder

Everyone experiences anxiety sometimes, and everyone has certain thoughts that emerge repetitively, causing distraction. People with clinical anxiety or OCD experience these things long term, to a degree that impairs day-to-day functioning. These conditions are treatable with medication and therapy. Managers can help these workers address their limitations through accommodations, while also leveraging their strengths.

Anxiety Disorders

Anxiety disorders occur when someone experiences intense, excessive, and persistent worry and fear in everyday situations. Although we all experience anxiety some of the time, to qualify as a disorder the anxiety must be long-lasting, be difficult to control, interfere with daily activities, and be disconnected from the actual level of threat in the environment. Anxiety can take many different forms, and people may experience some of or all the following symptoms:

- Feeling nervous, restless, or tense much of the time

- Feeling a sense of impending doom

- Excessive worrying, combined with an inability to control worrying

- Difficulties concentrating

- Avoidance of anxiety triggers, including people and places

- Selective mutism, that is, people with anxiety may occasionally and involuntarily lose the ability to speak

- Physical symptoms such as increased heart rate and breathing, excessive sweating, uncontrollable trembling, feeling weak and tired, and problems with sleep and appetite

(Selective mutism is discussed in more detail in Chapter 5 in the section on autism.)

For people with what is referred to as *generalized anxiety*, the symptoms are broad based, occurring in varied circumstances and settings. Others have more specific forms. For example, people with social anxiety experience symptoms when anticipating or engaging in social interaction. Their anxieties focus on fears about being embarrassed, viewed negatively, or judged by others. People with agoraphobia, by contrast, fear being in situations in which escape may be difficult or help unavailable. In extreme cases, some patients with agoraphobia are confined to their homes because of this fear. Phobias, such as an intensive and irrational fear of spiders, are also a form of anxiety disorder. Given the variation in symptoms and functional limitations that occur, tailoring accommodations strategies for the individual is especially important.

Some people with anxiety disorders experience panic attacks. While any person may suffer a panic attack, panic disorder is a form of anxiety in which panic attacks are the central and defining symptom. Panic attacks have sudden and unpredictable onsets that are not necessarily related to what is happening in the immediate vicinity. Many times, panic attacks do not have any clear external cause or trigger. The person having the panic attack experiences intensive fear, as if a dire threat were present, and a sense of doom. These feeling are accompanied by a physiological stress response that includes sweating and chills, shaking, a pounding heart, difficulty breathing, and head and chest pain. Sufferers often report that panic attacks feel like a heart attack, or like they are about to die. The primary symptoms generally only last 5–10 minutes, although the lingering physical and psychological aftereffects can last much longer. Panic attacks, although not physically dangerous under normal circumstances, should be treated as medical crises that require an immediate response.

Obsessive-Compulsive Disorder

OCD is a form of anxiety disorder that results in repeated, intrusive, unwanted thoughts that cause anxiety (the *obsessions* part of OCD) and the urge to engage in certain repetitive behaviors (the *compulsions* part of OCD). The obsessions and compulsions are usually interrelated, although a small portion of affected people only experience one or the other. For example, someone may demonstrate unusual levels of concern about germs and touching objects others have touched since they are afraid of being contaminated. They may therefore wash their hands dozens of times a day for seemingly little reason, or they may engage in elaborate cleansing or safety rituals before and after taking part in shared activities. For other people with OCD, the way in which objects are organized may become a point of obsession, with a compulsive need to have items arranged in a particular (usually symmetrical) order. Engaging in the compulsive behavior helps resolve the anxiety that was generated by the obsessive thoughts. However, this relief is temporary because the cycle then begins anew, with the thoughts reappearing. Since the compulsive behavior is an anxiety-relieving device, any interference with it can cause significant mental distress. OCD-related behaviors are not rational, cognition-driven responses, but rather they are emotion-driven. Rational approaches to stopping the behavior (e.g., generating objective evidence that an item is sterile and could not possibly contaminate anyone) are therefore singularly ineffective and unhelpful.

Many people experience intrusive thoughts sometimes. For example, one might leave the house and wonder if they remembered to turn off the stove or lock the door. Many people also engage in repetitive rituals, including ritually double- and even triple-checking stoves and doors, to comfort themselves. Diagnostically, to be qualified as OCD, those thoughts and behaviors would need to take up at least an hour of time each day, be beyond the control of the person engaging them, and they must interfere with work, school, or other aspects of daily life. They must also not be done for pleasure or enjoyment. OCD is treatable, and there are several medications on the market that are commonly prescribed to help people manage or even break the cycle of intrusive thoughts, anxiety, and unwelcome compulsive behavior.

Functional Limitations and Accommodations Associated With Anxiety and OCD

Anxiety and OCD have negative impacts on stress tolerance, focus, concentration, memory, ability to manage distractions and meet deadlines, and social functioning. These conditions often result in overall higher levels of fatigue and irritability, which is partially a biochemical response to the excessive levels of cortisol (the stress hormone) that are released when people experience anxiety. Many people with anxiety and OCD are perfectionists and their need to perform perfectly can contribute to excessive stress and further anxiety, creating a self-reinforcing negative spiral. It can also prevent them from moving from one task to another because they may be unwilling to leave a task until it is perfect, which can be functional or nonfunctional for the organization depending on the nature of the tasks in question.

Common accommodations for anxiety and OCD include stress-reducers such as flexible scheduling, the ability to work from home as needed, positive supervisory practices, peer understanding (through training), and support for healthy lifestyles and work–life balance. In addition, providing written instructions about tasks, policies, and procedures can be helpful because anxiety interferes with information processing and memory. Extra help with time management may be required, either in the form of coaching or by providing supports such as alarms and electronic reminders, day planners, and other standard time management tools. A quiet space to calm oneself when experiencing extreme anxiety, such as a designated room with comfortable couches that is painted in soothing colors, can also make self-regulation of symptoms easier.

Certain social and communication practices can also make the workplace more accessible for workers with anxiety and OCD. For example, some people with social anxiety or phobias about public speaking may need to be excused from doing presentations in front of large groups, and instead they can provide needed information in written or video formats. Similarly, in important group meetings there should be an option to ask questions via text or in another written format that does not require the worker to speak in front of the entire group. For more generalized forms of anxiety, providing reassurance to help mitigate excessive self-doubt and providing feedback about when something is good enough and the person should move on to another task can be helpful. The tendency toward perfectionism can lead to individuals becoming intensely focused on very narrow issues that are of minor importance or are unimportant. A pre-planned, subtle visual signal can be helpful for letting them know that they need to move on from a point in a meeting, perhaps to pick it up again later in a different setting or with different people. As another social concession, some of the rituals that comfort people with OCD are completely harmless to both themselves and others. For example, needing to ritualistically check that a door is locked four times over does not interfere with work activities. Coworkers should be actively discouraged from interrupting these harmless personal rituals and, of course, should refrain from teasing, bullying, or harassing the individual engaging in them.

Importantly, coworkers should be trained on how to identify and respond to a panic attack. Some interventions recommended by healthcare professionals include remaining calm (because agitated people can negatively impact the individual suffering from a panic attack), and validating their distress by actively and empathetically listening to their feelings and perspectives. Some people experiencing a panic attack fear being judged or perceived negatively for getting distressed without the presence of an overt threat, which is often a significant additional stressor in and of itself. Providing reassurance by telling the person they are safe, assuring them that nobody is judging them, and letting them know you will not leave is helpful (although, do ask them if they would prefer you to leave). Remind them that the most intense symptoms of panic attacks generally do not last more than about 5 minutes to 10 minutes. Remind them to breath, and slow your own breathing to encourage mirroring, and perhaps engage in light conversation (unless they do not want to). Use techniques that help ground people in the present such as physical touch, like a comforting arm around a shoulder, but only after asking if doing so is okay. Some people will not want to be touched during a panic attack. Giving the person a textured object to handle may also help the panic attack subside, as well as encouraging repetition of soothing or helpful phrases such as "this cannot hurt me." Avoid dismissively comparing normal stress and fear to panic attacks, shaming or blaming the person for their response, minimizing their experience by saying things like, "It's not really that bad," and giving advice (other than a reminder to breathe). Also, do not take comments made mid-attack personally because people are not rational when experiencing a panic attack, but rather they are experiencing an intensive fight-or-flight response and may say and feel things they would not normally say or feel.

Respect for after-attack care is essential because panic attacks are mentally and physiologically exhausting and most people will require some recovery time even after the primary symptoms go away.

Developmental Delays, Intellectual Disabilities, Memory Impairments, and Brain Injuries

In the past, developmental delays and intellectual disabilities were sometimes referred to as *mental retardation* within the medical community. This term is no longer in favor due to toxic evolutions in the colloquial usage of the word. The term *retardation* and all variations are now considered slurs and should not be used in respectful conversations.

There are many forms of developmental delay and intellectual disability, and many different genetic or epigenetic conditions that can cause it. Covering every form of developmental delay is beyond the scope of this book, but two of the most impactful forms (as measured by percentage of the population affected) are examined here as representatives of the type. Those two conditions are Down syndrome and fetal alcohol spectrum disorder (FASD). When accommodating workers with any form of developmental delay, including those not explicitly mentioned here, collect information about their individual symptoms and needs to arrive at useful accommodation strategies. Making assumptions is likely to lead to a biased perspective because underestimating the abilities of people with intellectual disabilities in the workplace is common, a fact that has been verified in academic studies and through self-reports of individual job seekers (e.g., Hewitt, 2022).

Understanding and Accommodating People With Down Syndrome

Down syndrome is a genetic developmental disorder caused by the existence of an extra chromosome. Chromosomes carry genetic information, and typically each cell in the human body contains 23 chromosomes. However, people who are born with Down syndrome have an extra copy (either partial or complete) of chromosome number 21. Down syndrome impacts intellectual functioning, meaning that people with Down syndrome may process information more slowly and have some executive functioning limitations. (For a detailed definition and discussion of executive functioning, refer to the section on autism in Chapter 5.) Short-term memory may also be impacted, particularly for information that is presented verbally. The degree of intellectual impairment varies from individual to individual and generally ranges from mild to moderate. Despite myths to the contrary, many people with Down syndrome are literate and able to fully participate in educational and training opportunities. AnnaRose Rubright, who has Down syndrome, is one such example. She was profiled in *Forbes* magazine after graduating with a bachelor's degree from Rowan University in New Jersey in May 2020. Similarly, Dylan Kuehl, who also has Down syndrome, graduated from Evergreen State College in Washington with a bachelor of arts degree in 2022.

Down syndrome also impacts adaptive behaviors, meaning everyday social and practical skills such as interpersonal relations and communication, social problem solving, time management, daily personal care, and safety management. Down syndrome affects physical development as well, and people with the condition have distinctive facial features that often make their condition immediately recognizable. They also tend to have poor muscle tone, shorter than average stature, and an increased risk of (often treatable) congenital heart defects.

Since people with Down syndrome tend to process information more slowly, there are several accommodations that can help maximize communication effectiveness. They may require extra time and repetition when training. Supervisors and colleagues should make sure that they give instructions in a quiet environment that is free from distractions. Speak slowly with frequent pauses, using clear short sentences while avoiding unnecessarily complex vocabulary. Ask the worker to paraphrase back instructions to ensure understanding and allow extra time for them to formulate questions. Since short-term memory for verbal information is sometimes impacted, supervisors could also consider providing recorded or written directions (using simple language and sentence structure in the written content) or visual prompts to help remember needed tasks. For the subset of people with Down syndrome who may struggle with literacy, color coding is often a useful solution to act as a reminder to complete certain tasks. Text readers can also be helpful. Form generating software that directs people to fill in the blanks, word prediction and completion software, and human assistance with proofreading and copyediting can help those with partial literacy or lower literacy who need to complete written tasks.

Challenges with adaptive behaviors can be accommodated with a variety of methods depending on the nature of the individual's limitations. Issues with communication and social problem solving can be ameliorated with an appropriately trained coach or, in some settings, peer assistance. (Peers should receive appropriate training, too.) Time management can be buttressed through standard techniques such as increased use of day planners, formal reminders, and alarms that indicate when to switch tasks. Safety management may require special attention, especially when the individual's job puts them in regular contact with clients or the public. People with Down syndrome are often quite trusting, which makes them vulnerable to various forms of exploitation and ill treatment. They may need more explicit warnings and action scripts than other employees to help them recognize and address customer behaviors that are not acceptable, such as sexual harassment or the varied subterfuges commonly used to obtain illegitimate, inappropriate discounts or free items.

Workers with Down syndrome and other intellectual disabilities sometimes work in a supported employment setting. Supported employment refers to work in the community that is formally supported on an ongoing basis by an agency or coach that is external to the employer and provides the service professionally. These agencies or coaches act as guides and mediators between the worker and the employer as required. They help direct the employer in appropriate accommodation practice as well as directly support the worker, and as such they are often used by small and midsize companies who lack in-house HR expertise in this area. Generally, these programs receive some form of government funding and are operating by not-for-profit agencies, although some are supported by fees paid by the employer. Supported employment is a good option for workers who require more ongoing support, but it is not required to have a successful employment relationship. Many workers with Down syndrome can acquire and keep their jobs in competitive labor markets without participating in formal supportive employment programs, so, as always, individual needs should be considered.

Understanding and Accommodating People With Fetal Alcohol Spectrum Disorders (FASDs)

FASDs are permanent brain injuries caused by exposure to alcohol while in the womb. They are considered developmental disorders with physical, cognitive, intellectual, emotional, and behavioral impacts. In North America, it is one of the leading causes of preventable developmental delay. Severity levels and symptoms vary considerably from one individual to the next and required accommodations will therefore also vary considerably.

Symptoms potentially associated with FASDs include deformities of the limbs and fingers, vision and hearing issues, restlessness or hyper-activity, poor coordination and balance, and heart and kidney problems. People with FASDs often have intellectual disability, including some or all of the following: low IQ; learning disabilities; poor memory; problems with attention, focus, and information processing; and difficulties with reasoning and problem solving. They may have trouble switching between tasks and adapting to change, combined with issues with time perception. They may display poor judgment, lowered impulse control, poor social skills, or have difficulty identifying the consequences of their actions. Their moods may change rapidly.

FASDs are commonly divided into four subtypes.

- Fetal alcohol syndrome (FAS): This represents the end of the continuum with the broadest degree of involvement (i.e., there are physical, cognitive, intellectual, emotional, and behavioral symptoms). People with FAS may struggle with learning, attention span, memory, communication, social skills, vision, and hearing.

- Alcohol-related neurodevelopmental disorder (ARND): This variation is typified by intellectual and learning disabilities and is often accompanied by poor impulse control.

- Alcohol-related birth defects (ARBD): People with this variation experience only physical symptoms such as problems with their heart, kidneys, bones, or hearing.

- Neurobehavioral disorder associated with prenatal alcohol exposure (ND-PAE): This variation is typified by difficulties with cognition, behavior, and life skills. It generally presents as having problems with planning and memory, behavioral problems such as severe tantrums or mood instability, and trouble completing the tasks required for daily living such as personal hygiene, dressing appropriately for the weather and social setting, and self-care.

Given the wide range of symptoms associated with FASDs, there are a wide array of potential functional limitations and accommodations.

For example, people with hearing impairments generally require online meeting tools with closed captioning to fully participate in remote meetings. They may need either sign language interpreters or social concessions that enable lip reading, such as remembering to face the person who is Deaf when speaking, for in-person meetings. Supervisors may be required to deliver written rather than verbal task instructions, and safety alarms need to be perceptible, with visual as well as auditory signals. People with sight impairments may require text-to-voice software to access work documents, and they may need hallways and other thoroughfares to be kept uncluttered and barrier free. And people with limb differences may require specialized hand tools, carts to help carry objects, or custom-made personal protective equipment. These are only the most obvious accommodations, and a more thorough discussion of accommodations for sight and hearing impairments and limb differences appears in Chapter 4.

Problems with attention, focus, time management, and information processing can require accommodations such as quiet, distraction-free workspaces, extra time to complete tasks, help prioritizing tasks, very clear step-by-step written instructions for complex processes, and technological tools for time management, such as electronic calendars with reminders. Social limitations may require peer support and understanding, an adjustment in expectations for nonwork-related levels of casual peer interaction, or even a job coach to help navigate and interpret unstated social and political workplace expectations. People with learning disabilities may require information presented in an alternate format, for example video as opposed to text-based training materials, or they may require more time to fully learn new processes. These accommodations for attention, focus, information processing, social limitations, and learning disabilities are just the beginning. Chapter 5 provides more in-depth information about each subtype of disability and appropriate interventions.

People who struggle with mood instability and problems with emotional self-regulation may benefit from the introduction of positive supervisory practices, flextime, and work-from-home options. Peer understanding and attentiveness to the physical environment, such as the color of paint used on the walls, can also have positive impacts. (For more information on accommodations for mood disorders, refer to the earlier content in this chapter. Also, Chapter 8 more fully discusses the psychological impact of interior design.)

Finally, intellectual disabilities can be accommodated through modification of training strategies—often involving more repetition and hands-on practice—using simple language and pictures or graphics for written instructions, providing tools like calculators and spellcheckers, simplifying needed forms, and providing templates for forms that actively prompt the person to complete them properly. (For more accommodation suggestions for intellectual disabilities, refer to the earlier content found in this chapter under Down syndrome.)

Memory Impairments, Brain Injuries, and Concussions

There are a very wide range of conditions that cause memory impairments. Covering all of them is beyond the scope of this book, but the accommodations used for memory impairment are similar regardless of the cause. These accommodations include regular training refreshers, written policy and procedure manuals that are searchable by keyword, applications and alarms specifically designed to act as a reminder, use of personal organizers, recorded or written directions, visual prompts to complete tasks (such as Post-it notes), and having a support person who checks in to verify all tasks have been remembered.

Brain injuries are the result of trauma, such as being hit in the head with an object or striking one's head while falling. Strokes and aneurisms can also cause brain injuries. The symptoms associated with brain injuries vary tremendously depending on the region of the brain that is impacted. People may experience cognitive problems, short- or long-term memory loss, and issues with physical coordination and gross or fine motor skills. They may lose the ability to understand or use speech or lose the ability to engage in emotional self-regulation. Previously acquired skills and knowledge may be less obtainable or, in severe cases, disappear almost entirely. They may even have their entire personality permanently transformed. Given the extraordinarily wide array of potential impacts, providing a list of all possible accommodations here is not practical. Instead, each symptom will need to be addressed individually, using guidance from the content on disabilities that bear the closest resemblance to the worker's symptoms. (For example, if gross motor skills are impacted, refer to the chapter on mobility impairments. If emotional stability is impacted, refer the content on mood disorders.) But there is one form of brain injury that is more commonly seen and for which symptoms and accommodation strategies are more consistent: the concussion.

Concussions are caused by an abrupt blow or jolt to the head such that the head and brain move rapidly back and forth, causing the brain to bounce around in the skull. This not only leads to direct damage to the brain cells but also generates problematic chemical and metabolic changes inside the brain. Concussions are both common and serious, frequently occurring in team sports such as football, soccer, hockey, and rugby, as well as resulting from falls and accidents. Sometimes concussions are acquired at work, especially in higher risk industries such as construction. Concussions, if not treated properly, can result in long-term cognitive issues, so responding appropriately to workplace head injuries, having people who are trained to recognize the symptoms, and respecting treatment protocols is important. Having additional concussions after an initial one significantly increases the potential for long-term problems. Some people who have had multiple concussions experience permanent issues with concentration, memory, headaches, and balance. At the most severe end of the continuum, people who experience repeated serious concussions, such as professional boxers and football players, may acquire chronic traumatic encephalopathy (CTE), a serious brain disease that can cause changes to personality, mood, and cognition that interfere with daily life. The signs of a concussion include the following:

- Inability to recall anything immediately prior to or after being hit or falling
- Appearing dazed or stunned
- Confusion or forgetting what was said moments ago
- Moving clumsily and appearing sluggish or groggy
- Loss of consciousness, even if only briefly
- Answering questions unusually slowly
- Abrupt changes to mood or behavior
- Reporting a headache or pressure in the head
- Nausea, vomiting, balance issues, dizziness, or double vision
- Unusually bothered by light and noise
- Reporting "just not feeling right"

A concussion is a temporary health issue that under normal circumstances should improve with treatment, although people who have very severe concussions or multiple concussions may experience long-term symptoms. Standard treatment for a concussion involves stopping all activities right away and taking medication for pain relief, followed by a period of rest. The length of rest should be determined by a doctor based on severity but is generally 48 hours at an absolute minimum. It is often longer. An extended leave of several weeks may be required in some cases. Recognizing that this rest period includes rest from cognitive activities such as reading and writing is important. Expecting a concussed person to work from home is neither medically advisable nor reasonable. Physical activity will need to be avoided as well. Cognitive and physical tasks should be reintroduced gradually, at a physician-supervised pace that does not result in triggering renewed symptoms. Avoiding activities that may lead to another head injury until symptoms are fully resolved, which can take weeks or months, is critically important. Employees may need to be reassigned or put on light duties during the period of healing if their job is physically or cognitively strenuous or involves any risk of further head injury. Paid leaves and the ability to work light duties will help prevent employees from pushing themselves too hard prematurely, potentially compromising their long-term health due to financial need.

Accommodation or Just Good Management Practice?

A significant proportion of the potential accommodations for psychiatric disabilities represent well-validated best practices for all employees. For example, changing policies to permit the banking of unused sick days and permitting usage of sick days to manage mental health would benefit all employees experiencing significant stressors. Flexible schedules are associated with higher productivity, job satisfaction, and affective commitment and lower rates of absenteeism. Flexible schedules are not only helpful for people with disabilities, but they are also helpful for parents, working students, newly arrived immigrants who need to attend immigration-related appointments, people juggling two part-time jobs, and people who want to avoid peak commuter traffic. Similarly, positive supervision benefits all employees. Having supervisors who exhibit supportive behaviors is associated with improved levels of employee engagement, job satisfaction, organizational commitment, subjective well-being, and job performance. Even the types of cognitive supports frequently requested by employees with psychiatric disabilities simply represent good communication practices. Lack of effective communication negatively impacts many organizational outcomes. Providing written rather than verbal instructions for complex multistage tasks, clearly delineating organizational priorities, and providing clear and concise performance standards are practices that have obvious value for all workers.

FURTHER READINGS ●————————————————————

Bastien, M. F., & Corbière, M. (2019). Return-to-work following depression: What work accommodations do employers and human resources directors put in place? *Journal of Occupational Rehabilitation, 29*, 423–432. https://doi.org/10.1007/s10926-018-9801-y

Malo, M., & Rodriquez, V. (2022). Sheltered employment for people with disabilities: An international appraisal with illustrations from the Spanish case. *Rivista Internazionale di Scienze Sociali, 2*, 125–144. https://doi.org/10.26350/000518_000093

Szeto, A. C., & Dobson, K. S. (2010). Reducing the stigma of mental disorders at work: A review of current workplace anti-stigma intervention programs. *Applied and Preventive Psychology, 14*(1–4), 41–56. https://doi.org/10.1016/j.appsy.2011.11.002

Williams, A., Fossey, E., Corbière, M., Paluch, T., & Harvey, C. (2016). Work participation for people with severe mental illnesses: An integrative review of factors impacting job tenure. *Australian Occupational Therapy Journal, 63*(2), 65–85. https://doi.org/10.1111/1440-1630.12237

Zafar, N., Rotenberg, M., & Rudnick, A. (2019). A systematic review of work accommodations for people with mental disorders. *Work, 64*(3), 461–475. https://doi.org/10.3233/WOR-193008

REFERENCES ————————————————————

American Psychiatric Association. (2022). *Diagnostic and statistical manual of mental disorders* (5th ed., text rev.). https://doi.org/10.1176/appi.books.9780890425787

An, S., Roessler, R., & McMahon, B. (2011). Workplace discrimination and Americans with psychiatric disabilities: A comparative study. *Rehabilitation Counseling Bulletin, 55*(1), 7–19. https://doi.org/10.1177/0034355211410704

Angst, J. (2013). Bipolar disorders in *DSM-5*: Strengths, problems and perspectives. *International Journal of Bipolar Disorders, 1*(12). https://doi.org/10.1186/2194-7511-1-12

Bhandari, S. (2022, January 12). *Faces of schizophrenia you may know*. WebMD. https://www.webmd.com/schizophrenia/ss/slideshow-schizophrenia-famous-names

Buchanan, A., Sint, K., Swanson, J., & Rosenheck, R. (2019). Correlates of future violence in people being treated for schizophrenia. *American*

Journal of Psychiatry, 176(9), 694–701. https://doi.org/10.1176/appi .ajp.2019.18080909

Centers for Disease Control and Prevention. (2019, February 12). *Concussion signs and symptoms.* https://www.cdc.gov/headsup/basics/ concussion_symptoms.html

Centers for Disease Control and Prevention. (2023, January 24). *Fetal alcohol spectrum disorders (FASDs).* https://www.cdc.gov/ncbddd/fasd/ index.html

Chow, C. M., & Cichocki, B. (2016). Predictors of job accommodations for individuals with psychiatric disabilities. *Rehabilitation Counseling Bulletin, 59*(3), 172–184. https://doi.org/10.1177/003435521558

Concussion Legacy Foundation. (2023). *What is a concussion?* https:// concussionfoundation.org/concussion-resources/what-is-concussion

Evans, J., Bond, G., Meyer, P., Kim, H., Lysaker, P., Gibson, J., & Tunis, S. (2004). Cognitive and clinical predictors of success in vocational reha- bilitation in schizophrenia. *Schizophrenia Research, 70*(2), 331–342. https://doi.org/10.1016/j.schres.2004.01.011

Fabian, E., Waterworth, A., & Ripke, B. (1993). Reasonable accommo- dations for workers with serious mental illness: Type, frequency, and associated outcomes. *Psychosocial Rehabilitation Journal, 17*(2), 163– 172. https://doi.org/10.1037/h0095591

Granger, B., Baron, R., & Robinson, S. (1997). Findings from a national survey of job coaches and job developers about job accommoda- tions arranged between employers and people with psychiatric dis- abilities. *Journal of Vocational Rehabilitation, 9*(3), 235–251. https://doi .org/10.1016/S1052-2263(97)10006-X

Hewitt, F. (2022, November 18). People with Down syndrome 'over- looked' in the job market. *Hamilton Spectator.* https://www.thespec .com/business/2022/11/18/people-with-down-syndrome-overlooked- in-the-job-market.html

Huff, S. W., Rapp, C. A., & Campbell, S. R. (2008). "Every day is not always Jell-O": A qualitative study of factors affecting job ten- ure. *Psychiatric Rehabilitation Journal, 31*(3), 211–218. https://doi .org/10.2975/31.3.2008.211.218

Huppert, J. D., Simpson, H. B., Nissenson, K. J., Liebowitz, M. R., & Foa, E. B. (2009). Quality of life and functional impairment in obsessive- compulsive disorder: A comparison of patients with and without comorbidity, patients in remission, and healthy controls. *Depression and Anxiety, 26*(1), 39–45. https://doi.org/10.1002/da.20506

Job Accommodation Network. (2023). *Obsessive compulsive disorder (OCD)*. AskJAN. https://askjan.org/disabilities/Obsessive-Compulsive-Disorder-OCD.cfm

MacDonald-Wilson, K., Rogers, S., & Massaro, J. (2003). Identifying relationships between functional limitations, job accommodations, and demographic characteristics of persons with psychiatric disabilities. *Journal of Vocational Rehabilitation, 18*(1), 15–24.

MacDonald-Wilson, K., Rogers, S., Massaro, J., Lyass, A., & Crean, T. (2002). An investigation of reasonable workplace accommodations for people with psychiatric disabilities: Quantitative findings from a multi-site study. *Community Mental Health Journal, 38*(1), 35–50. https://doi.org/10.1023/A:1013955830779

Mayo Clinic. (2018a, January 10). *Fetal alcohol syndrome*. https://www.mayoclinic.org/diseases-conditions/fetal-alcohol-syndrome/symptoms-causes/syc-20352901

Mayo Clinic. (2018b, May 4). *Anxiety disorders*. https://www.mayoclinic.org/diseases-conditions/anxiety/symptoms-causes/syc-20350961

Mayo Clinic. (2018c, May 4). *Panic attacks and panic disorder.* https://www.mayoclinic.org/diseases-conditions/panic-attacks/symptoms-causes/syc-20376021

Mayo Clinic. (2020, January 7). *Schizophrenia*. https://www.mayoclinic.org/diseases-conditions/schizophrenia/symptoms-causes/syc-20354443

Mayo Clinic. (2022, October 4). *Drug addiction (substance use disorder)*. https://www.mayoclinic.org/diseases-conditions/drug-addiction/symptoms-causes/syc-20365112

McHugo, G., Drake, R., Xie, H., & Bond, G. (2012). A 10-year study of steady employment and non-vocational outcomes among people with serious mental illness and co-occurring substance use disorders. *Schizophrenia Research, 138*(2), 233–239. https://doi.org/10.1016/j.schres.2012.04.007

Miller, K. (2022, August 24). Man becomes first graduate with Down syndrome from his college. *My Modern Met*. https://mymodernmet.com/dylan-keuhls-down-syndrome-graduates-college/

National Health Service. (2019, November 18). *Symptoms - Obsessive compulsive disorder (OCD)*. https://www.nhs.uk/mental-health/conditions/obsessive-compulsive-disorder-ocd/symptoms/

Norlian, A. (2020, May 21). The first degree: Woman is first person with Down syndrome to graduate from Rowan University. *Forbes*. https://www.forbes.com/sites/allisonnorlian/2020/05/21/the-first-degree-woman-is-first-person-with-down-syndrome-to-graduate-from-rowan-university/?sh=4fec5fdd2e6d

Raypole, C. (2020, January 27). *How to help someone having a panic attack.* Healthline. https://www.healthline.com/health/how-to-help-someone-having-a-panic-attack

Sparkles, I., Riley, E., Cook, B., & Machuel, P. (2022, February 10). *Outcomes for disabled people in the UK: 2021.* Office for National Statistics. https://www.ons.gov.uk/peoplepopulationandcommunity/healthand-socialcare/disability/articles/outcomesfordisabledpeopleintheuk/2021#employment

Statistics Canada. (2020, January 29). *A profile of Canadians with mental health-related disabilities.* https://www150.statcan.gc.ca/n1/daily-quotidien/200129/dq200129b-eng.htm

Intermittent
Disabilities

Intermittent disabilities are disabilities that are episodic, meaning symptoms come and go at unpredictable and largely uncontrollable intervals. These types of disabilities require special consideration when planning accommodations because accommodations may be needed on an ongoing daily basis or sporadically, and needs may evolve and shift as severity levels fluctuate. There are several broad categories of intermittent disease:

1. *Progressive degenerative conditions* that worsen over time, but at unpredictable intervals with long periods of either complete remission or reduced and changeable symptoms. Examples include multiple sclerosis (MS), cystic fibrosis, and some forms of cancer. Needs associated with these conditions change over time.

2. *Chronic conditions with highly unpredictable but brief flare-ups* that are often completely disabling in the moment but only last minutes, hours, or a couple of days. Examples include migraines and anxiety attacks. These conditions may require ongoing accommodations to minimize the probability that symptoms will emerge and short-term accommodations when an attack occurs.

3. *Chronic conditions with unpredictable, lengthier flare-ups* that are often disabling and may last days, weeks, or months. These conditions are not degenerative, so they typically do not worsen significantly over time, which distinguishes them from the first category. Examples include some forms of depression, certain autoimmune diseases, and some chronic pain disorders. These conditions may require ongoing accommodations and are also more likely to require the worker to take a temporary leave of absence for treatment and symptom management when flare-ups occur.

4. *Chronic conditions that flare-up at somewhat more regular intervals* (although still not completely predictable) and are impairing

but not usually completely disabling, such as digestive disorders like Crohn's disease and asthma. These conditions are less likely to require a temporary leave of absence for treatment and symptom management (although it is still possible) but may require day-to-day accommodations.

These categories are loose, and there may be overlap between them. Each type of intermittent disability may require a slightly different accommodation approach, and even workers with the same condition may experience different symptoms and differing levels of severity and may have varied accommodation-related needs. For example, irritable bowel syndrome or Crohn's disease both vary significantly in severity and frequency of symptoms between individuals. As such it may require an extended leave for one worker while another may be able to work effectively with other accommodations. Flexibility and attention to individual needs is key.

The need to employ people with intermittent disabilities is not only a social justice issue, but also a practical issue for employers given the demographic realities of today's labor market. Establishing the percentage of the population with intermittent disabilities is difficult because there is such a wide variety of disability types included; however, we do know the number is increasing. This increase is in part due to the aging workforce, leading to higher incidents of age-related impairments such as osteoarthritis. The increase is also directly related to the COVID-19 pandemic, which created a large cohort of "long haulers" who are experiencing ongoing symptoms such as extreme fatigue, breathlessness, and brain fog. In June 2022, the Centers for Disease Control and Prevention (CDC) in the United States reported that 1 in 5 people who had COVID reported they were still experiencing symptoms more than 3 months later. Since approximately 40% of people had reported having COVID, that means that 7.5% of all adults sampled reported long-haul COVID symptoms. If that trend holds, there will continue to be large numbers of workers experiencing long-haul COVID symptoms in the workforce for the foreseeable future. Very little is known about the long-term prognosis for these COVID long-haul patients, but early findings suggest accommodation needs may exist for a long time—or may even be permanent. All this is occurring against a backdrop of pre-existing labor scarcity in many occupations, and underutilized workers could help address those gaps. Some people with intermittent disabilities prefer part-time work, yet part-time work has not conventionally been offered in many high-skill professional and trade roles, leading to a pool of underemployed skilled individuals. The social norm of requiring professionals and skilled tradespeople to work full time requires amendment to address this problem.

Special Considerations Related to Intermittent Disabilities

There are several special considerations when supporting workers with intermittent disabilities. In addition to providing workplace accommodations to support completion of day-to-day tasks, employers may also have to address unpredictable absences and associated staffing issues. These absences may be brief, for example, someone taking an afternoon off due to a migraine, or they may be lengthy, such as someone taking several months off for cancer treatments or to stabilize their psychiatric medication regime. Employees may require a continuous leave for a designated period, their return date may be uncertain, or they may require intermittent leaves as symptoms flare up. For example, a person with arthritis or gastrointestinal issues may require a couple days off on short notice when symptoms are especially bad, and that may occur several times per year. Since coworkers can be impacted by unplanned absences, there are broader workload, fairness, and perceptual issues that require careful attention. Employers need to ensure that workers with disabilities do not experience unfair social sanctions or negative performance evaluation impacts because of their medical conditions while also ensuring that other employees do not face undue stress, inconvenience, or excessive workloads during periods of absence. While this may sound challenging, there are concrete strategies to achieve these goals, which are discussed shortly.

A major barrier often encountered by workers with intermittent disabilities is the myth of control over symptoms. Since many of the symptoms associated with intermittent conditions (most notably pain and fatigue) are invisible, some colleagues may be predisposed to perceive workers who report flare-ups as fakers or malingerers who are merely seeking to avoid undesirable work tasks or go home early. This impression can be heightened by the fact that stress magnifies the symptoms of many intermittent disabilities, including digestive pain and psychiatric disorders, meaning that affected workers have an increased probability of experiencing flare-ups during busy periods in which everyone is overwhelmed. Ironically, the fear of peer judgment and censure is a significant stressor that can magnify symptoms independently, creating a negative spiral of social censure, stress, worsened symptoms, and increased accommodation needs that lead to further social censure. Disabilities that are poorly understood, such as addictions, depression, and eating disorders, can be erroneously perceived by some peers as signs of moral weakness, and individuals with these disabilities experience even more social censure and judgment and are more likely to be targets of peer resentment that creates negative spiral effects.

This leads to the next major barriers encountered by workers with intermittent disabilities: peer attitudes, equity concerns, and feelings of guilt. When an employee is absent, other employees often must work a little harder. This can create feelings of guilt and inadequacy that add to the absent worker's existing stress load and undermine their healing. It is well established in the organizational behavior literature that employees compare their inputs (i.e., effort and work completed) and their outputs (i.e., rewards) with those of their peers. If there is a perceived disparity, for example, a coworker is perceived as putting in less effort and receives an equal or higher reward, then important workplace attitudes such as job satisfaction, organizational commitment, and even turnover intentions are negatively impacted. These negative consequences should be mitigated with careful planning that minimizes the impact of a given employee's absence on other workers. If strategies to balance workloads are not implemented the result may be stress, burnout, and impaired performance for all workers and unwarranted resentment and hostility directed at the worker with an intermittent disability.

Employers can mitigate these interrelated negative impacts in several ways. Strategies that reduce stress are a good place to start because symptoms of many ailments are less likely to arise in the first place in lower stress workplaces. A lot of the interventions related to mitigating stress represent general evidence-based best practice in management. For example, stress related to work tasks can be mitigated by ensuring assigned tasks are realistic. Specifically, managers can ensure that the employee has the needed training and skill to complete the task or tasks, and completing them in the time allotted is possible. Tasks should be clearly explained, and employers should provide the needed resources to complete them. Performance goals should meet the SMART criteria, meaning they are specific, measurable, agreed on, realistic, and time-bound. Positive supervisory practices, such as getting to know workers individually, providing social support to them, and highlighting positive aspects of performance and areas for improvement, can also help lower stress.

To lessen stress related to work-life conflict and symptom management (as opposed to tasks), employers can offer flexible scheduling, modified work hours, and work from home options whenever possible. Some employees may prefer part-time hours either temporarily or permanently, especially if fatigue is an issue. This is commonly referred to as a reduced work schedule. The ability to switch between part-time and full-time hours as needed is a particular boon when employers can offer it. Flexible scheduling and work-from-home options are particularly good for people with intermittent flare-ups because they allow more flexibility to manage symptoms (e.g., some may find their symptoms are worse immediately upon waking or later in the evening) and to attend medical appointments. However, simply having a work-from-home accommodation is not a panacea. The conditions that ensure successful work from home must be present. Various researchers who examined employees' experiences during the COVID-19 pandemic, for example, identified that people working from home require a suitable workspace, appropriate technological tools, digital social support, and an effective monitoring mechanism for working from home to be effective, productive, engaging, and satisfying.

Stress and anxiety about medical needs and associated financial vulnerability can be significantly reduced through the provision of a benefits plan that offers short- and long-term disability leaves. These benefits reassure employees by giving them the security of knowing that illness will not financially devastate them. Ironically that peace of mind alone can reduce stress, improve health, and thereby lessen the probability of needing the leaves in the first place! Employee assistance plans, commonly included as part of standard benefits packages, are also helpful for reducing stress because they offer free, confidential access to a range of helpful services such as therapy, addictions counseling, financial planning, and basic legal advice for things such as divorce and child custody cases. However, part-time workers are often excluded from benefit plan participation, which not only eliminates an important source of support, but it also pressures workers into working full time to keep benefits, which may further compromise their health. Employers may want to rethink which employees qualify for benefits since those benefits, while they do add extra expenses, also help ensure employee well-being and therefore have many positive impacts. Provision of benefits to part-time workers is increasingly viewed as an indicator of corporate social responsibility and a differentiator used to attract workers in competitive labor markets.

To lessen stress related to interpersonal dynamics within the workplace, employers are encouraged to provide diversity training that helps create empathy. Training that focuses on a combination of knowledge and skill development and that allows for the sharing of personal stories and perspectives is generally the most successful. This type of training should help mitigate negative fallout an individual might experience from disclosing that they have a disability. Since diversity training is not always popular, making it a standard part of orientation training and other regularly scheduled annual training offerings is best rather than only offering it once a disability-related need has been identified. Otherwise, the individual impacted may find themselves blamed for "making everyone take the training," thus making their social situation worse, not better! While in theory nobody should know who the person with a disability is, in practice when coworkers need to assist with accommodations, this standard is not always met; sometimes, it is not even a possibility. Some disabilities are visible. Chapter 3 digs more deeply into effective diversity training. Personality tests, such as the Myers Briggs Type Indicator, can also be used to create teams with more inherently compatible personalities.

The most effective way to avoid interpersonal conflict and associated stress is to minimize the impact of an unplanned absence on other employees. Careful job design and amended job descriptions can help, especially if critically time sensitive tasks are either assigned to someone else or can be completed from home. In fact, amended job descriptions are the most frequently requested accommodation among workers with intermittent disabilities. Some creativity may be required. For example, in an accounting department with multiple accountants, the employee with an intermittent disability triggered by stress may be assigned internal budgeting and variance analysis tasks—which tend to be less time sensitive—while another employee focuses on external financial statement reporting, which must be completed within Securities and Exchange Commission (SEC) time lines that offer no flexibility. In another example, a human resources (HR) person who is part of a recruiting team may focus on résumé reviews or reference checks that can be done from home, while a colleague performs the in-person interviews. Similarly, when there are options available, supervisors may want to minimize the frequency with which they schedule workers who experience intermittent disabilities to work alone. For example, if a retail outlet typically has three staff members except for the early morning (i.e., the first hour) after opening, when only one works, they may wish to schedule the worker with an intermittent disability during the core hours when three staff members are onsite. Job description changes and flexible scheduling are helpful in many contexts, but they are not a panacea. There will be a limited number of circumstances in which people with unpredictable intermittent disabilities cannot meet the bona fide occupation requirements for jobs in which consistent attendance is critical to fulfilling basic task requirements or is required to meet minimum workplace safety standards. The number of jobs that legitimately necessitate certain task requirements is likely much smaller than the number of jobs that people *assume* necessitate them. Properly executed, scientific job analysis procedures should be used to determine legitimate bona fide occupational requirements to avoid indirect discrimination because of faulty assumptions.

In addition to thoughtful job design, cross-training can also help mitigate the negative impact of temporary absences because more employees are trained in each task, lessening the potential for process bottlenecks during absences. Job sharing achieves the same thing and may be a good option if two employees both want to work part-time hours, especially if one has the flexibility to sub in when the other is ill. Finally, employers may wish to use placement agencies to hire temporary workers during extended absences. (This option is more practical for some jobs than others due to skill scarcities in the temporary labor pool for some occupations.) When temp workers are not an option, then employers should develop a plan to handle extended absences. That plan may involve shifts in responsibilities of other workers (which may require training them in advance), minor process adjustments, temporarily automating some tasks, and postponing noncritical tasks. One especially helpful tactic is to have key documents and projects in process on a shared drive such that key information is not inaccessible on someone's password protected computer. Advance planning for absences prevents a crisis, with all the stress, anxiety, and guilt associated with it.

Accommodations for Workers With Intermittent Disabilities

There are a wide variety of intermittent medical conditions, and the specific accommodations needed vary considerably. Broadly speaking, there are four intermittent disability types that tend to be seen in workplaces more frequently: digestive disorders, pain disorders, long-haul COVID, and addictions. But there are some common threads and approaches that benefit almost all workers with intermittent disabilities. As previously discussed, flexible schedules and work from home options are common accommodations when the job role allows for it, and job description adjustments can also be helpful. Additionally, modifying work pace expectations may be required, particularly during times when symptoms are more acute. This may also require modifying associated performance expectations for some workers to ensure fairness and make sure performance goals are obtainable. Professional ergonomic assessments are also frequently requested because proper workspace design can mitigate pain and fatigue. Ergonomic experts and occupational therapists may be able to recommend special desks, chairs, workstation arrangements, and tools that can assist workers based on their individual needs.

Another common accommodation relates to processes for justifying absences. Many employers require a doctor's note for each absence exceeding a day or two. This expectation is unreasonable for people with diagnosed chronic conditions because it not only requires the ill worker to travel to a doctor (assuming one is accessible), but it also wastes scarce healthcare resources. In addition, depending on their location and health insurance coverage, workers may need to pay out of pocket, creating financial barriers. Even in places that have government funded healthcare, such as Canada, acquiring doctor's notes for employers often involves paying fees. Once the nature of a chronic condition has been documented by a physician, employees should not be required to produce medical evidence of every flare-up, especially when absences are brief (e.g., hours or a few days). Furthermore, employers should avoid *attendance management incentives*, which provide team bonuses based on overall attendance rates, because these programs set up workers with intermittent disabilities for negative peer pressure and hostility should their attendance impact the bonus payments of team members. Rigid attendance management policies that punish or discipline employees after a preset number of absences also should not be applied when workers are absent for medical reasons. (Although, absences unrelated to medical needs could still be a disciplinary issue. Simply having an intermittent disability does not excuse nonmedical absenteeism, and the distinction needs to be clear to both employer and employee.)

Importantly, employers should not impose continuous leave on an employee who asks for an accommodation consisting of intermittent leave. Continuous leave implies that the employee will not return to work until the health issue is resolved, and that is often not a realistic expectation for chronic conditions. Instead, intermittent leave, in which the employee takes time off as needed, is a more appropriate accommodation. In the United States, there have been court cases in which employers who tried to force employees into continuous leave in lieu of intermittent leave were found liable for improper behavior, including the precedent setting case of *Brown v. Gestam* (2018). In that case, a materials-handling employee working at an auto parts manufacturing plant who had flare-ups of gout, hypertension, and arthritis had their right to intermittent leave supported after the employer attempted to impose continuous leave instead (Waltemath, 2018).

Some companies have tried providing access to health self-management programs, offered either as part of a benefits plan or through the training and development branch of the HR department, to assist workers with intermittent disabilities. These programs consist of training, either online or facilitated in person, on topics such as health self-management, self-efficacy, ergonomics, and communication. A U.S. research team led by William S. Shaw, Robert K. McLellan, and Elyssa Besen conducted a study in which they collected data from 119 workers with intermittent disabilities who participated in a five-session health self-management facilitated program. They found that participation was associated with increased work engagement, decreased incidents of extended sick leaves (absences of more than 10 consecutive days), and decreased turnover intentions. The program did not impact perceived work limitations, perceived self-efficacy, overall job satisfaction, or level of work fatigue. While these programs are still being assessed, these early results suggest that they have some benefits; in particular, they help communicate a sense of support and inclusion that sets a positive cultural tone.

Other relevant accommodations have already been described in previous chapters. For example, workers with MS or cerebral palsy who are wheelchair users or have impaired upper limb functioning would need similar accommodations to other wheelchair users and people with upper limb impairments, and workers with arthritis would also benefit from the mobility and agility accommodations discussed in Chapter 4. Accommodations for severe depression, which can be intermittent, are covered in Chapter 6. And long-haul COVID is complex and variable; however, fatigue is a major symptom and so the accommodations recommended below would also be useful for a wide variety of other conditions for which fatigue is a primary symptom.

Accommodations for Digestive Disorders

Digestive disorders include conditions such as irritable bowel syndrome, Crohn's disease, and colitis. These conditions can cause gastrointestinal pain, which is sometimes severe, as well as the need to use the bathroom urgently and frequently, extreme flatulence, diarrhea, nausea, vomiting, and constipation. These disorders can be chronic or episodic, and symptoms are generally magnified by stress. Personal dignity is a significant consideration because using a shared bathroom or a bathroom located very near the workspaces of coworkers when experiencing severe digestive issues can be a deeply humiliating experience. Common accommodations include moving the affected person's workspace closer to the bathrooms in case of a sudden and urgent need to go, provision of a private bathroom, permitting work from home as needed, and avoidance of policies that monitor bathroom breaks or punish people for what the employer considers to be excessive bathroom breaks. Flexible scheduling can also help employees manage their day-to-day schedules such that they are at work at times when they are less likely to experience symptoms.

Minor job restructuring may be helpful when trying to make a job more suitable for working from home. Special attention may have to be paid to ensure that bullying and harassment do not occur related to either the need to use the bathroom frequently or the perceived perk of having work from home, flexible scheduling, or unmonitored breaks. Employers may wish to consider whether allowing all employees to have these accommodations would be a good strategy because flexible scheduling and voluntary work from home have evidence-based advantages including improvements in job satisfaction, productivity, and organizational commitment. Furthermore, the monitoring of bathroom breaks is considered inappropriately intrusive by most workers and creates gendered issues for menstruating employees, who may need more frequent breaks to attend to personal hygiene needs.

Accommodations for Pain Disorders

Pain disorders include a wide variety of conditions for which pain is a primary symptom. This includes migraines, fibromyalgia, endometriosis, nerve damage, Lyme disease, chronic back conditions, and many other diagnoses. Accommodation needs vary considerably depending on the source, frequency, and intensity of the pain experienced. Professional ergonomic consultations and associated adjustments to physical workspaces are common accommodations because the placement of chairs, screens, keyboards, and other tools can play a significant role in muscular and skeletal strain. In addition to placement, ergonomic consultants may recommend the purchase of special chairs, standing desks, desks with adjustable heights, or similar office furniture tailored to the individual needs of the affected worker. (Read more about ergonomics in Chapter 8, which covers inclusive design.)

Workstations can also be relocated to provide easier accessibility to elevators, copy machines, or other work tools. This is especially helpful for employees for whom movement and walking create pain. Adjusting work hours and increasing the frequency of breaks are also common accommodations. Frequent breaks, even if they are short, can provide significant relief for many individuals with chronic pain. Some individuals may prefer, for example, to have three different 10-minute breaks instead of a single half an hour break. This also enables compliance with medication regimes because many pain medications must be taken with food, so can only be taken when employees are able to snack. Additionally, minor changes to job descriptions can eliminate specific tasks that are especially problematic and are likely to cause or increase pain.

There are a wide variety of specialized anti-pain tools for specific contexts. For example, people required to stand for long periods of time may benefit from anti-fatigue matting. These soft mats absorb shock while encouraging subtle leg and muscle movements as feet adjust to the soft, slightly irregular, grooved surface. This prevents the muscles from constricting and limiting blood flow, which lessens pain in the feet, legs, and back. In another example, many power tools can be rendered more useable by using anti-vibration tool wraps, which lessen the vibrations impacting the person holding the tools, leading to less muscle strain and pain. Given the wide range of options, a comprehensive list of every pain minimization device available is beyond the scope of this text. Managers and HR personnel should consult with ergonomic professionals about devices unique to their industry, context, and required tasks.

Pain-related disabilities are often subject to gendered stereotyping by coworkers. Awareness and education about these gendered challenges can help supervisors and managers prevent inappropriate peer responses and mitigate toxic effects when they do occur. Specifically, women who experience pain due to invisible ailments are more likely to be considered mentally unstable, that the pain is all in their heads, which harkens back to a long patriarchal history of dismissing women as *hysterical*, a word whose Greek root meaning is *suffering in the womb*. This condescending attitude can make coworkers less compliant with accommodation needs, and less empathetic. Men, by contrast, are often still expected to maintain tough or macho attitudes, particularly in historically male dominated industries. Those outdated, toxic gender norm expectations lead people to punish and devalue males who admit to experiencing pain or needing help, which can negatively impact how they are treated by coworkers and their willingness to request needed accommodations in the first place. Managers should be aware of the potential for these types of attitudinal barriers so that interventions and corrective actions can be implemented as needed.

Accommodations for Long-Haul COVID and Fatigue

In early 2020, the world experienced a major pandemic, which at time of writing was still ongoing. As millions of people around the world became infected with the COVID-19 virus, many found themselves struggling to recover. Medical science is still catching up, but statistics released by the CDC in June 2022 suggest that almost one in five (19%) people who catch COVID will experience long-haul symptoms, meaning symptoms that continue for more than 3 months after initial exposure. There are already a small proportion of patients who have reported symptoms lasting more than a year, and those symptoms may or may not be permanent. The most common symptoms of long-haul COVID include extreme fatigue, shortness of breath, and cognitive issues such as brain fog and difficulties with memory. Some people also experience dizziness, headaches, heart and kidney complications, or the loss of taste and smell.

Accommodations for long-haul COVID depend on the presenting symptoms. For example, if brain fog and memory issues are the primary symptoms, then the suggestions made for addressing executive functioning limitations and memory impairments in Chapter 6 would be relevant. If headache pain is an issue, then the suggestions found under pain impairments in this chapter would be most helpful. Shortness of breath can be accommodated by minimizing unnecessary physical demands and increasing the frequency of breaks. For example, placing their workstation closer to areas the worker needs to go to frequently throughout the day can make a difference. Wheeled carts can also prevent excessive physical strain because of needing to carry items from one place to another.

Fatigue is one of the most commonly occurring symptoms of long-haul COVID and is also a significant component of other intermittent conditions, such as fibromyalgia and chronic fatigue syndrome. Accommodations for fatigue may include flexible scheduling, working part-time or restricted hours, taking more frequent breaks, and working from home. Adjustments to work pace can make a big difference; a slower pace is not only more manageable, but it can also help prevent *crashes*, which occur when a chronically fatigued person pushes themselves too hard, resulting in the need to take an extended break of days or weeks to recover. Positive, supportive, and nonjudgmental supervisory practices help indirectly by minimizing the stress associated with experiencing variable energy levels. Finally, there are industry and occupation specific tools that can minimize fatigue such as the anti-fatigue matting and anti-vibration tool wraps. Ergonomic experts can assist with identifying appropriate devices from among the overwhelming and ever-evolving array of options tailored to specific work tasks and occupational roles.

Addictions

Addictions require special consideration. Addiction is a disease, with measurable impacts on brain chemistry and structure. While people can be addicted to many things, including video games, generally drug and alcohol addictions are of the most concern to employers. The National Institutes of Health (NIH) National Institute on Drug Abuse and its director, Nora Volkow, state,

> [W]hen you're becoming addicted to a substance, that normal hardwiring of helpful brain processes can begin to work against you. Drugs or alcohol can hijack the pleasure-reward circuits in your brain and hook you into wanting more and more. Addiction can also send your emotional danger-sensing circuits into overdrive, making you feel anxious and stressed when you're not using the drugs or alcohol. At this stage, people often use drugs or alcohol to keep from feeling bad rather than for their pleasurable effects.

> To add to that, repeated use of drugs can damage the essential decision-making center at the front of the brain. This area, known as the prefrontal cortex, is the very region that should help you recognize the harms of using addictive substances.

> "Brain imaging studies of people addicted to drugs or alcohol show decreased activity in this frontal cortex," says Dr. Nora Volkow . . . When the frontal cortex isn't working properly, people can't make the decision to stop taking the drug—even if they realize the price of taking that drug may be extremely high . . . . (NIH News in Health, 2015)

Employers cannot discriminate based on disability, and they are also responsible for ensuring safe workplaces. These priorities can appear to conflict with each other, particularly when an individual with an addiction is in a safety sensitive job, such as heavy equipment operator. Yet there are evidence-based best practices that preserve the rights of the disability community while also respecting employers' need for safe, functional workplaces. Before exploring those options, developing a better understanding of addiction in general is helpful.

Using a substance does not mean an individual has an addiction. Distinguishing between employees who are caught using a substance such as alcohol or marijuana at work as an irregular occurrence and employees who have an addiction is important. The former is a disciplinary matter, particularly when formal policies forbid consumption at work or when levels of consumption result in impairment, while the latter is a disability accommodation issue. Distinguishing a casual user from a person with an addiction will usually require professional medical evaluation, and employers should avoid making unsupported assumptions. According to the *Diagnostic Manual of Mental Disorders* (*DSM-5-TR*), which is used by physicians, psychiatrists, and psychologists, addiction involves the following:

- Taking more of a substance than recommended or taking it for longer periods of time than intended or recommended.

- Wanting to cut down usage but finding oneself unable to do so.

- Spending much of one's time acquiring, using, or recovering from use of the substance in question.

- Experiencing intense cravings and urges to use the substance.

- Inability to complete regular work, school, or home-based tasks due to excessive substance usage.

- Ceasing activities that were previously valued to focus on substance usage.

- Continuing substance usage even when it has clear negative impacts (impacts may include health, relationships, psychological well-being, and daily functioning).

- Using substances even when it creates active danger.

- Requiring more and more of a substance to gain the desired effect and developing a tolerance.

- Experience of withdrawal symptoms when not taking the substance.

The management of addictions in the workplace is also rendered more complex due to significant differences in law between jurisdictions. For example, random drug testing of employees is permissible in some, but not all, U.S. states, while Canada does not generally permit it but has a small number of exceptions for particularly sensitive industries and occupations (e.g., some elite military and aviation roles are subject to random testing). Covering all the jurisdictional legal differences in this book is not possible, especially because different states and provinces often have different rules. Rules may also vary by job type and risk level. Even the specific circumstances can have an impact on legal rights. For example, in Canada drug testing employees after a workplace accident or if they show clear signs of impairment is permissible, even if under regular circumstances they could not legally be tested.

Managers and HR practitioners researching their specific legal context before proceeding with any drug testing initiatives or related policy development is critical. Importantly, HR practitioners and managers must comply with the laws in the places their employees work rather than their headquarters. For example, an employer headquartered in one U.S. state that permitted random drug testing could not legally randomly test employees who work in states in which it is not permitted. Given the complexity and relevance of situational variables, seeking expert legal opinions before proceeding with any drug testing initiatives or developing formal policies on the matter is prudent.

Employers have the right to have functional workers who are not impaired on the job, and employers have the responsibility to ensure safe workplaces for all. It is, for example, perfectly acceptable—and even required—to send an actively impaired employee home if they pose a safety risk, although the employer must ensure that the employee does not drive themself. Workers with addictions have a legitimate medical disability whose symptoms include extreme difficulties in stopping using the intoxicant. This disconnect is generally addressed using a combination of accommodations and a formal disability management plan, sometimes referred to as a *return-to-work plan*.

Accommodations for addictions are generally centered around creating an environment that is conducive to treatment and recovery. This may involve short- or long-term sick leaves, temporary reassignment of the individual to jobs that are not safety sensitive during their recovery, and adjustments to the schedule or flexible scheduling to permit attendance at recovery meetings such as Alcoholics Anonymous (AA). The techniques to lessen stress described earlier in this chapter are also helpful since stress leads to a heightened probability of relapse. During initial recovery periods, many people with addictions will experience withdrawal symptoms ranging from body pain, difficulty focusing, headache, and hand tremors to irritability. The specific symptoms and their duration vary depending on the substance used. Temporary accommodations may be needed, such as more frequent breaks, written instructions in lieu of verbal ones, or social consideration and empathy when exhibiting unusual irritability. Social support from supervisors and peers also goes a long way since many people with addictions suffer from self-esteem issues. Knowing that others value them despite their oft-stigmatized medical struggles can have a significant positive impact. Hope is an important recovery tool, and meaningful social support helps create hope.

Disability management plans are a nonpunitive, supportive way of addressing problematic behaviors and disability-related needs while maintaining employment. They are sometimes called return-to-work plans; however, that name can be somewhat misleading because they can be used for employers who never left the workplace. For example, a worker who falls and injures their back may be provided with a disability management plan that allows for four weeks off followed by shorter hours or light duties while they recover. That would be termed a return-to-work plan. Meanwhile, a worker with an addiction who has been actively impaired on the job may be provided with a disability management plan that provides access to treatment and requires them to be sober at work; however, they might continue working without interruption while undergoing treatment (excepting for the day they were actively impaired because they would be sent home).

Disability management plans can be used for any condition but are most frequently and commonly used for individuals managing addiction. In the context of addiction management, they are fundamentally an enforceable contract in which both parties acknowledge disability-related issues, and the worker promises to meet certain reasonable behavioral and work standards in exchange for support and accommodations to help them get well. For example, a disability management plan may state that the employer will offer time off and pay for an in-patient rehabilitation program and will then offer accommodations such as flexible scheduling to attend recovery meetings (such as AA). In some cases, the employee also may be temporarily reassigned from a safety sensitive job to another role. For example, in a warehouse workplace, they may be taken off forklift driving duties and be assigned the tasks of a picker-packer instead. In return the employee promises not to use alcohol or drugs while at work and not to show up for work intoxicated. Consequences for failure to meet one's commitments are written into the contract; however, because relapse is a very common part of recovery from addictions, most disability management plans allow for two to three relapses before punitive actions, such as dismissal, are considered. Again, the law varies significantly from one jurisdiction to another regarding how many relapses, if any, are legally required prior to a dismissal. The amount of support offered will also impact the permissibility of any subsequent dismissals, so expert legal advice should be consulted. The employer's goal, however, should be support and recovery, with dismissal considered only as a last resort after significant, sincere, evidence-based efforts have been made to help the employee overcome their addiction and perform to an acceptable standard.

The actual design and completion of a disability management plan is covered in more depth in the Appendix, which offers checklists for managers and HR personnel. When designing plans for workers with addictions, there is one issue that requires special attention. Importantly, employers can specify the need for treatment but not the actual treatment plan itself. A treatment plan is within the purview of the worker's physician, not that of their employer. As such, it would be inappropriate to name a specific treatment or recovery group in the disability management plan. One of the most common conditions employers require is continued participation in a recovery group such as AA. Yet specifically naming AA in the disability management plan is inappropriate; instead, the plan should highlight the physician's recommendations for ongoing treatment and leave the choice of actual support group to the individual and their medical team. There are many reasons that someone may choose an alternate to AA. First, AA requires acknowledgement of a *higher power*, something to which many people, particularly atheists, have a religious or spiritual objection. Also, AA is fundamentally structured around a highly social group-sharing model that may not work for people with severe social anxiety, autism, or other forms of neurodiversity. Finding AA groups suitable for those with hearing impairments can also prove challenging; although online groups are emerging that help address this barrier through use of closed captioning. Enabling choice ensures that workers can select the recovery plan that is most suitable for their personality, beliefs, and circumstances.

Examples of Successful Interventions With Workers With Intermittent Disabilities

The following examples are based on unpublished research interviews I (the author) conducted with workers with disabilities between 2019 and 2021. Names and employers have been disguised to protect privacy.

Accommodating Arthritis: Maria Sanchez's Story

Maria Sanchez worked in HR as an occupational health and safety specialist for a large, multibuilding pharmaceutical research company. Her job tasks included conducting regular safety inspections of all offices and laboratories to identify, eliminate, or mitigate workplace hazards, conducting employer safety training, ensuring compliance with safety standards (e.g., the wearing of personal protective equipment), verifying safety equipment maintenance duties were performed (e.g., cleaning chemical exhaust hoods), and overseeing the storage of hazardous chemicals. Maria developed osteoarthritis, which worsened as she aged. She began experiencing significant hand and wrist pain when writing and typing, and she found that walking across the corporate campus to conduct inspections in different buildings created hip pain. On two separate occasions she required short-term leaves lasting 2 to 3 weeks because her symptoms flared up and the pain was excessive. Both times she observed that she had known her symptoms were worsening but she felt pressure to attend to her duties anyway until it reached a point at which she could no longer perform at all. To minimize the likelihood of her pushing herself beyond her limits again, Maria and her employer developed the following accommodations:

1. Maria was provided with voice-to-text software on a smartphone that was connected to the health and safety inspection application they used. This allowed her to verbally make notes during inspections instead of having to write, which provided significant relief for her wrist and hand pain. This software was also installed on her workstation so she could dictate emails and reports instead of being required to type.

2. All the buildings already had elevators, so stairs were not an issue; however walking around their sprawling corporate campus was often painful. Maria was provided with a used golf cart to help her travel between buildings. This lessened her hip pain considerably because some days walking between buildings could amount to 2–3 kilometers over the course of the day.

3. Peers were asked to cooperate with efforts to schedule regular laboratory inspections by floor and building. (Previously they had been scheduled based solely on the personal convenience of the lab manager.) This eliminated the need for excessive walking and associated hip strain and made the inspection process more efficient.

As a result of these accommodations, the severity of Maria's symptoms decreased significantly. Occasionally, however, she still struggled with some of her duties due to pain. She noticed that symptoms were generally worse in the morning, a common occurrence with arthritis. She occasionally had to cancel safety inspections first thing in the morning because movement was too painful. Canceled inspections created inconvenience for coworkers because the lab managers needed to be to physically present when their labs were being inspected. After consulting her, her employer then decided to revisit this rule about lab managers being present. Inquiries revealed that the rule was in place in case Maria had questions for them. They observed, however, that her smartphone enabled her to ask lab managers questions even if they were away, and she could send them photos of areas of concern. The rule had been put in place decades ago and had not been updated with changes in technology—it had not occurred to anyone that it was no longer particularly functional. After having this realization her employer initiated flexible scheduling for Maria. This allowed her to come in later in the day, once her symptoms were under control. She could even complete her duties in the evening, although she was directed that she needed to be done by 9:00 p.m. because it was not permissible to phone a lab manager any later than that. Lab managers were also informed when their inspections would take place, so they only needed to watch for after-hours calls on that day. Furthermore, Maria was free to come in on weekends should she need to catch up because of missing a day of work earlier in the week. (Essentially, she could trade regular workdays for a weekend workday as needed.) Attendance was monitored monthly rather than day-to-day, such that if she worked the appropriate number of days in the month there was no need to report an absence.

This combination of accommodations significantly improved Maria's ability to perform her work tasks. While she still had occasional work absences due to excessive pain, the overall frequency of those absences did not exceed the norm for other employees and she was able to complete her duties to everyone's satisfaction.

Accommodating Crohn's Disease: Joel McDermott's Story

Joel worked as a sales representative for an organization that sold enterprise resource planning software tools. These complex tools generally required 9–18 months to complete the sales cycle because detailed process analysis was required to customize the software appropriately for the client's needs. Relationship development and management made up a large part of the job, and it was not unusual for a sales rep to need to visit a client half a dozen times in person before making a sale, on top of regular phone consultations and the generation of technical specification documents. Joel was assigned to accounts in the food manufacturing sector, which meant he needed to travel throughout the country to make these visits—he may be in Seattle one day, New York the next, and Phoenix the day after that.

Joel began to develop gastrointestinal issues after about 2 years of employment with his organization. This caused him to miss several key sales appointments and, on one occasion, a nonrefundable flight. His employer had to purchase a second plane ticket at full fare prices. As a result of this embarrassing incident, Joel took a short-term leave of absence to address his health. Joel was eventually diagnosed with Crohn's disease, which is magnified by stress. This posed problems because the unpredictability of symptoms made it difficult to travel and difficult to guarantee he could interact with customers with appropriate dignity.

His employer, in consultation with Joel, reassigned him to a sales role that would not require as much travel. He was taken off food manufacturing and assigned government accounts instead. This lessened the need for travel because the government accounts tended to be clustered in and around Washington, DC. Because he did not have to travel by plane, Joel experienced less general stress, which helped him better manage his symptoms. It created another unexpected problem though: mealtimes with clients. There was a well-established norm of conducting business over restaurant meals in Washington, DC., and the richness of much of the food and lack of control over ingredients tended to worsen Joel's symptoms. He addressed this by creating a list of *safe restaurants*, that is, restaurants with menu items that he knew would not trigger his medical condition. His employer was flexible and allowed him to use establishments that were slightly pricier to guarantee he would have appropriate meals.

Despite these accommodations, Joel did still occasionally need to miss a client meeting due to illness. Yet he was also a high-performing sales representative who had closed deals that others had not been able to close. In an unusual and creative solution, his employer modified the job description of another (willing) worker to address this issue. Every sales rep traveled with a technical consultant. The sales rep managed the sales cycle and the relationship aspects of the deal, the technical analyst ensured the technical specifications were exactly right and would write any custom code required. (Pretty much all accounts required some customizations.) Generally, sales reps were considered the client management people and technical analysts were considered the engineering people. Joel's employer asked for a volunteer among the technical analysts to do some cross-training with sales to learn some client management skills. While Joel would still have primary responsibility for the sales cycle, the analyst could step in at the last minute for a client meeting as needed. This solution was satisfactory to all concerned—the volunteer analyst had the opportunity to learn a new skill and increase their promotion potential, and the employer retained a talented worker who brought in profitable accounts. Joel was able to experience lower stress knowing that, when needed, he had reliable and competent backup and support available to cover his medical absences.

FURTHER READINGS

Gignac, M. A. M., Bowring, J., Jetha, A., Beaton, D. E., Breslin, F. C., Franche, R-L., Irvin, E., Macdermid, J. C., Shaw, W. S., Smith, P. M., Thompson, A., Tompa, E., Van Eerd, D., & Saunders, R. (2021). Disclosure, privacy, and workplace accommodation of episodic disabilities: Organizational perspectives on disability communication-support processes to sustain employment. *Journal of Occupational Rehabilitation, 31,* 153–165. https://doi.org/10.1007/s10926-020-09901-2

Lysaght, R., Krupa, T., & Gregory, A. W. (2022). Employer approaches to recognizing and managing intermittent work capacity. *Equality, Diversity, and Inclusion: An International Journal, 41*(5), 739–759. https://doi.org/10.1108/EDI-02-2021-0046

REFERENCES

American Psychiatric Association. (2022). *Diagnostic and statistical manual of mental disorders* (5th ed., text rev.). https://doi.org/10.1176/appi.books.9780890425787

Anakpo, G., Nqwayibana, Z., & Mishi, S. (2023). The impact of work-from-home on employee performance and productivity: A systematic review. *Sustainability, 15*(5), 4529. https://doi.org/10.3390/su15054529

Arthritis Society Canada. (2023). *Workplace accommodations for people with arthritis.* https://arthritis.ca/support-education/arthritis-and-work/i-m-an-employer/workplace-accommodations-for-people-with-arthritis

Boston Scientific Corporation. (2017). *Workplace accommodations for office workers with chronic pain*. PainScale. https://www.painscale.com/article/workplace-accommodations-for-office-workers-with-chronic-pain

Canadian Human Right Commission. (2017). *Impaired at work: A guide to accommodating substance dependence*. https://www.chrc-ccdp.gc.ca/sites/default/files/impaired_at_work.pdf

Centers for Disease Control and Prevention. (2022, June 22). *Nearly one in five American adults who have had COVID-19 still have "long COVID."* https://www.cdc.gov/nchs/pressroom/nchs_press_releases/2022/20220622.htm

Clair, J. A., Beatty, J. E., & Maclean, T. L. (2005). Out of sight but not out of mind: Managing invisible social identities in the workplace. *Academy of Management Review, 30*(1), 78–95. https://doi.org/10.2307/20159096

Chung, T., Morrow, A. K., Parker, A., Mastalerz, M. H., & Venkatesan, A. (2022, June 14). *Long COVID: Long-term effects of COVID-19*. Johns Hopkins Medicine. https://www.hopkinsmedicine.org/health/conditions-and-diseases/coronavirus/covid-long-haulers-long-term-effects-of-covid19

Gignac, M. A. M., Lacaille, D., Beaton, D. E., Backman, C. L., Cao, X., & Badley, E. M. (2014). Striking a balance: Work-health-personal life conflict in women and men with arthritis and its association with work outcomes. *Journal of Occupational Rehabilitation, 24*(3), 573–584. https://doi.org/10.1007/s10926-013-9490-5

Hesse, K. A., & Ehrens, D. R. M. (2003). ADA, FMLA—inability to perform essential functions of job, reasonable accommodation, intermittent leave. *Benefits Quarterly, 19*(1), 63–65.

Job Accommodation Network. (2023a). *Chronic pain*. https://askjan.org/disabilities/Chronic-Pain.cfm

Job Accommodation Network. (2023b). *Gastrointestinal disorders*. https://askjan.org/disabilities/Gastrointestinal-Disorders.cfm

Job Accommodation Network. (2023c). *Myalgic encephalomyelitis/chronic fatigue syndrome*. https://askjan.org/disabilities/Myalgic-Encephalomyelitis-Chronic-Fatigue-Syndrome.cfm

Lloyd, E. P., Paganini, G. A., & ten Brinke, L. (2020). Gender stereotypes explain disparities in pain care and inform equitable policies. *Policy Insights from the Behavioral and Brain Sciences, 7*(2), 198–204. https://doi.org/10.1177/2372732220942894

National Institutes of Health. (2015, October). *Biology of addiction: Drugs and alcohol can hijack your brain*. News in Health. https://newsinhealth.nih.gov/2015/10/biology-addiction

Niebuhr, F., Borle, P., Börner-Zobel, F., & Voelter-Mahlknecht, S. (2022). Healthy and happy working from home? Effects of working from home on employee health and job satisfaction. *International Journal of Environmental Research and Public Health, 19*(3), 1122. https://doi.org/10.3390/ijerph19031122

Shaw, W. S., McLellan, R. K., Besen, E., Namazi, S., Nicholas, M. K., Dugan, A. G., & Tveito, T. H. (2022). A worksite self-management program for workers with chronic health conditions improves worker engagement and retention, but not workplace function. *Journal of Occupational Rehabilitation, 32*(1), 77–86. https://doi.org/10.1007/s10926-021-09983-6

Smith Fowler, H. (2011, March 31). *Employees' perspectives on intermittent work capacity: What can qualitative research tell us in Ontario?* Social Research and Demonstration Corporation. https://www.srdc.org/uploads/IntermittentWork_report_EN.pdf

Van Eerd, D., Bowring, J., Jetha, A., Breslin, F. C., & Gignac, M. A. (2021). Online resources supporting workers with chronic episodic disabilities: An environmental scan. *International Journal of Workplace Health Management, 14*(2), 129–148. https://doi.org/10.1108/IJWHM-08-2020-0137

Waltemath, J. (2018, July 20). Forcing continuous leave when employee sought intermittent leave may violate both FMLA, ADA. *Westlaw Today.* https://today.westlaw.com/Document/I784e1b298c5611e8a-5b3e3d9e23d7429/View/FullText.html?contextData=(sc.Default)&transitionType=Default&firstPage=true

Yu, J., & Wu, Y. (2021). The impact of enforced working from home on employee job satisfaction during COVID-19: An event system perspective. *International Journal of Environmental Research and Public Health, 18*(24), 13207. https://doi.org/10.3390/ijerph182413207

Inclusive by Design

Thus far, this book has largely focused on accommodations, which are intended to eliminate or mitigate barriers to job performance for workers with disabilities. But what would happen if those barriers never existed in the first place? What if the world was inherently accessible for a wide range of body types and physical and cognitive abilities without any intervention being needed? What if the workplace and the broader world was inclusive by design? Let's explore the answers to these questions with a discussion of inclusive design.

Inclusive design is an emerging field in architecture, interior design, urban planning, and product design that considers this exact question. The British Standards Institution defines inclusive design as "the design of mainstream products and/or services that are accessible to, and usable by, as many people as reasonably possible without the need for special adaptation or specialized design" (Keats, 2005). This could include products such as software or hand tools but also entire buildings, city blocks, and interior spaces. Curb cuts are a simple example. Curb cuts are small ramps built into the curb of a sidewalk, making the curb navigable for wheelchair users and others who struggle with stepping up. Installing curb cuts when a sidewalk is first installed is comparatively simple. Reengineering spaces to add them afterward, while still possible and worthwhile, creates more cost, effort, and disruption. As such, it makes sense for cities and towns to add curb cuts to all curbs during installation of sidewalks since that would eliminate an important barrier to mobility. Yet this frequently isn't done, which creates significant and unnecessary mobility problems for people who are wheelchair users as well as for other members of the community. In fact, when curb cuts first became a prominent feature of American cities, a study of pedestrian behavior was conducted in Sarasota, Florida, that found that the curb cuts were widely used by a broad range of people including wheelchair users, people with walkers, parents with strollers, travelers with luggage, workers pushing carts or wheelbarrows, and even skateboarders. In fact, fully nine out of 10 pedestrians went out of their way to use the curb cuts (Blackwell, 2017). The results highlighted that improving the accessibility of spaces often benefits all community members, not just those with disabilities.

Making inclusive design the default position ultimately improves the lives of many while eliminating barriers to full community participation, including participation in the labor market. Inclusive design results in a more equitable society and reduces the collective and individual social, psychological, and financial burdens associated with unemployment and underemployment.

Inclusive design is broad and is still evolving. This chapter explores the aspects of it that are most relevant for fostering equitable employment, including the design of buildings, interior spaces, and work tools as well as attentiveness to transportation-related needs, work processes and policies, and social environments.

Building Design

The suggestions that follow assume that the employer is constructing a new facility and can control the building specifications. Not all suggestions will be possible to implement in pre-existing buildings, although many can be addressed with renovations. Three primary considerations when designing buildings are accessibility for people with mobility limitations, navigability for people with vision impairments, and acoustics for everyone, but particularly for those with hearing impairments. There are additional considerations related to levels of privacy, stimulation, and psychological well-being, some of which are covered under building design while others are discussed under interior design.

Accessibility Design

Designing buildings to enhance accessibility for people with mobility impairments, especially wheelchair and scooter users, are among the more obvious concerns that need addressing. As a result, the criteria and standards required by governments have been documented and, in most legal jurisdictions, formalized with legislation, formal building code standards, and extensive official regulations. Those regulations cover the need to provide ramps at building entrances, elevators within the building, automatic door openers, and similar accessibility aids. The rules are precise and extremely detailed to ensure safety. For example, wheelchair ramps must have a maximum slope consisting of a 1-inch rise for every 12 inches of length, resulting in a 4.8-degree angle and an 8.3% grade. The minimum width of the inside rails must be 36 inches, although 48 inches is better due to the extra width of some motorized chairs and scooters. Specifications for items such as handrail placement, size, and type; automated door opener requirements; and accessible washroom dimensions are equally well documented in most jurisdictions such that employers can request that architects and builders simply comply with regulations. (Those wanting to view a sample of recommendations can consult the links under Further Readings at the end of this chapter, as well as searching local building codes.) But just meeting minimum requirements is not the goal, but rather exceeding regulations. For example, wider bathroom stalls than the minimum requirement are helpful to maximize comfort and flexibility to accommodate emerging mobility aids.

One common need that is often overlooked is access to electrical outlets. Since outlets are usually placed low on the floor, they can be difficult for people in wheelchairs to reach, so planning for some at waist height is helpful. (Some legal jurisdictions do regulate outlet placement, so consult local building codes before proceeding.) Another commonly overlooked area is the spacing between entry doors when double doors are used. People who need to push the automatic door opener buttons to have doors open for them sometimes find that there is not enough space between the doors to allow them to rotate sufficiently to reach the second button that opens the inner set of doors. This problem can be solved by allowing extra space or having both sets of doors open with a single button. Extra thought should also be given to the specific, local environmental conditions. For example, in hot and sunny climates, handrails should not be black to avoid experiencing burns in summer, while in wintery climates, rail materials that lessen the transfer of cold to the hands should be used (e.g., wood rather than metal).

In addition to complying with basic accessibility regulations and laws regarding ramps, handrails, accessible bathrooms, and the provision of elevators, employers should also be attentive to how people will move in the interior spaces. Wider hallways and doorways are helpful, as are lowered sinks and having at least one of the bathroom mirrors placed at a height suitable for a wheelchair user. Public spaces in which people tend to stop and converse, such as lobbies, should have space for benches such that people who become engaged in conversation with colleagues who are using wheelchairs can sit at eye level with them, which is generally more comfortable for both parties. Cafeterias and other spaces that accommodate crowds should have clear paths wide enough for wheelchairs to pass even when at capacity. Display cases in the cafeteria, coffee makers in break rooms, printers, cupboards containing personal protective equipment, and other office community resources must be reachable by people in wheelchairs without requiring special assistance. Some of these issues, such as cafeteria counter or built-in cupboard heights, may need to be addressed during the construction or renovation phase, while others, such as printer placement, could be addressed post-construction.

Vision Impairment Design Accommodations

People with vision impairments also have predictable difficulties navigating physical spaces. (Suggestions for mitigating these difficulties can also be found in Chapter 4.) Inclusive design focuses on minimizing the existence of the difficulties rather than mitigating them. For example, a general layout that focuses on straight lines with turns, such as hallways, at 90-degree angles helps people with low vision or no vision to maintain their spatial orientation. The layout of each floor should be consistent to enable easier navigation. For example, washrooms should be at the same location on each floor. Protrusions should be detectable by a person using a cane, which means that objects or signs mounted less than 2.030 mm (0.07 of an inch) above the walking surface should have a leading edge no higher than 680 mm (26.7 inches). (Note that these dimension guidelines assume an adult is using the cane; in buildings frequented by children, adjustments will need to be made.) Stairs can be made safer by having handrail extensions at the top and bottom of the stairs in a high contrast color (compared to the walls), and by having slip resistant high contrast strips at the edge of each step. Similarly, clear paths through busy spaces such as lobbies can be signaled with high contrast colors built into the floor coverings themselves. For example, dark blue tiles against white tiles could be used to indicate a safe path to an information booth or escalator. The installation of tactile floor stripes (i.e., textured floor coverings that have, for example, small bumps on them) can be used to signal location and as a warning that hazards such as a staircase are nearby.

The use of braille signage and braille elevator buttons should be included at the design stage. Signs and doorways can also be highlighted using contrasting colors. Color usage should be consistent throughout the building and have meaning. For example, having washroom doors in one consistent (but different) color based on gender is helpful, easily distinguishing men's, women's, and gender-neutral facilities.

Security solutions should also be scrutinized before being installed. Access cards, for example, are easier to use if they can just be waved in front of a reader rather than having to be inserted in a specific direction or orientation. The card readers should be consistently located and be a high contrast color compared to the wall. Furthermore, having an audible cue that they have been activated, not just a visible one, is helpful.

Acoustic Design and Echolocation Accommodations

Less obvious is the need to design spaces to enable the use of echolocation. Echolocation is a technique used by many people with vision impairments. A sound, such as snapping fingers or tapping a cane, is generated and the reflected sound that bounces back is assessed to establish physical characteristics such as the size of a room, the presence of structural barriers such as poles, and the presence of hallways. Attention should be paid to the placement of noise-generating components of a room to ensure they provide useful information. For example, escalators produce a distinctive noise, which should help identify a central location in the building, or a water feature may indicate an area for rest such as a garden or reception space. Ventilation ducts, by contrast, may be useful for wayfinding or simply mask and block other important sounds depending on placement. Echolocation is more difficult in large rooms with high, open ceilings, which tend to have more *sound glare*, meaning a high level of reflected and ambient sound. Double glazed glass is an effective sound buffer, and it can be strategically used to lessen ambient noise to better enable echolocation. Carpets and acoustic ceiling tiles also dampen sound and should be used strategically. (But too much sound dampening interferes with echolocation because reflected sound is minimized, while not enough sound dampening ensures confusion due to the cacophony of noises competing with echolocation techniques.) Since the way sound travels and is reflected off structures and materials is complex, the assistance of specialized acoustic engineers is recommended.

Management of sound is also an important consideration when designing structures that minimize barriers for the hearing impaired. People with partial hearing can participate more fully when rooms are designed with acoustics in mind. Ideally, speakers at the front of a given room can be easily heard while ambient and background noises are muted, and conversations can be held in any space within the room. The shape of rooms heavily impacts acoustics, with rectangles being the preferred shape to ensure sound waves travel effectively from the front of the room to the back. Room size, ceiling height, and wall, floor, and ceiling materials also have an impact. There are devices that can be placed throughout a room to aid in sound dispersal (e.g., a curved diffusor can direct sound waves to parts of a room where they otherwise would not reach) and sound suppression (e.g., sound absorbing ceiling tiles can minimize ambient background noise). The correct combination for a given space is a task that is generally beyond the expertise of the average layperson, requiring a formally trained acoustics engineer, who could also be consulted preconstruction to prevent the emergence of problems in the first place.

Finally, furniture placement should be given careful attention. To read lips, workers need to be able to see the speaker(s), so tables and chairs that allow one to rearrange the room at need are preferred over seating that is permanently fixed in place, such as that found in some lecture halls.

Mental Health and Well-Being Design

Building design can even assist with mental health needs, reducing the symptoms associated with stress-related ailments and improving the health of all workers, with and without disabilities. Psychological well-being is enhanced and stress is reduced when people can see outdoor spaces, particularly when those outdoor spaces include natural environments, plants, and trees rather than other buildings, parking lots, and similar urban views. A 2001 meta-analysis of numerous studies that was sponsored by the Canadian Institute for Research in Construction found that access to a window with a view of nature increased job satisfaction, job engagement, positive perceptions of working conditions, and life satisfaction, and it reduced turnover intentions. From a building design perspective, this means that maximizing access to windows is important. There are several ways this can be achieved, including narrower buildings, placing washrooms, kitchens, and other community spaces that are not primary workspaces in the center of the building, and increasing the overall number and size of windows. Interior, outdoor courtyards are also an excellent way to maximize window space, especially if the courtyard is planted with shrubs, trees, and flowers and is accessible to employees on breaks. Buildings can also be placed further away from the street and parking lot to enable planting of trees that screen urban views, or parking lots can be underground such that they do not impair the view. Adding a rooftop garden space can lessen the carbon footprint of the building while providing employees without windows an outdoor view during breaks. Many people find spending time in a garden relaxing, which further improves psychological well-being and ability to manage stress.

Finally, building design can assist with mental health and foster a disability-friendly environment by considering privacy and levels of unwanted stimulation experienced in workspaces. Many people with conditions such as attention deficit disorder and autism struggle with open floor-plans that contain many densely packed cubicles because they tend to be bustling, noisy environments with many distractions that lead to sensory overwhelm. Designing smaller office spaces for individual workers, preferably with doors, is ideal but often cost-prohibitive. But there are compromises that can keep costs in check while ensuring that employees have fewer distractions. For example, building designers could plan to have cubicles in a few distinct, smaller rooms, perhaps sorted by job function, rather than have one giant open-plan *cubicle farm*. Areas that will include a larger number of cubicles should use sound dampening construction materials in walls and ceilings and be placed away from main thoroughfares, cafeterias, break areas, and bathrooms, which create additional bustle and potential for distraction. Cubicles can also be placed such that people's voices are directed away from each other rather than toward each other. For example, cubicle walls and a desk would be placed such that the worker faced the window when speaking rather than the wall of the adjacent cubicle.

Bathroom privacy is also a key support for people with medical conditions that involve gastrointestinal issues, and that privacy is appreciated by people without disabilities, too. Having some private, one-person bathrooms in a facility to serve a range of needs is helpful, including supporting the dignity of people experiencing gastrointestinal distress and providing a comfortable space for those going through gender affirmation transitions due to gender dysphoria.

Interior Design

The interior design of buildings also has implications for inclusion. Some areas of concern include signage type and placement, furniture and shelf placement, degree of involuntary exposure to irrelevant sensory input, privacy needs, and the psychological impact of color.

Signage Design

The placement of signs is important, particularly for workers who are vision impaired. Signs need to be placed such that they do not create an obstacle to people who are blind and use canes to navigate. They also need to be in large print and clearly delineated (e.g., a white sign against a white wall would be harder to see than a sign outlined in red or black), and the sign itself should use contrasting text and background colors such that people with impaired vision can easily perceive and read them. Colors on the opposite ends of the color wheel, such as blue and orange, create the best visual contrast.

Furniture and Shelving Placement

Similarly, furniture should be placed with care and be in contrasting colors compared to the wall and carpet and should always be kept in the same location. There should be clear, wide paths between furnishings that enable the passage of a scooter or wheelchair even when people are seated at couches and tables. (Designers often forget to account for the space that will be taken up by peoples' legs once a space is populated.) Using tactile strips or different colored or textured flooring to delineate those paths can also assist people with vision impairments to navigate the space, and it discourages others from casually moving furnishings.

Shelving units used to hold important work tools such as reference books and printers need to be at a level that can be readily reached by a person in a wheelchair. Coffee pots, microwaves, and similar devices also need to be placed such that they can be reached easily by workers in scooters and wheelchairs without having to request assistance every time.

Privacy Design Considerations

Privacy can be improved and involuntary exposure to excessive sensory input (e.g., noise and visual distractions) can be reduced through placement of interior décor that also acts as screening, such as large plants and bookshelves. Plants are an especially good choice because exposure to plants has both physical and psychological benefits, reducing stress and even lowering blood pressure (Lee et al., 2015). Spiky cacti, however, are not recommended due to the risk they pose to those with limited vision, or simply people who are clumsy and likely to brush against them inadvertently. Flowering plants also have more potential to trigger allergies, making leafy green plants such as ferns and small, nonflowering trees the best choices. Bamboo grows especially quickly and creates particularly robust screening. The placement of cubicles and the material they are made from can also have a dramatic impact on the level of distraction experienced. Cubicles should be soundproof and placed such that noise is directed away from coworkers rather than toward them.

Color Design

Researcher Faber Birren (1900–1988) devoted his career to studying the psychological impact of color in the workplace, publishing more than 40 books and 250 articles on the subject and serving as a consultant for industry giants such as General Electric and DuPont. Birren found that color impacted the safety behaviors, morale, and productivity of workers.

The following insights are from his seminal book titled *Colour and Human Response*, which was originally published in 1978 and reprinted in 1991.

Red colors tend to raise blood pressure, pulse rate, and respiration and excite brain waves, and orange and yellow have similar effects, although the impact is reduced. Blue colors, by contrast, have the opposite effect, lowering blood pressure and pulse rate, and purples operate in a similar manner to blues, although with lesser impact. Greens engender largely neutral reactions. This indicates that stress reduction is best supported with blue tones. Meanwhile, those who experience excessive fatigue may occasionally benefit from the extra stimulation of red colors, especially for tasks requiring higher levels of mental alertness or activity. Note that these physiological responses to color operate largely independently of personal preferences. For example, someone's favorite color may be red, and they may dislike blue, but their body will still have a nonconscious relaxation response to blue tones. (There may be individual exceptions for people who strongly associate a color with a prior life experience. For example, someone who was lost in a forest for an extended period as a child may react differently to [normally neutral] shades of green if they associate the color with the fear and anxiety of that negative experience.)

Shades of color matter, too. Cooler colors such as blue, green, and violet tones are best for workspaces, and warmer colors such as red, orange, and yellow tones are best for areas devoted to rest and relaxation. This can be somewhat confusing, since it was just explained that blues are calming and reds exciting, but any color can have a warm or cool tone. For example, a yellower shade of green such as neon green will be warmer, while a bluer shade of green such as the color of a spruce tree will be cooler. So, when creating a dining space in which the hope is for people to relax and shed stress, it may be prudent to use blue to lower blood pressure and pulse rate, but a warm shade of blue that includes more yellow rather than a cold shade of blue.

Accent colors can reduce monotony, helping people stay more alert throughout the workday. Colors such as those used for doorways, window frames, and baseboards can be used to create an optimal blend of stimulating and relaxing colors in a given space based on the primary purpose of that space.

High gloss paints create glare, which causes physical, mental, and emotional discomfort, especially when highly lit. Matte finishes on walls are preferable. Similarly, brightness can be a source of distraction when engaged in sedentary tasks such as sitting at a desk reading and writing. Muted blue green tones are ideal to support focus and concentration.

This can assist all employees but may especially benefit those who experience problems with focus and concentration, such as workers with attention deficit disorder. Context, of course, is everything. Bright colors such as yellow, coral, and orange improve alertness, and therefore safety, in physically demanding and hazardous work settings. These colors are recommended for walls and even machinery in contexts such as manufacturing. Orange may also lessen hostility and irritability, improving the social environment. Brown and gray, however, seem to have a stifling, depressive effect. Research studies conducted by Henner Ertel (quoted in Birren's book) have shown brown and gray rooms even lowering IQ scores slightly among school children as compared to rooms painted light blue, yellow, yellow-green, and orange.

Color can have surprising health and psychological impacts in specific contexts. Researcher Helen Varley documented some of these in her book *Colour* (1991). In one example, workers in a lipstick factory were suffering from nausea and dizziness because of green afterimages caused by staring at red lipstick all day. The illnesses disappeared after the walls were painted green. Production in another factory improved after the boxes that materials were shipped in were changed from black to light green. Workers had perceived the black boxes as heavier even though they weighed the same as the green ones. This perception slowed them down when moving the black boxes. Some shades of yellow are avoided on airplanes because they tend to induce or worsen nausea. Vivid colors in hallways and corridors have also been demonstrated to increase the speed with which people travel through those spaces. Given these examples, if an employee states that they believe a color change may improve their ability to work or lessen the impact of a disability, they may just be right!

Work Tool and Software Design

Inclusive design is not limited to buildings and workspaces. The principle can be applied to anything. For example, power tools, hand tools, software, uniforms, and safety equipment can all be intentionally designed to be usable and safe for a wider variety of body types and medical conditions. During the early days of the COVID-19 pandemic, the firsthand consequences of a lack of inclusive design were obvious. Large number of female healthcare workers reported that many of the masks and respirators they were expected to use in pandemic wards were not appropriately sized for smaller female faces, creating gaps that exposed them to the virus to a degree not experienced by their larger female colleagues and their male colleagues (Porterfield, 2020). This life-threatening workplace safety issue was entirely preventable had the masks and respirators been designed with inclusive principles in mind.

Work Tool Design

The Canadian Centre for Occupational Health and Safety has several recommendations related to tools. Power tools, for example, should be made using materials that reduce the vibrations experienced by the user. Anti-vibration tools should be the standard default to reduce repetitive strain injuries and ensure tools are more useable for people with fatigue issues, limb conditions, or other disabilities. A longer trigger mechanism that allows the user to activate the tool using two or three fingers rather than one also lessens muscle strain and enables people with limb differences or missing digits to use it more readily. Hand tools should be equally useable for left- and right-handed users, and in some cases a left-handed version and a right-handed version may be required. The tool handles should be slightly contoured for easier grip. When the direction of the force being applied is in line with the forearm and wrist, then tools should have a bent handle to prevent the need to awkwardly flex or hold the wrist at an unnatural angle; however, if the direction of force is perpendicular to the forearm and wrist, then a straight handle will lessen fatigue and strain. Handle diameters influence the degree of force needed to control the tool and should be within 30–50 mm (1.1 to 1.9 inches) for power grips and 8–16 mm (0.3 to 0.6 inches) for precision tasks. Handles should also be made of nonslip and nonconductive materials. By buying tools that meet these standards as the default, employers are less likely to find themselves needing to make additional tool purchases to accommodate a disability (although that may still occur sometimes).

Personal protective equipment is another area that may require special attention. Here, inclusive design and making one product suitable for all may not be possible or appropriate. For example, custom-tailored gloves and other protective clothing may be required for people with limb differences or dwarfism to ensure that it is sized appropriately and can be worn comfortably. Safety goggles may need to be fitted over glasses or contain prescription lenses. The nature of hearing protection used may need to be adjusted to accommodate people using hearing aids—for example, sound-canceling headphone-type devices that go over the ears may be more suitable than ear plugs intended to go in the ears.

In this context, inclusive design would mean having a wide range of options (e.g., different styles of hearing protection) available in existing inventory, and a formal and consistent process whereby such needs are identified and addressed before the employee is asked to complete the task, ensuring that the equipment is there when needed without having to make a special accommodation request. A similar process can also be used for custom workstation modifications. The best time to make such inquiries is after an offer to hire has been signed and before the individual's first day of work, although there should also be a follow-up check after the individual has started working because they may not be aware of all needs beforehand.

Documents and Software Design

Written materials are often an important work resource. Understanding them is important for all employees, including those with intellectual and learning disabilities or literacy issues. Written materials may include everything from safety instructions, work task assignments, and policy and procedure manuals to human resource forms and software applications used for day-to-day tasks. These documents and applications should be designed for the lowest level of reading skill that is practical respective to the content. Simple words and phrases should be used, and documents that are not intended for technical experts should avoid using overly technical language or abbreviations. Most word processing programs now have embedded tools that allow you to assess the level of literacy required to read the text, and this information can provide guidance about when you may need to simplify your language. In addition, key instructions, such as critical safety information, can be communicated graphically in addition to using text-based instructions. In some instances, video content can replace text-based task instructions, especially within software applications. Standard forms, such as expense reimbursement or vacation request forms, can be rendered more readily useable by people with literacy issues or cognitive impairments using visual or auditory prompts that help them complete the forms more accurately. For example, hovering over a blank field could bring up a tooltip element with an explanation and an example highlighting what is required. Dropdown menus that allow one to select from a short list of appropriate options may be easier than typing original text into a blank space, and there should be both visual and auditory alerts when a required field has not been completed.

Software can also be designed with different needs in mind. The Web Content Accessibility Guidelines (WCAGs) are detailed guidelines that, when followed, ensure web-based content is accessible for people with a wide variety of disabilities, including auditory, cognitive, physical, speech, and visual disabilities. The guidelines are extensive, and a full accounting is beyond the scope of this text. A link to the full guidelines appears in the Further Readings at the end of this chapter. Key elements, however, include having the ability to turn text into speech and vice versa. This allows people with visual impairments to hear written content, people with hearing impairments to see spoken text, people with speech impediments to type and have their written input converted to the spoken word, and people who are unable to type or have literacy issues to have their spoken words converted into printed text. As such a person who is blind, a person who is Deaf, a person who has profound dyslexia, a person who is nonverbal, and a person with a double arm amputation could all meet online and communicate readily.

Other aspects of the WCAGs standards deal with barriers that are less obvious to the average layperson. For example, color contrasts between the background and foreground are important for visual processing, and thus standards are specified. Some disabilities render the use of a mouse difficult or impossible, so keyboard commands must be available for each function normally achieved by clicking a mouse. Content also should not flash more than three times per second to avoid triggering visual processing issues or epileptic seizures. The size of the target for pointer inputs should be large enough for people with unsteady hands to click. Employers purchasing software—even if hosted locally and not, strictly speaking, web-based— should ask about compliance with WCAGs guidelines. Employers building web applications and software in-house should have their developers comply with the guidelines.

When making inquiries, employers should be aware that there are three levels to the WCAGs standard: A, AA, and AAA. The A level is the most basic, and while it ensures access for many users who experience common barriers such as sight and hearing impairments, some barriers may still exist. The AA level is the most targeted performance level, suitable for most users including those using assistive technology. It is the level that is frequently cited in the development of formal regulations and in legal cases. The AAA level is the highest conformance level, accommodating an extremely wide variety of disability types and unique barriers associated with them. This level is not necessarily practical or achievable because it accounts for every possible disability and barrier. As such, this level is seldom holistically achieved; however, organizations often pick and choose specific criteria to comply with based on the needs of identifiable individuals in their organization.

Many companies find themselves designing and developing their own specialized tools, workflows, software, and policies. The tips about things like tool grips and WGAC standards are equally applicable when designing tools in-house, but the overall creative process also needs to be inclusive. The design team should be aware of inclusive design principles and embed them in their methods right from the beginning. For example, a wide variety of diverse end-users should be consulted during the initial design phase and the testing phase, with special attention paid to the needs of users of differing abilities and body types. When doing this, be aware of the time and labor involved and make sure employees who participate are provided some relief from other tasks. Do not continually tap the same person. For example, if there is only one employee who is a wheelchair user, they may find it exhausting to be consulted by every team for every issue related to wheelchair accessibility. In cases like that, hiring outside expertise on a short-term contract basis may be preferable. Having diverse members on the design team is also helpful because this expands the range of issues (i.e., potential barriers) they will consider and will foster creativity.

While all members should be encouraged to consider these priorities, there should be a designated, appropriately trained individual on the team whose formal role is to monitor inclusion. Accountability is an important driver of behavior, so holding someone personally accountable using appropriate formal performance metrics will help ensure the issue gets the attention it deserves. Finally, employers themselves need to be open to taking additional time to find optimal tools rather than creating artificial deadlines that require teams to rush a solution out the door without full consideration. This is particularly relevant in the software design world, which often embraces a *get it out the door and fix it later* mentality that can limit the thought and care put into inclusion and access.

Transportation

Getting to and from work can pose a significant barrier for people with many types of disabilities. In a community designed with inclusion in mind, public transportation would be fully accessible to all. Unfortunately, this is not the case. For example, in many cities and towns, wheelchair users need to prebook specialized transportation rather than take city buses, and the number of trips per week is limited, as are the hours in which the service is provided. Furthermore, many workplaces are not located in areas in which public transportation is available, meaning employees rely on their own cars, bikes, or walking to get there.

People with mobility impairments, vision impairments, fatigue, and pain, and people impacted by sensory issues can find public forms of transportation such as buses and subways difficult to use and unduly stressful. Employers can help by advocating for more inclusive forms of public transportation and by filling in the gaps by providing their own transportation options. Some large companies invest in their own small buses or private taxis, while smaller, less well-resourced companies can arrange carpools, provide funding for private transport, and even directly compensate employees for helping a colleague who lives nearby get to and from work each day. When public transportation is not an option, those kinds of alternatives become even more attractive.

Attention should also be paid to the needs of employees with disabilities who are able to self-drive to work or who have another party drive them to work. Parking lots should be as close to the building as possible, and the closest spaces should be reserved for employees with disabilities. Both the lots themselves and the pathways to the building need to be maintained. Snow removal during winter should be done in a timely manner, before workers are arriving for their shifts. Moving a wheelchair through deep snow is both extraordinarily difficult and dangerous, but slippery surfaces also impact employees with a range of other conditions, and controlling ice around the building entrance should be a priority. Furthermore, parking areas should be well lit and, if underground, there should be clear signage indicating where to exit as well as elevators available with braille buttons.

Policies and Procedures

Policies and procedures are also subject to inclusive design priorities. Policies and procedures become problematic when they create disadvantage based on disability. Whenever possible, inclusive design ensures that policies and procedures do not include embedded disability-related barriers, rather than fixing the barriers later through exceptions and accommodations. Attendance and tardiness policies are an excellent example. Many attendance and tardiness policies are punitive, with disciplinary consequences for absences or being late. Others focus on positive reinforcement by offering financial incentives for perfect attendance. Both are problematic for the members of the disability community who experience unpredictable flare-ups of symptoms, have symptoms that are more active at specific times of day (such as increased pain and stiffness in the morning), or require ongoing medical monitoring at regular doctor's appointments.

Whenever possible employers are encouraged to offer flexible scheduling, which eliminates the issue of tardiness entirely, and work-from-home options that will allow some people to work even when experiencing mild symptoms that prohibit in-person attendance. When that is not possible employers must ensure that any tardiness or absences that are related to the disability are not counted for disciplinary purposes. Requiring a doctor's note for each permissible absence is not practical, and employees with documented disabilities should not be asked to produce one every time. It becomes more reasonable to ask for a note for longer absences (more than 3 days, perhaps). Finally, group-based attendance bonus incentives should be avoided completely. These incentives provide an entire work team with a financial bonus if the entire team has no absences in a given period of time. These incentive plans create enormous peer pressure to show up for work even when ill, and they often result in bullying and harassment of workers who supposedly let the team down by requiring an absence. Other policies that are likely to be problematic are policies that require travel for specific training in order to receive promotions, policies that require a minimum number of hours worked a week to access supports such as benefits, policies that require working full-time hours to be eligible for promotions, and policies that impose mandatory overtime under certain conditions.

One of the most controversial policies that some employers have introduced recently is a disclosure policy related to drug and alcohol addiction. Some employers, realizing that they cannot fire employees for having addictions, have created policies that make a failure to proactively disclose an addiction a fireable offense. (Technically the employee is being fired for the lack of disclosure, not the addiction itself, creating a legal loophole.) The employers doing this argue that disclosure is required to provide appropriate supports and ensure a safe workplace. The problem is that denial of addiction is so common that it is one of the diagnostic criteria for addiction, rendering the expectation of voluntary self-disclosure unrealistic at best. These policies are therefore not advisable and are not in the spirit of inclusion. Approaches to addictions in the workplace vary significantly from one legal jurisdiction to the other such that legal responses to these policies are unpredictable. For example, in Canada, the case of *Stewart v. Elk Coal Company* (2017 SCC 30) went all the way to the Supreme Court. The employer had instituted a policy requiring employees to proactively disclose addictions before the occurrence of a drug-related incident. The employee did not disclose his addiction and was subsequently involved in an accident involving a loader while impaired by cocaine. He was terminated due to violating the policy, which he challenged because denial is a symptom of addiction. When the complaint went to the Supreme Court, the termination was upheld by a slight majority of the judges. A minority of the judges considered the termination to be discriminatory but felt it was justified due to undue hardship related to accommodation needs. One judge wrote an impassioned dissenting opinion arguing that this decision represented an unacceptable and highly discriminatory outcome that would seriously disadvantage members of the disability community. It is worth noting that this dissenting opinion was held even though the setting (a coal mine) is a workplace in which safety concerns are much more central than in typical office environments. The differences of opinion displayed in the highest courts in Canada serve as a useful reminder that these policies have uncertain legal standing in many jurisdictions and it may be prudent to avoid them entirely, especially if the workplace is not especially safety sensitive.

Social Environment

Inclusive design extends to the social environment in the workplace. Formally sanctioned social activities that are used to build a sense of teamwork often revolve around either sport, dining, or drinking, which can all be problematic for members of the disability community. Informal social activities are even more likely to be centered around drinking in many workplace cultures. Managers should be attentive to designing sanctioned activities that are accessible for people of all body types and abilities. This does not mean that every single activity needs to be fully accessible—although that would be nice—but there should be meaningful ways for people with various needs and preferences to participate. For example, a company-sponsored family picnic in a park that includes a casual softball game could also include fun activities that are more accessible and that run simultaneously, such as a trivia challenge or learning how to make balloon animals for the children in attendance. Managers should also be sensitive to varied dining needs and should plan both formal and informal activities that do not involve drinking. (For more information on making dining inclusive, explore the scenarios presented in Chapter 3.)

One of the faulty assumptions often made when social activities are planned is that everyone is an extrovert. Extroverts prefer high stimulation settings, and they are energized when there is a great deal going on at once. For example, a crowded party with many small clusters of conversations and multiple activities would be exciting. Introverts, by contrast, prefer settings with less stimulation. Introverts are often mischaracterized as disliking human interaction, but that is not true. They do, however, find that having to pay attention to a wide variety of stimuli simultaneously is exhausting. They may well enjoy the same busy party that energizes the extrovert, but after an hour they will be exhausted and in need of a quiet space to take a break. Social events are almost always planned with an *extrovert assumption*, that is, the nature of social events tends to lean more toward the boisterous and busy. This can create issues for people with many types of disabilities including fatigue and autism (the latter due to sensory overload). Planning some quieter events that are focused on only one or two activities may make introverts more likely to participate while also making participation easier for some members of the disability community. Time limited events that are scheduled to last only an hour or two also are more accessible because there is no need to fear social sanctions for leaving early.

By expanding the definitions of inclusive design into the social and policy world as well as the physical world, the spirit of inclusion that the movement intends to foster can truly be embraced. Employers also save themselves time and effort by designing a workplace that avoids the creation of disability-related barriers in the first place. Inclusive design is, therefore, a winning formula for employers, employees, and the broader community.

FURTHER READINGS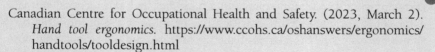

Canadian Centre for Occupational Health and Safety. (2023, March 2). *Hand tool ergonomics.* https://www.ccohs.ca/oshanswers/ergonomics/handtools/tooldesign.html

Canadian National Institute for the Blind. (2019a). *Acoustics.* https://www.clearingourpath.ca/2.4.0-acoustics_e.php

Canadian National Institute for the Blind. (2019b). *Layout.* https://www.clearingourpath.ca/2.1.0-layout_e.php

Canadian National Institute for the Blind. (2019c). *Protruding objects and other obstacles.* https://www.clearingourpath.ca/3.2.0-protruding-objects_e.php

Chang, F. (2020, October 19). To build more inclusive technology change your design processes. *Harvard Business Review.* https://hbr.org/2020/10/to-build-more-inclusive-technology-change-your-design-process

Keates, S., Clarkson, P. J., Harrison, L. A., & Robinson, P. (2000, November). *Towards a practical inclusive design approach.* In Proceedings on the 2000 Conference on Universal Usability, 45–52. https://doi.org/10.1145/355460.355471

University of Cambridge. (2023). *Inclusive design toolkit.* https://www.inclusivedesigntoolkit.com/

REFERENCES

Birren, F. (1978). *Colour and human response.* Van Nostrand Reinhold.

Blackwell, A. G. (2017). The curb-cut effect. *Stanford Social Innovation Review.* https://ssir.org/articles/entry/the_curb_cut_effect

Demming, A. (2020, February 4). Acoustics in architecture. *Physics World.* https://physicsworld.com/a/acoustics-in-architecture/

Farley, K. M. J., & Veitch, J. A. (2001, August 15). *A room with a view: A review of the effects of windows on work and well-being.* Institute for Research in Construction. https://citeseerx.ist.psu.edu/document?repid=rep1&type=pdf&doi=d61e3be90835118f12f35d586c0bc38cae858180

Jeamwatthanachai, W., Wald, M., & Wills, G. (2019). Indoor navigation by blind people: Behaviors and challenges in unfamiliar spaces and buildings. *British Journal of Visual Impairment, 37*(2), 140–153. https://doi.org/10.1177/0264619619833372

Keates, S. (2005). Standard BS 7000-6:2005: "Design management systems - Managing inclusive design". British Standards Institution.

Lee, M. S., Lee, J., Park, B. J., & Miyazaki, Y. (2015). Interaction with indoor plants may reduce psychological and physiological stress by suppressing autonomic nervous system activity in young adults: A randomized crossover study. *Journal of Physiological Anthropology, 34*(21), 1–6. https://doi.org/10.1186/s40101-015-0060-8

Northeast Rehabilitation Health Network. (2008, July 25). Wheelchair ramp information. *BrainLine.* https://www.brainline.org/article/wheelchair-ramp-information#:~:text=Maximum%20slope%20for%20hand%2Dpropelled,(48%22%20is%20ideal)

Porterfield, C. (2020, April 29). A lot of PPE doesn't fit women—and in the coronavirus pandemic, it puts them in danger. *Forbes.* https://www.forbes.com/sites/carlieporterfield/2020/04/29/a-lot-of-ppe-doesnt-fit-women-and-in-the-coronavirus-pandemic-it-puts-them-in-danger/?sh=19464389315a

Sánchez, J., Sáenz, M., Pascual-Leone, A., & Merabet, L. (2010, April 10). Navigation for the blind through audio-based virtual environments. In *CHI'13 Extended abstracts on human factors in computing systems* (pp. 3409–3414). https://doi.org/10.1145/1753846.1753993

Sorensen, M. (2012, July 1). *Small room acoustic size and shape.* Acoustic Fields. https://www.acousticfields.com/small-room-acoustic-structure/

Varley, H. (1991). *Colour.* Marshall Editions.

World Wide Web Consortium. (2018, June 5). *Web content accessibility guidelines WCAG 2.1.* https://www.w3.org/TR/WCAG21/

World Wide Web Consortium. (2023, April 19). *WCAG 2 overview.* https://www.w3.org/WAI/standards-guidelines/wcag/

9

Case Studies
A Glimpse into the Real World

While there are best practices in disability accommodation, it remains true that every case is individual. Human resources (HR) personnel, managers, and business owners need to apply guidelines and best practices in a variety of complex situations in which the needs of the organization, customers, peers, the worker with a disability, subordinates, and in some instances a support animal, all require consideration. It is not possible to just open a book and find a perfect solution to every situation requiring accommodation—common sense, good judgment, clear communication, an awareness of the specific work flow and tasks required, creativity, and empathy are all needed to reach optimal solutions. The following cases are intended as practice. They describe real situations, but the names of individuals, organizations and businesses, and locations have been changed.

Working through these cases will allow the reader to practice their applied accommodation skills using real-world examples that reflect the complexity of actual workplaces. Read through each case and then stop and reflect: What would you do if you were the key decision maker in this scenario? You can then compare your solution to a recommended solution, keeping in mind that there can be multiple valid ways to approach any given accommodation need.

Farid's Story: Intermittent Disability in a Team Warehouse Setting

This case involves a warehouse picker-packer job and an employee with Crohn's disease. The symptoms associated with his Crohn's disease are intermittent and unpredictable, leading to inconvenient absences and associated peer resentment. The incentive system and managerial policies of the organization inadvertently magnify these problems directly and indirectly through heightened stress. The case explores issues centered around managing the unpredictability of intermittent disabilities, as well as the impact of organizational policies and peer attitudes on inclusion outcomes.

The Case

Farid's heart sank. He knew he would have to call in sick again. He didn't want to, but his Crohn's disease was flaring up, and he had spent the last 20 minutes in the bathroom. He wasn't sure what had set off his symptoms this time, but he knew from experience that it would only get worse as the morning progressed. He couldn't face the embarrassment of running to the bathroom multiple times throughout his shift, never mind the humiliation of having to use a shared bathroom with his coworkers. Regretfully, he called his supervisor, Ling, and explained that he would be absent that day. It was an especial blow because it meant he would lose his perfect attendance bonus for the month. The stress of losing the bonus was, ironically, making his gastrointestinal symptoms worse, as did stress of any kind. While the $50 bonus may seem small, Farid was always cash-strapped because he was supporting family members in India, sending them any extra money he had. In their village, $50 in American funds represented about a week's worth of wages, so it made a difference. He was particularly stressed because he feared the loss may impact the family's ability to afford his mother's prescription medications.

Shift supervisor Ling hung up from Farid's call with a sigh. His absence would create inconvenience. Ling liked Farid. He was a hard worker, and, on a personal level, Farid was one of the employees who always took care to use Ling's preferred pronouns (them and their), a form of acknowledgement and respect that Ling appreciated because not everyone was as careful. That said, Ling wasn't sure how to address Farid's occasional absences, which generally lasted 1 to 2 days and, while unpredictable, occurred on average once every 4 to 6 weeks. Sometimes absences were spaced more closely together (once he was absent for 4 days in a 10-day period), while other times Farid would go for 2 or 3 months without symptoms before needing to call in again. Absences created issues for everyone because they were very busy and the company had a standing promise to deliver all orders within 48 hours, or discounts would be applied. This promise was one of their competitive advantages, making them a preferred vendor in their field and generating repeat business. It was so important to the company that they had generated two incentives to ensure they reached their goal. The first was the monthly bonus for perfect attendance, which would ensure an adequate number of workers were available. The second was a team-based monthly performance bonus, which rewarded the entire warehouse staff as a group if a minimum of 98% of orders arrived on time. The company also tried to ensure efficiency by tightly monitoring breaks. People who took overly long on breaks of any kind could be disciplined, but it was seldom necessary because their peers would often informally intervene before it got to that point, resenting anyone who was perceived as slowing down the team and singling them out for mockery or ostracism.

Farid was one of 16 picker-packers in a medical supply warehouse, meaning he would fulfill orders by pulling the needed stock from the shelves and packing it up in boxes. In addition to the picker-packer roles, the warehouse also employed the following: a forklift driver; two shift supervisors, one each for the 6:00 a.m.–2:00 p.m. and 2:00 p.m.–10:00 p.m. shifts; a customer service representative who took phone orders, verified online orders, and handled inquiries about shipments and product availability; and a shipper-receiver who received new stock from suppliers, verified the accuracy of shipments, created bills of lading, and used software to generate the complex documents needed to ship medical supplies across international borders. Business was booming, and all employees were very busy. Overtime was not uncommon, and while compensated fairly, some employees grumbled about being asked to work extra hours too often—especially those who were the only ones fulfilling their role such as the customer service agent and the shipper-receiver.

Ling went to their team and explained that they would be one person short that day. "That's not fair," complained picker-packer Marissa. "We have lots of orders today and without him we'll have to work late. I'm supposed to go to my daughter's softball game tonight." Oscar, another picker-packer, also grumbled. "I don't know why we keep him on the team. Farid is so unreliable," he voiced loudly. Ling, not knowing what to say, did not respond to the comments and just told everyone to get to work. But Ling could still hear muttered complaints throughout the day, which they also ignored. Ling knew that Farid could not be disciplined for a disability but also felt the coworkers had a point about the negative impact on them. Everyone was already under considerable stress during busy times, which seemed to be all the time, and everyone already had to work overtime so often that it wasn't surprising that someone with frequent absences was looked down upon. Ling thought about the respect and consideration that Farid had always provided to them. It was much appreciated, especially because not all their coworkers were equally considerate. In fact, Ling had taken to using the family bathroom at the coffee shop across the street after having dealt with too many odd looks and hostile reactions when using either of the gendered washrooms in the warehouse. Ling felt a nagging sense that they might not be meeting the same bar of respect and consideration for differences that Farid had shown. "I wonder what I should or could be doing," Ling wondered to themself, "in order to better accommodate Farid's Crohn disease in the workplace."

Assessing Ling's Next Steps

Ling is correct to be concerned about the degree to which Farid is receiving appropriate accommodation. There are also warning signs about inadequacies in the broader culture in this workplace as relates to inclusivity. Some well-intended policies have actively contributed to a less accommodating workplace. Ling should reconsider each of the following policies:

- *The monthly team-based on-time delivery bonus,* which magnifies both the perceived and actual negative impact of Farid's absences on his coworkers. Not only does colleague resentment cause Farid stress that exacerbates his symptoms, but on-time order delivery is outside the control of warehouse staff once orders leave with third party shippers. It would be more appropriate to reward individual order fulfillment rate, along with individual order accuracy metrics.

- *The monthly perfect attendance bonus,* which is difficult for Farid to obtain for disability-related reasons. Not counting disability-related absences would be a better option. The organization may also want to consider less punitive ways to meet their productivity targets, such as developing a long-term relationship with a temp agency that can provide experienced picker-packers when employees are unexpectedly absent.

- *The policy of monitoring bathroom breaks,* which both embarrasses and punishes those who need more frequent bathroom breaks. It also sends a message of distrust that is ill-suited to development of a positive and psychologically safe workplace culture. Alternate incentive plans should be sufficient to motivate individual performance without monitoring the bathroom habits of employees.

Additionally, Ling should address the bullying and disrespectful attitudes that have been allowed to emerge and develop unchallenged. A respectful workplace policy should be introduced along with associated training based on evidence-based best practices (such as focusing on both skills and knowledge and introducing storytelling). The policy then needs to be enforced. Employees who are openly disrespectful about the needs of others (including disrespecting pronoun preferences) should be corrected using a progressive disciplinary process, with the behavioral expectations made clear. Furthermore, leaders should model that respectful behavior. Finally, if Farid and the current job incumbent are open to the idea, Ling may want to consider cross-training him for the customer support position, which could be done from home relatively easily. That would give Farid the flexibility to be able to work from home as needed while lessening overtime burdens for the current customer support representative.

FURTHER READINGS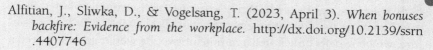

Alfitian, J., Sliwka, D., & Vogelsang, T. (2023, April 3). *When bonuses backfire: Evidence from the workplace.* http://dx.doi.org/10.2139/ssrn .4407746

Daniel, T. A. (2020). What causes toxic workplace situations? A focus on the individual, situational, and systemic drivers. In *Organizational toxin handlers: The critical role of HR, OD, and coaching practitioners in managing toxic workplace situations* (pp. 17–35).

Oladele's Dilemma: When Accommodation Needs Conflict

This case features an HR manager overseeing two office employees who work for an insurance company. They have conflicting accommodation needs. One requires the presence of a service dog at work due to epilepsy, while the other has a severe allergy to pet hair. The manager must determine how to address both sets of needs while taking into account organizational constraints.

The Case

Oladele sat glumly at her desk staring out her window at the parking lot. She had worked in HR for a midsize insurance firm for a long time and was the senior member of the HR Department, but she had never encountered an issue like this before. She knew she needed to accommodate disabilities in the workplace, but she had never had two employees with incompatible accommodation needs. She had no idea how to resolve the dilemma she found herself in.

Oladele's inclusion challenge arose when a newly hired employee, Joshua, indicated that he had a service dog. Joshua had epilepsy, experiencing seizures at unpredictable intervals. He generally experienced one or two seizures per month. The seizures were relatively mild, but there was always a risk that he would fall or injure himself in some way if they occurred unexpectedly. The triggers for them were not clear, but Joshua's service dog, Odin, could detect an upcoming seizure by smell, giving Joshua between 10 to 15 minutes warning before it struck. That gave Joshua several minutes to find a safe space in which to lie down before the seizure started, as well as find a person to monitor him during the seizure in case extra assistance was needed. (While very rare, any seizure that lasted more than 5 minutes would require emergency medical attention.) After the seizure, which usually only lasted a minute or two, he would generally need a couple of hours of rest to recover, but he would otherwise be fine.

Joshua had been very open about his medical condition after signing his offer to hire, and before he started Oladele had already taken some steps to ensure he would be accommodated. For example, she arranged for an unused private office to be turned into a safe space for seizures, with a comfortable futon placed low to the ground, soft pillows, and no hazardous objects or hard furniture that could bruise or injure. With Joshua's written permission, she also explained his condition to coworkers and trained them about appropriate responses to seizures. It seemed everything was ready—until the first day he started. Oladele had forgotten to mention the service animal to the staff, and within minutes, an employee of long-standing named Amelie came to speak to her. "I don't mean to be a bother," Amelie said, sniffling noticeably, "but I have to go home right away. I can't be near Odin. He is triggering my allergies. My breathing already feels tight, and if he actually brushes against me it will be only a matter of minutes before I break out in hives!" Amelie quickly left for the day, but it was clear a solution would need to be found.

Oladele considered her options. Both Joshua and Amelie were benefit claims administrators. Their job role involved both processing benefit claims and answering calls from clients checking the status of their claims. Given the sensitivity of the information handled, data security was a priority and as a result there were extensive cybersecurity protections, sophisticated firewalls, identity verification protocols for clients calling in, and other precautions in place. Phone calls with clients were also recorded as a standard practice. The job required workers to know a complex legacy software system well, and there were many small details that impacted whether a claim would be accepted or not.

New hires were generally paired with a long-tenured worker who served as their formal mentor for the first 4 months so that they could get guidance easily without fearing annoying or disrupting their colleagues. The new employee would be assigned a cubicle beside their mentor for that training period to enable communication flow. Oladele had observed that this mentoring relationship, intended primarily as on-the-job training, also had positive social impacts. Workers assigned a mentor tended to make friends and become part of the office community, quickly becoming team players. People in other job roles that lacked formal mentoring seemed to take longer to socially integrate. Joshua had been assigned to Mitchell for mentor support. Mitchell sat in a cubicle directly across from Amelie. It was an unfortunate coincidence, especially since the benefits administration team was spread out over three rooms on the same floor. (While the organization rented two floors of their downtown office tower, the second floor was reserved for the executive team. Working on the executive floor was considered a significant status symbol and perk because the workspaces were larger and more luxuriously furnished.)

Oladele decided to consult with Amelie to collect more information. She called her at home to discuss the situation. "There's nothing I can do," Amelie explained. Her initial comment was followed by a huge crashing noise, then, "Guys, just stop for a minute and BE QUIET. Work is on the phone!" There was more crashing noise, followed by a child's cry, and a quickly cut-off, "But Mom—." A moment later, Amelie returned to the phone. "Sorry about that," she said, "with three kids at home, it is hard to hear myself think never mind have a quiet phone call. To answer your question, I've tried allergy medications in the past and they don't work. I simply cannot be near a dog. Even being in a space that recently held a dog can trigger my allergies if their fur and dander is still present. It's terrible!"

Oladele considered everything she had learned. Physical separation of the two employees seemed like the only option, but how could they achieve that while also ensuring an appropriate onboarding experience for Joshua and a healthy working environment for Amelie. She needed to decide on the best course of action.

Assessing Oladele's Next Steps

Oladele's only viable option is physical separation of the two employees. Given the extreme sensitivity displayed by Amelie, simply having them in separate rooms or working slightly different hours is unlikely to be sufficient. If one of them wished to work from home, that would solve the problem; however, that option is not suitable for Joshua because he is still training and integrating into the team, and is it not suitable for Amelie because her home environment is not conducive to working. The organization has two floors, creating the opportunity to place Joshua and Amelie on different floors. Since placement on the executive floor is considered a status symbol, there may be social consequences for receiving a perk that colleagues do not get. In addition, the employee who is moved may feel isolated from their team. It would therefore be better to move half of the benefits administration team to the other floor rather than just one individual, with a "no dog" floor and a "dog" floor. This would likely require workspace modifications to make the workspaces on each floor equivalent in quality.

An unintended benefit of this solution is that some members of the executive team would likely need to switch floors to make room, which will create more organic opportunities for communication between workers and executives. Improved bottom-up communication offers competitive advantage because executives have a better idea of customer or client issues when they speak with frontline workers.

While working on different floors solves the most pressing issue, there will also be conflicting needs during group meetings of all benefit administrators. Conducting such meetings over Zoom or similar online meeting tools, even when workers are in the office, would mitigate this problem. There should also be at least one group meeting room that is designated a "no dog" room so that Amelie can meet colleagues without fearing exposure to dog hair. Since Amelie and Joshua are of different genders, bathrooms are not an issue, but if they were the same gender or the company had gender-neutral washrooms, there would need to be a similar agreement in which at least one facility was left completely dog-free. Similarly, if the building has multiple elevators, they should reach an agreement about which elevator the dog will use such that Amelie can avoid any exposure.

FURTHER READINGS ●───────────────────────

HR Reporter. (2016, July 7). *Assistant dogs at work: What you need to know.* https://hrnews.co.uk/assistance-dogs-at-work/

Foreman, A., Glenn, M., Meade, B., & Wirth, O. (2017). Dogs in the workplace: A review of the benefits and potential challenges. *International Journal of Environmental Research and Public Health, 14*(5), 498. http://dx.doi.org/10.3390/ijerph14050498

Natasha's Day: The Challenges of Getting From A to B

This case explores multiple physical barriers experienced by an office worker who is a wheelchair user. The harm of those physical barriers is magnified by the attitudes and lack of understanding displayed by managerial personnel. Consider how the employer can address these inadvertent barriers in a comprehensive manner, preventing problems before they arise.

The Case

Natasha was hurrying along the pathway, strong biceps bunching as she navigated the slope of the ramp. Despite the slight nature of the incline, it was rough going because snow clogged the route, adding considerable resistance to the forward momentum of her wheelchair. Finally, she got to the front door, pushing the button to automatically open it. As she wheeled inside, her wheels got caught up in the mat, which had gotten bunched up because of people scrapping damp snow off their boots as they entered the building. She reached down awkwardly but could not reach the mat to tug on it. Happily, a colleague entering behind her was able to straighten it, giving her extra momentum with a quick push. She appreciated the help but felt frustrated that it had been necessary. Snow days were always difficult.

Her next stop was the bathroom. There was only one wheelchair accessible bathroom in the building, and it was on the main floor while her office was on the sixth floor, so she always tried to use it before heading up to her workstation. She worked in a cubicle with the other junior marketing staff. Management preferred to keep team members together to foster a sense of cohesion, so each floor *belonged* to one functional department. It wasn't the most convenient arrangement given the limited appropriate bathroom facilities, but Natasha didn't want to make a fuss, so she dealt with it.

She waited to use the bathroom that morning because someone without disability-related issues was using the only wheelchair accessible stall, explaining that she "liked more space." After emerging from the bathroom, Natasha found herself in even more of a rush. She had to make an important presentation today and needed to get her things from her desk, prepare herself, and get back down to the first floor meeting room as early as possible. Natasha knew that if she got to her meeting early, she would have time to rearrange things so that she wasn't hidden behind a high speaker's podium, and she could reach the microphone.

In her hurry to get to the elevator, she did not notice the sign at first. It was taped to the elevator and said "Out of Order" in big letters. "AGAIN??" Natasha gritted her teeth in frustration. It was the third time in a month that the elevator had broken down. It was old and required an excessive number of repairs, but budgets were tight, and the employer was not willing to replace the decades-old device because they were prioritizing other capital improvements, such as a new roof. As she stared at the closed doors in frustration, she heard a ding and checked her cell phone. Her boss, Chris, had just text messaged her asking why she wasn't there yet. "Remember," the text message warned, "if you are late more than three times per month, then you cannot get the highest performance rating. I need to treat you the same as everyone else. You want your quarterly bonus, don't you?" All Natasha could think was "really?" Her frustration, already peaking, threatened to take over entirely, and she had to wait a couple of minutes, taking deep breaths like in yoga class, before texting back to make sure she held her temper in check.

After she contacted Chris, he apologized for not realizing the elevator was out. (He had arrived very early that morning, and it had been working then.) Natasha got him to collect her things from her desk and bring them down to her. She arrived in the meeting room still feeling rather aggrieved by the situation. Natasha saw immediately that the equipment setup wasn't going to work for her. Despite her reminders to Chris (her manager), the audio-visual (AV) technicians usually forgot about her wheelchair when setting up the equipment. They were always apologetic and even embarrassed afterward, but that didn't seem to result in improvements the next time. This time, the mystery was solved when the technician told her that the setup information they received on their standard forms did not identify who the meeting was for, only the AV equipment needed, so they didn't actually forget her needs; they simply didn't get the requisite information. It seems her manager, who had numerous direct reports, often failed to convey the necessary reminder because it wasn't part of the standardized form. It was the last straw of a difficult morning. Not wanting colleagues to see her cry or lose her temper, Natasha once again retreated to the bathroom, hoping for privacy to collect herself. She knew tears and anger would not help her, but it seemed that her employer made things much more difficult than they needed to be. She felt as if she just didn't matter to them. Otherwise, why would she have so many struggles without other people even noticing? Also, how could anyone expect her to perform well, never mind at her best, under these conditions? She felt as if she were being set up for failure.

Chris's Accommodation Efforts

Chris was enjoying his latte as he sat at his desk. He was reviewing notes prior to Natasha's big presentation. He couldn't help but feel somewhat self-satisfied by all he had done for Natasha. She was his first direct report with a disability, and he thought he had done a good job of accommodating her and making her feel welcome. He had ordered a special desk that was better suited and sized for wheelchair users and had proudly directed her to it on her first day. He had felt a little let down when she didn't comment positively on the desk, but that was okay. He also arranged for her to have a designated parking spot for her wheelchair accessible vehicle, and the spot was very close to the ramp into the building. When discussing things with her, Chris always made sure to sit so he didn't loom over her. He even made sure the boardroom table in the main meeting room was positioned to allow a wheelchair user to take a seat comfortably.

All in all, he felt he was very enlightened and deserved kudos for being so attentive to her needs. That was why he felt so hurt when the complaints started. First, it had been the broken elevator, which he could not control. He had sent requests to the facilities team but had no influence on repair priorities. Then it had been the snow outside on the ramp, which he also could not control because snow was cleared by an independent contractor. Then there were the AV team issues, when he had no alternative but to use the standard form.

He understood why Natasha was complaining, of course, and the company could be liable for the accommodation-related issues she faced. He felt strongly that it wasn't his liability though; he was doing his best. He wondered why she couldn't see how much he was trying. Didn't effort count? He tried to maintain his open and friendly demeanor but increasingly found himself considered responsible for accommodation failures in other departments. His resentment began to fester, and even though part of him knew it was unfair, Natasha was the apparent source of all these conflicts and stress.

Over time, it became more difficult to be compassionate, and he found his frustrations getting directed at Natasha. This was magnified when she began complaining about the lateness policy. She seemed to want special treatment, and that seemed wrong to him. He was beginning to wonder if Natasha was a good fit for the organization.

Assessing Differing Perspectives and Next Steps

Natasha and Chris have very different perspectives about the degree to which the organization has engaged in appropriate accommodation. Chris had good intentions, but he does not understand many of the daily challenges Natasha faces. Barriers that are very clear to her are largely invisible to him. He did several things incorrectly. For a start, he made assumptions about Natasha's accommodation needs and preferences, instead of using a consultative process, and he also failed to proactively ask her about emerging needs and new problems after she started employment. He also failed to advocate for his employee with other departments or address root causes of barriers. For example, Chris made no effort to propose new forms for the AV team that would identify disability-related needs. Saying that a solution is "not my department" is not an acceptable response to accommodation needs. Egregiously, Chris also expected gratitude for basic accommodation. Nondisabled employees are not expected to be grateful merely for being given work tools they can use, and employees with disabilities should not be treated differently. Making it about himself and his ego, Chris seems more concerned with signaling that he is a good, virtuous person than with genuinely accommodating an employee.

But not all failures in this case belong to Chris. To improve diversity outcomes at this company, the organization should engage in inclusive design processes. Such processes would identify inadvertent barriers created by situations such as the AV forms and the late policy. The executive team also should realize that some things (such as elevator repairs) need to be addressed right away because they create significant safety issues as well as accommodation issues, creating unacceptable levels of risk and potential legal and moral liability. For example, Natasha could become stuck on the sixth floor during a crisis, such as an active shooter or chemical spill, if the elevator is not working, with potentially fatal results. Most of the issues Natasha faces, such as the entry mat getting bunched up or snow not being cleared early enough, have very simple and obvious solutions. The issue here revolves more around the employer's unwillingness to listen and be responsive due to overconfidence that they already have accommodation covered. Ongoing discussions, check-ins, and surveys with employees with disabilities can help prevent this problem.

FURTHER READINGS

Maisel, J. L., Steinfeld, E., Basnak, M., Smith, K., & Tauke, M. B. (2017). *Inclusive design: Implementation and evaluation.* Routledge.

Sahoo, S. K., & Choudhury, B. B. (2023). Wheelchair accessibility: Bridging the gap to equality and inclusion. *Decision Making Advances, 1*(1), 63–85. https://doi.org/10.31181/dma1120239

Courtney's Emails: The Communication Conundrum

This case takes place in a university academic department. It addresses differences in perceptions of what constitutes appropriate communication between a member of the faculty who is autistic and their coworkers. These differences in perception eventually lead to formal HR complaints. HR initially fails to recognize that the communication problems represent a disability-related issue rather than a disciplinary matter. Readers are encouraged to assess the appropriateness of the organizational response and the mental health impacts of communication-related conflicts.

The Case

Courtney sat in the meeting with HR, hardly believing what she was hearing. She stared at her hands, trying to sharpen her focus despite the familiar, sinking feeling of dismay that threatened to drown out the voices around her. "Look up," she thought to herself with a sense of panic, "otherwise they'll think you aren't paying attention." She tried, lifting her head to look Janice, the HR representative, in the eye. The words Janice spoke disappeared into a soft haze as Courtney tried to maintain the expected level of eye contact, tried to be "normal," tried to fix her face into a suitable expression. After a moment, realizing she had no idea what had just been said, Courtney, feeling trapped and desperate, gave up and returned her gaze to her hands. It felt like grade school all over again. Courtney could almost hear the schoolyard taunts, the long-ago voices mocking her and asking why she had ever been so stupid as to imagine anyone would be her friend.

Courtney had begun working as a chemistry professor in a small midwestern college 10 years previously. She had come to the occupation late, doing her PhD in her mid-30s after a 14-year career in product development labs working on new chemical formulations for consumer-packaged goods such as household cleaning products and batteries. Courtney had enjoyed working in labs but had always coveted a career in academe, which provided the freedom to pursue a wider range of research interests and the joy of sharing her knowledge with students. One of her favorite things was helping students become excited about chemistry and seeing their confidence increase as they became more comfortable with the lab equipment and experimentation process. Courtney had also enjoyed developing relationships with the other faculty in the chemistry department. She had always felt nerdy, awkward, and odd. She had always struggled to be part of the group, and at the university she felt, for the first time in her life, like she just might fit in. Her colleagues were just as excited about arcane chemistry as she was, and nobody ever criticized her for using overly big words. Nobody ever misunderstood her passionate enthusiasm for "thinking she was better than them." Nobody told her to "just be quiet already, because nobody else cares." She felt she had come home.

The feelings of acceptance she experienced encouraged Courtney to reflect on earlier social problems and exclusion she had experienced. She began discussing these issues in private Facebook forums in her spare time, a process that eventually, through a long chain of contacts and referrals, led to the realization that she was autistic. At the age of 46, Courtney sought and received a formal diagnosis of level one autism (often previously referred to as Asperger's syndrome, a label no longer used due to associations with the Nazi medical experimenter Hans Asperger). Suddenly, many patterns in her life made sense to her, and problems she had experienced with social interaction and communication had a legitimate cause. Prior to her university career she had been told so often there was something "off" or "wrong" about her—and it was a source of comfort and relief to know her differences had a cause, and that there were other people like her in the world.

Armed with this new knowledge, Courtney felt ready to take on the world. Unfortunately, the world was about to change. Shortly after her realization, the COVID-19 pandemic struck. All classes and meetings were moved online, and email largely replaced the informal hallway conversations in which department matters had previously been discussed. Courtney knew she was in trouble. While she often struggled to interpret broader social cues, Courtney had a gift for reading micro expressions and body language. Many people with autism struggle with these two forms of nonverbal language, Courtney was not among them. She could read such cues expertly. Her difficulty was in anticipating emotional reactions before the fact and making appropriate attributions about their cause after the fact. Put another way, she could not necessarily anticipate when a comment would cause offense or determine why it caused offense, but she could read the offense on someone's face and body as if they were a book. That gave her the chance to correct and clarify when she inadvertently offended someone—a not uncommon experience because she tended to be blunt, direct, and tell the full truth when asked. She was continually surprised that purely factual statements such as "This program is not working effectively based on the metrics" or "That practice is not functional and was chosen based on incorrect information" were often considered offensive.

The pandemic-driven move to primarily email communication concerned Courtney deeply. At this point, she had worked at the university for just over 8 years. She was not worried about interactions with students. There were very clear communication expectations and norms when it came to student-teacher interactions such that Courtney had an informal script that she could follow to ensure appropriate communication. The same was not true of peer interactions and departmental and committee communications. Fearing that the lack of nonverbal cues would magnify her pre-existing issues with social interaction and communication, Courtney decided to proactively tell department members she was autistic. She hoped this would engender some understanding and tolerance for any communication missteps, and she explicitly asked people to come to her if they had concerns about her emails. Initial responses to her message were largely positive and supportive, and Courtney felt good about her decision to disclose her neurodiversity.

As the new pandemic reality continued over the next 2 years, many of the university's processes and procedures were altered, creating significant administrative confusion. Courtney found herself frequently sending messages inquiring about the *why* behind new processes, many of which seemed illogical or inefficient to her. These messages were generally ignored by her chair and dean, which she found both frustrating and inexplicable. She seldom received a response, and when she did, the process itself was reiterated but the why was never explained. Courtney was at heart a logical person. Not understanding the logic behind the new processes, she often struggled to remember and comply with them. Then came the vote. The vote that started her slide into disillusionment and isolation. The vote that changed everything.

It wasn't even a central, important issue at the end of the day. The Chemistry Department, anticipating the end of in-person gathering restrictions related to the pandemic, decided to have a vote about whether or not to host an academic conference at their institution. If the conference proceeded, every member of the department would be required to contribute labor, including helping arrange the conference itself, reviewing submissions, and leading sessions. Since this would create a lot of work, the acting chair, who had been in the role for 6 months while the regular chair was on leave, determined that a minimum of half the department would need to vote yes to hosting the conference. Sometimes individual faculty members chose not to vote on a given issue. The chair explicitly explained that the motion would need to be supported by half the department, not half the people who voted. After the voting was completed, more than

50% of those who voted had supported the conference, but due to several people failing to vote at all, that still did not reach the threshold required for half the department. The chair announced that the department would not, therefore, sponsor the conference. About an hour later, another email arrived from the regular chair who was on leave. That email overturned the results of the vote, stating that since half the voters supported the initiative, it would go ahead.

This result stunned Courtney. She was appalled that the rules had been broken in two different ways: First, the voting parameters had been changed, and second, a chair who was on leave and therefore had no standing or authority had interfered in the decision. Still in disbelief, she sent an email to both the acting chair and the chair asking them to explain and justify their decision. Her email read:

> I formally object. As our leader, you stated that if less than half the department supported the initiative, you would not proceed. Now that you didn't get the vote you hoped for, you are changing the rules. That is fundamentally unfair, especially when we will be required to participate. What was the point of a vote with preset standards for approval if you are just going to ignore it? I thought you said we had a voice but that does not seem to be true. This is extremely upsetting.

After sending this message, Courtney received a two-sentence reply that confirmed the department would move forward with the conference. The message did not provide an explanation for the change in approach. Once again, Courtney sent an email complaining. She again reiterated, "Agreed-upon voting parameters are changed when management gets an answer they don't like." She also said, "After a lengthy stint of leaders who ignored our wishes, YOU were supposed to be the ones who were better than that. What happened? This is exactly the type of leadership behavior you used to rail against."

Courtney did not receive an answer to her email, but 5 days later she did get a call from their HR representative asking her to come into their office to discuss a disciplinary matter. Initially she was confused. What disciplinary matter? When she came to the scheduled appointment the HR representative explained that a half dozen of her colleagues had come as a group to complain about her "rude" and "belligerent" communication style, particularly her emails. In fact, they had brought a large file folder of emails that had caused offense, emails that went back a full 8 years! They complained that she frequently violated the Respectful Workplace Policy, using the emails as proof. Courtney was stunned. In the entire 10 years she had been working there, nobody had ever commented on her communication style. Nobody had ever suggested she had given offense. She thought she had found a safe community. She thought she had made friends, friends who could trust her with difficult truths. Yet, clearly, she was mistaken. While she had thought she was getting along well with everyone, it appeared that her colleagues felt quite differently. She had been offending and alienating them all without even realizing it. Furthermore, they had ignored her pleas to discuss any communication problems with her and had gone directly to HR despite knowing she was autistic. Courtney felt the cold, familiar numbness of depression slide over her, threatening to drown her. Every friend she thought she had made was now, in her eyes, fictional. Awash in hopelessness, she began to think through the implications of her situation. HR had called her in for a disciplinary discussion, but that didn't seem fair to her. She asked if she could see the offensive emails so that she could better understand what she had done wrong, but the HR representative responded that the complainant's identities were to be kept private, so the emails could not be shared. Courtney again felt a sense of despair. "How can I fix a problem," she thought to herself, "when I don't even understand it?"

Courtney approached her union representative with some of her concerns. The union shared many of her concerns about the complaint process. With their assistance, the disciplinary discussion was canceled and a formal disability accommodation process was launched. Since the formal accommodation process included procedural negotiations with union representatives and medical consultations with experts who had extensive waiting lists, it ended up being a lengthy process that took more than 9 months. Numerous accommodations were granted, including changes to the process by which suggestions and critiques could be submitted, a communication coach for Courtney, and training on neurodiverse communication styles for her colleagues. In the meantime, however, the amount of time it took to resolve the issue contributed to worsening interpersonal tension within the department. By the time she had an accommodation plan, Courtney no longer felt that a friendly reconciliation with her colleagues was possible, and she remained socially isolated and guarded around her peers for the remainder of the employment relationship.

What Went Wrong?

The situation faced by Courtney and her coworkers was entirely preventable with consistent application of organizational policies, proactive supervisory feedback, and basic disability management efforts. First, the triggering incident revolved around misuse of a formal voting process, a problem that was never actually addressed by HR. Changes to documented policies and procedures should be rare, well-justified, and clearly explained to avoid the appearance of impropriety. A perceived lack of justice can be especially triggering for people on the autism continuum, who may have extreme difficulty letting go of unresolved inequities and moving on.

Creation of an inclusive culture encourages disclosure of a disability before an employee has problems because it lessens fears of stigmatization. That then allows for relevant coaching and training prior to conflicts emerging. Courtney was not comfortable disclosing until she was struggling. When she first revealed she was autistic, her dean or chair should have approached her about developing a formal accommodation plan with HR right away. Instead, they expressed verbal support but did nothing else to ensure her success.

There seems to have been missed opportunities for constructive supervisory feedback because Courtney did not receive complaints about her communication style. The complaints from her colleagues should have been brought up and addressed when they happened, not years later. Courtney was not given an opportunity to even realize that her behavior was problematic, or correct it. The situation made it inevitable that Courtney would feel ganged up on and bullied, even if that was not the intent of the others, whereas one-on-one conversations when communication issues first occurred would likely have been perceived as gentle and friendly corrections. The HR department also responded inappropriately when it, with advanced knowledge that the employee was autistic, failed to consider an accommodation process and moved directly into a disciplinary process.

FURTHER READINGS

Booth, J. (2016). *Autism equality in the workplace: Removing barriers and challenging discrimination*. Jessica Kingsley.

Hayward, S. M., McVilly, K. R., & Stokes, M. A. (2018). Challenges for females with high functioning autism in the workplace: A systematic review. *Disability and Rehabilitation, 40*(3), 249–258. https://doi.org/10.1080/09638288.2016.1254284

Networking While Hard of Hearing: Bruno's Job Search Story

A job candidate with a hearing impairment struggles with typical campus networking events that are meant to introduce graduating students to employers. Using insights from these experiences, readers should consider how recruitment events can be made more accessible.

The Case

Bruno left the networking event feeling frustrated. He had expected difficulties when he decided to attend, but he didn't realize that participation would be all but impossible. For him, the evening had been a discouraging waste of time. He was starting to think that the campus events designed to help members of his graduating class find employment just wouldn't work out for him. He wondered what to do next.

Bruno was in his final term of a social work degree. There was a strong demand for social workers in the large city he lived in, yet it was still challenging to find full-time, permanent placements. Many of the entry level jobs offered were precarious contracts or part-time work. His college tried to help by sponsoring on-campus networking events for those seeking regular full-time employees. Each event was similar: Employers would come to meet and mingle with large numbers of students who would soon be in the job market. Wine and cheese would be served in a huge, echoing reception room, and new connections would be forged informally, without any particular system for introducing candidates and employers. Each job candidate was responsible for putting themselves out there and being seen and heard. Brief conversations turned into requests for résumés, which turned into interviews and job offers. To participate, however, one needed to be part of those brief introductory conversations. That is where Bruno's problems started.

Bruno was hard of hearing and used hearing aids. The hearing aids were effective in many settings. For example, he was generally able to hear teachers lecturing in classroom—if nobody was chatting in the back of the class or otherwise creating distracting noise—and he was able to have one-on-one conversations in quiet spaces. His hearing aids were much less effective when there were multiple conversations going on simultaneously, especially in small, tightly packed spaces or very large echoing spaces. When sound came from all directions at once, the result would often be an unintelligible cacophony. While he had some small skill in lip reading, his ability to do so was impaired in settings in which people were eating and drinking at the same time. He also struggled if people had mustaches or beards. Three years into the COVID-19 pandemic, some employer representatives still chose to wear masks in public and that completely eliminated his ability to read their lips. Making matters worse, occasionally someone started speaking to him when he wasn't directly facing them, and with all the background noise, he might not even be aware they were talking to him. In one instance, another student had told him a couple minutes later that an employer had tried to talk to him, and Bruno hadn't even noticed! The employer seemed to think they were being deliberately ignored because they quickly turned and walked away. Even when he could hear a little of what was being said, he often needed to ask people to repeat themselves and speak up. He could see the frustration on their faces as he struggled to converse, and his conversations tended to end quickly when the other party sought to escape the awkwardness. Over the course of the evening, he had not collected a single business card or arranged to send his résumé to anyone. He decided to go discuss his difficulties with the school administrators to see what could be done to help him.

Fixing the Issue: Next Steps in Recruitment

The next day, Bruno went to speak to Gia Wang, the staff member who was responsible for recruitment events. He explained the difficulties he had experienced. "I am so sorry," said Gia. "It never occurred to me that networking would be such a problem for the hard of hearing. Thank you for letting me know." Gia then asked Bruno a few questions about his needs and sat down to make a short-term plan and a long-term plan. Her short-term plan sought to help Bruno right away, while the long-term plan aimed to avoid similar disability-related barriers in the future.

Gia's short-term plan involved a more personal career placement service than was normally offered. Since she had no immediate solution for the networking events taking place that week, she took it upon herself to collect Bruno's résumé and match him with suitable employers who were holding recruitment events on campus. She then arranged for him to meet them privately for a couple minutes in a quiet room just before the main event started. While this was an imperfect solution, it did fill the gap in service while Gia made more substantive changes to remove barriers.

Gia's long-term solution began with the realization that since she had failed to identify one disability-related barrier, she may also have overlooked others. She surveyed all 4th-year students, asking about the accessibility of recruitment events. She learned that many people found the busy nature of traditional networking events problematic for various disability-related reasons. The next year, she retained some traditional networking events but also found other ways for students to interact with potential employers. For example, very brief private meetings with each employer were arranged using a model similar to speed dating, in which candidates rotated between rooms in a long hallway every 5 minutes, having one-on-one conversations with up to 10 potential employers in an hour. She also created a video résumé library searchable by degree being obtained and career interest, which employers could browse at their leisure. This option was popular because students could rerecord their videos as many times as they wanted to get them perfect. Finally, she arranged for a written-case competition in which students were asked to present their solutions to a business problem faced by organizations who were hiring. The employers then assessed the caliber of the solutions to decide whom to interview, making disabilities that impact verbal communication and social presentation skills irrelevant at that stage of selection.

Gia also continued her student survey every year, acting on feedback she received, to ensure no inadvertent barriers cropped up again. By taking these steps Gia ensured that her school met legislative requirements requiring equal access to education-related services for students with disabilities. This was not only the right thing to do, but it also lessened risk of liability due to indirect (inadvertent) discrimination.

FURTHER READINGS

Bowe F. G., McMahon, B. T., Chang, T., & Louvi, I. (2005). Workplace discrimination, deafness and hearing impairment: The National EEOC ADA Research Project. *Work, 25*(1), 19–25.

O'Connell, N. (2022). "Opportunity blocked": Deaf people, employment, and the sociology of audism. *Humanity & Society, 46*(2), 336–358. https://doi.org/10.1177/0160597621995505

What's in a Lunch: Mealtimes, Disability, and Inclusion

An employee in the high-tech sector who works directly with customers is concerned that her inability to share in communal meals due to a severe allergy is having an unfair negative impact on customer perceptions, her performance evaluations, and her social status as a friendly team player. Her manager must determine if inadvertent discrimination is occurring and, if so, how best to respond.

The Case

Madison looked up as the lunch cart came clattering into their make-shift classroom. She had just been leaning over a desk to show one of her clients how to input a new product number into the inventory management component of the enterprise resource planning (ERP) system that her company had sold them. The intoxicating smell of freshly cooked pizza hit her almost immediately, causing her stomach to grumble at the same time as she sighed. Another day of reheated soup for her. "Look," the IT manager at the customer site stated proudly, "we heard that you don't eat wheat, so we ordered a gluten-free pizza for you." He seemed very pleased with himself. Madison cringed inside and braced herself for a discussion she had already had twice this month at other customer sites. She always felt bad when people went to extra effort for her and that effort was wasted, and in addition she did not want to offend anyone, least of all a customer. That said, she knew that *gluten-free* fast food pizzas were almost always prepared on the same surfaces as the regular pizzas. With her celiac disease, it just was not worth the risk of eating it. Even a small amount of cross-contamination, such as a few crumbs dropped from a regular pizza, would be enough to make her seriously ill for days.

"I'm so sorry," Madison explained, "but I really can't eat that." The IT manager looked confused and chagrined. Her five teammates (Sangita, Tyrone, Xander, Melissa, and Pham), who were also there to help with the new ERP system installation and training, looked embarrassed for her and quickly changed the subject. Madison, relieved that the conversation had been redirected, took the opportunity to make her way to the kitchen. After waiting in line almost 15 minutes to get access to the only microwave, she began heating up her soup. She could hear her colleagues, who were two rooms away, talking and laughing heartily with the customer, and she wondered what the joke was. By the time she returned, however, things had calmed down and people were eating quietly in groups of three or four. She joined her teammates, who were deep into a technical discussion. Madison wanted to help, but since she had missed the first part of the conversation, she was not entirely sure what problem they were trying to solve. Nobody seemed inclined to fill her in, so she focused on her chicken and vegetable soup instead, feeling somewhat left out and lonely. After they had been speaking for several minutes, getting increasingly frustrated with each other, she realized that she did recognize the issue they were talking about. It was one she had encountered previously and knew how to solve. She could have saved them time and aggravation if she had been part of the conversation earlier. Madison found herself feeling bad, even though she had not really done anything wrong.

Two weeks later, Madison sat with installation technicians Sangita, Tyrone, Xander, and Melissa, fellow trainer Pham, and their manager Ruth to conduct the standard debriefing that always occurred after the completion of new ERP installations at client sites. As per usual, the meeting was being held over the lunch hour. The trainers and installation technicians sent to each customer site were assigned to new teams on a project-by-project basis from a pool of 24 people (eight trainers, 10 junior installation technicians, and six senior technicians), all managed by Ruth. These temporary teams allowed Ruth to match her employees' skills with the unique requirements of each project and the preferences of each client. Since everybody had been reassigned to a new project team by now, the lunch hour was the only time they could all be reliably available.

Madison sat at the meeting watching everyone else dig into the lasagna and garlic bread that had been brought in for lunch. The whole team was raving about how good the lunch was. Apparently, the new Italian restaurant that had opened down the street was very authentic and made almost everything from scratch. Xander joked with Pham, saying that their afternoon garlic breath would scare off anyone in the office who was not "part of the team." Madison glanced down at the separate bag that had been provided for her, and the sad, gray-looking chicken salad sitting in its own little container. It was marked "gluten-free" and "Madison" in large black letters, and it was obvious that it was not among the items that the restaurant made fresh. On one level, she felt juvenile and silly that her lunch made her so sad. She should be happy that food was provided at all, and that people were attentive to her allergy. Even so, when comparing her meal to the feast her colleagues were enjoying, she just felt as if she was somehow worth less than the others. While they told stories of the best pasta dishes they had ever eaten, she sat quietly, not really part of the conversation.

The feeling was magnified when Ruth started the formal part of the meeting and began speaking about their performance at the last client site. Client reviews were formally collected after all projects and were an important component of their annual performance assessments. The client evaluations were combined with metrics about timely project completion and peer evaluations to derive a final performance rating. That rating was subsequently used to rank employees and determine raises, performance bonuses, task assignments, and promotions. The client had generally been happy with the overall team performance. The ERP installation had not gone perfectly smoothly (they never did), but the IT manager at the customer site had noted their professionalism and persistence in resolving any technical issues. The IT manager singled out Xander, Sangita, and Pham for being especially friendly and helpful, but reported that the lead trainer, Madison, had been "competent and agreeable in class but standoffish and often absent during casual social interactions. Some of the employees were put off by her attitude outside the classroom." The customer's employees apparently felt more comfortable following up with Pham for any future training needs—they felt like he was their friend and would bend over backward to help—whereas they were not sure about Madison. "Not that she did anything wrong," the IT manager reported, "she just didn't seem to connect with my team like Pham did."

Madison's heart sank when she heard this feedback. She remembered the laughter coming from the training room while she had been stuck waiting for the microwave. There had been several other socially awkward moments. For example, she had not been able to join in sharing a homemade cake that had been baked by the IT manager to celebrate the new software installation, and she had been forced to decline the handmade dumplings another employee had brought in to celebrate the Chinese New Year. Being excluded from consuming the food always seemed to leave her out of the associated celebration and social bonding, too. She thought again of the feedback accusing her of being "standoffish." "Well, that's not fair," she muttered to herself. "Just because I need to leave the group to make my own food, or I can't join their celebration in the same way, doesn't make me antisocial." Her next thought concerned her even more: "What if I don't get put on the best, most interesting projects with the biggest clients, even though I do my job well, because I am seen as less sociable?" Client reviews were such a large part of their annual evaluations, she worried that her literal inability to break bread with clients would hurt her career progression.

Madison wanted to know if her teammates thought she had been unfriendly. Maybe she was overreacting about the food? Maybe she was standoffish? Madison did not think so, but she was filled with doubts. She decided to ask Xander, Sangita, Pham, Melissa, and Tyrone to have a drink with her after work and discuss it. They looked embarrassed, glancing at each other uncomfortably. "We can't do it tonight," they said. "We have a trivia contest at the Iron Whistle pub. It's the finals so we need to go." "I didn't know you did trivia," Madison exclaimed. "I love trivia, can I come?" "Ummm, sure," said Tyrone, "but all they serve is beer and breaded wings, so you won't be able to eat or drink anything." "I don't care," enthused Madison, "as long as I can play. When did this start anyway?" "About four months ago," said Pham. "Remember when we all worked on the ACME account together with Mr.

Wiley? We got talking about trivia over pizza at lunch and decided to form a team. You must have missed it." Madison's heart sank yet again. She had wondered why her colleagues had all seemed friendlier together than the last time they had been on a team. Now she knew exactly why they all seemed to click, and she seemed, somehow, on the outside. All because she could not join them for pizza. Again. How many ways was her allergy impacting her job? Ways that she did not even realize! Something needed to be done.

Madison decided to ask for a one-on-one meeting with Ruth. At the meeting, Madison explained that she felt she was being excluded from important team and client bonding rituals during mealtimes. "Even though I do get my own food, it is different from the food of others, which sets me apart from everyone in a subtle way. It even seems to impact me at client sites. I am convinced that I am perceived as less friendly because I cannot participate in many of the food rituals. I think that for future meetings, you should start ordering in meals for everyone that are gluten-free so that I am not singled out anymore. It would be helpful if we could encourage clients to do the same when we work onsite. If we cannot get the clients onboard, then that should be considered when scoring and ranking my performance evaluations, since I get subtly devalued due to social issues created by my allergy."

Ruth heard everything that Madison said, but she had some concerns of her own. Ruth was concerned about whether people would enjoy gluten-free options. People liked pizza, pasta, and sandwiches. It was easy to accommodate vegetarians and religious dietary restrictions by changing the toppings, sauces, and fillings. Ruth was also very concerned about imposing menus on clients, who generally brought in whatever food they liked for the installation team. Finally, the meals that were brought in were selected based in part on affordability. Things such as pizza, pasta, and sandwiches tended to be cheap and filling. The alternatives, such as salads, grilled meats, and vegetables, were more expensive. Switching to gluten-free options would inevitably increase the cost of lunches, which would impact the overall budget used for staff entertainment, performance incentives, and rewards. That could mean fewer or smaller performance-based cash bonuses for everyone. That said, Ruth was concerned about equity and fairness and wanted to provide an optimal environment for team functioning.

Ruth's Next Steps

After several days of thought and some consultations with HR experts, she boiled down her decision to the following key considerations: Ruth did not have a legal obligation to fulfil Madison's accommodation request. While celiac disease is recognized as a disability, there is no duty to accommodate it in this situation because the request does not directly relate to Madison's ability to perform work tasks or fulfil her job description. Despite the absence of a legal obligation, Ruth still needs to consider the benefits and drawbacks of accommodation and make an ethical, as opposed to legal, decision. If Madison's request is denied, it is likely that Madison will experience escalating anxiety about her social exclusion, and her concerns about the fairness of her evaluations will persist. Under these conditions, it is likely that her motivation and job satisfaction will diminish, and the team members will continue in their current trajectories and subtle cohesion issues will remain. But a few other scenarios could play out. If the request is granted and the changes are made without explanation, then team cohesion is likely to increase because Madison will become better integrated into the team when she can share meals freely. Since most of her teammates will not be aware that the menu change was a result of her needs, they will not feel resentful of her "special treatment." It may create some friction with clients who resent being told what food to buy, but if put into the standard contract such that they have advance notice, that reaction should be manageable. If team members are told that they are getting different food to accommodate Madison (which would be an invasion of privacy), then the response may be mixed. Some people will like the change and credit Madison for it, while others will dislike it and resent her for it. As such, if the change is made, then the rationale and impact of other budgets should remain private.

Another option is to stop providing meals to all employees. This solution is not optimal because the employees are accustomed to having meals provided and may resent their employer for stopping the practice. No longer having meals provided at client sites may also directly negatively impact timely project completion since it would require employees to go offsite to eat, resulting in fewer casual problem-identification and problem-solving discussions with clients.

Ruth does have a legal and moral obligation to ensure that performance evaluation criteria are fair and free from inadvertent discrimination. Since the evidence for bias in performance assessment is currently tenuous and being personable with clients is a valid metric for these job roles, Ruth should investigate further to determine whether bias exists. Reviewing prior assessments and conducting statistical tests can determine if Madison receives lower evaluations in areas impacted by social behaviors when she is excluded from meals. Ruth could also consult relevant metrics such as project completion and subsequent calls for retraining to get a fuller picture. If there is evidence of bias or results are inconclusive (or if the research cannot be conducted due to poor data collection and retention practices), then the client satisfaction surveys should be evaluated with the goal of rewording questions to lessen social biases. For example, they could eliminate asking questions that confound social behavior with training effectiveness. Instead of asking, "How friendly was your trainer on a scale of 1 to 10," they could ask questions such as, "After the training was complete, on a scale of 1 to 10, how confident were you in your ability to use the new system."

FURTHER READINGS ●

Kniffin, K., Wansink, B., Devine, C., & Sobal, J. (2015). Eating together at the firehouse: How workplace commensality relates to the performance of firefighters. *Human Performance, 28*(4), 281–306. doi.org/10 .1080/08959285.2015.1021049

Thomson, D., & Hassenkamp, A. M. (2008). The social meaning and function of food rituals in healthcare practice: An ethnography. *Human Relations,61*(12),1775–1802. https://doi.org/10.1177/0018726708098085

Vanessa's Story: Addiction at the Animal Shelter

The senior manager at an animal shelter must address concerns about an employee who is consuming alcohol on the job and dealing with depression. The manager must determine how to balance the rights of the worker with an alcohol addiction and mood disorder with the need to provide safe and appropriate care for vulnerable animals.

The Case

Tyron sighed deeply as he watched Vanessa push her mop, stumbling noticeably. He could smell the rum from his desk. She had promised just a week ago not to drink at work, yet here she was, swaying on her feet. He approached her and gently asked her to come into his office. Her eyes widened in dismay, and she began to demur, pointing out that the floors weren't finished yet. He stared at her for a moment longer and she dropped her gaze, following him to his office quietly. After closing his office door, sitting down, and inviting Vanessa to take a seat, Tyron asked his one-word question. "Again?" Vanessa, head still down nodded. "I'm sorry," she murmured, "it has been a rough couple of days." "Well go home and rest," Tyron said. "We will discuss this more tomorrow. I'll call you a cab." He began to dial the taxi. A few moments later Vanessa left, and Tyron started to consider his next steps.

Tyron managed a small animal shelter that offered protection and adoption services for cats, dogs, reptiles, and other household pets in need. He was the only full-time worker, and he performed the duties of an executive director, such as managing staff and the budget, while also doing some of the hands-on work. The shelter had five part-time paid staff who each worked between 15 and 25 hours per week. Three of the paid staff members, including Vanessa, were veterinary assistants who had specialized but basic training in the care and handling of animals. The other two were veterinary technicians who had college diplomas in veterinary technology and could perform simple medical procedures such as giving vaccinations and taking blood samples. Tasks requiring a fully qualified veterinarian were performed by a local volunteer who was at the shelter one afternoon per week and was available to help with emergencies. They also had a number of community volunteers eager to spend time walking, petting, and playing with animals in care. The volunteers were critical because the overall staffing level was not sufficient to provide each animal with the attention they needed. This was especially true because the vet assistants, in addition to feeding, watering, grooming, and caring for animals, also had to clean cages and bowls, sterilize floors, prepare special foods from raw ingredients for a handful of animals with unique medical needs, attend to the cricket farm used to generate food for lizards and snakes, and perform other menial maintenance tasks critical to ensuring a clean, safe environment. They even took weekly pictures of the animals and put them up on the website to encourage adoptions. Furthermore, there were always some animals who were too weak, ill, skittish, anxious, or traumatized to be handled by casual volunteers. Those high-need animals often required extra attention and customized care and training programs to make them eligible for adoption, which the vet assistants could provide.

Tyron thought back to the conversation he had had with Vanessa the previous week. It had all started because one of the volunteers had reported that they saw her drinking behind the building during a break on her shift. Tyron had previously seen her looking "out of it" at work and once had even seen her stumble for no apparent reason, but he had attributed it to fatigue and then promptly forgotten about it. When the volunteer made their report, he thought harder, and he could remember other times she seemed less aware of her actions. For example, once she had failed to notice that the sleepy puppy she was cuddling was being held awkwardly, and it had almost fallen out of her arms onto a cement floor! Another time she had mixed up food bowls and given an elderly cat some food that triggered a known allergy. Tyron was unsure whether those things occurred due to drunkenness—what he had seen was subject to interpretation—but then a second volunteer also reported seeing her drinking 2 days after the first report. This time it was in her car before the start of her shift. Tyron decided to talk to her about it.

At first, she vehemently denied the problem. "Who told you I was drinking?" she huffed, eyes flashing angrily. Tyron refused to tell her but did emphasize that he was concerned rather than angry. He told her he had lost a good friend to alcoholism in his younger days, and he never wanted to see it happen to another person. That seemed to get through to her, and after some hesitation she confessed that she had been drinking every day. "It is something I am struggling with right now," Vanessa explained quietly. "I've been struggling with depression for a couple of years and drinking just takes it all away for a while. It's not like I'm an addict or anything. I mean I drink every day. I can't seem to help myself; it happens even when I don't want to drink. But I'm sure I'll get better. This has been embarrassing. I will try harder. It will be fine. You'll see."

Tyron hadn't felt particularly reassured, but since Vanessa seemed so certain that she could control her drinking, he decided to give her the benefit of the doubt and see what happened. Now, a week later, here they were. He looked over to the new litter of kittens who had just arrived. They had been badly neglected and two were injured and fragile, requiring careful handling. Tyron shuddered to think about how easily they could have been hurt further if handled improperly, without sufficient attention. He had gotten into his line of work because he felt a deep compassion for all creatures and people in need of help. He thought carefully about Vanessa and how best to approach the situation.

Tyron's Next Steps

Tyron had Vanessa come into his office the next day, once she had sobered up, to discuss next steps. He explained his concerns about her handling animals, and they agreed to temporarily assign her to tasks, such as cleaning cages, that did not involve direct contact with animals. In the meantime, Tyron would help her access alcohol addiction treatment services. Once she had her drinking under control, she would return to her regular duties. Vanessa chose a peer support program she felt comfortable with, and Tyron agreed to schedule her work hours to accommodate attendance at late afternoon meetings.

He also asked what supports she might need for depression. Vanessa wasn't sure what Tyron could do, but she did mention that being with the animals had always helped, and now that she wouldn't be handling them directly, she thought it might be harder. After considering this, Tyron came up with a compromise. He knew denial and hiding drinking were symptoms of alcoholism, so he could not completely trust her. He needed to control risk, but he also wanted Vanessa to find healing where she could. Her official duties would still be limited during her initial treatment period, but she was permitted to spend time directly interacting with the animals before and after her shift if she came to Tyron's office first showing no signs of impairment and if she was with other casual volunteers.

Tyron also realized that he might be able to help with her depression in more subtle ways. He moved her workstation so that it was beside a sunny window. He asked her about her life and demonstrated concern for her well-being when he saw her. He made a point of offering positive feedback when she did something well. Tyron also made sure that other employees and volunteers did not engage in gossip or bullying behaviors. He had an expert come in and deliver a general mental health and wellness training session that destigmatized addictions and depression, among other topics. Finally, he gave her an unpaid week off (which she did not technically have enough vacation time for) so that she could visit her mother in another state and receive family support. Unfortunately, despite these supports Vanessa still struggled with her drinking. Tyron knew of a 30-day residential program that could help her, but it was very expensive, beyond the means of a small not-for-profit. He decided to contribute a third of the amount, all the organization could afford, while also offering her a very low-interest loan for the remainder, all legally documented. Once she returned to work, 5% of her gross pay would be deducted to repay the loan, allowing her to repay it within 2 years. Reasonable provisions for repayment in the event the employment relationship ended were also included. Vanessa agreed to this solution and, with the support and compassion of her colleagues, was ultimately successful in her recovery journey.

Roche, A., Kostadinov, V., & Pidd, K. (2019). The stigma of addiction in the workplace. In J. D. Avery & J. J. Avery (Eds.), *The stigma of addiction: An essential guide* (pp. 167–199). Springer.

Van Eerd, D., Cullen, K., Irvin, E., Le Pouésard, M., & Gignac, M. (2021). Support for depression in the workplace: Perspectives of employees, managers, and OHS personnel. *Occupational Health Science, 5*(3), 307–343. https://doi.org/10.1007/s41542-021-00090-9

Raul's Team: Onboarding and Accommodation

An HR manager in a market research firm must decide how best to eliminate inadvertent barriers embedded in the onboarding and training process after hiring a worker with a vision impairment. The manager must consider barriers related to travel, content delivery, learning material accessibility, scheduling, and suitability of social activities.

The Case

Raul scratched his head, puzzled about how to proceed. He was the HR manager for a regional branch office that was part of a large multinational market research firm. They had recently hired five new people to work at their call center administering surveys. The new hires would call people in their homes at prearranged times to ask them survey questions. The people responding to the surveys were paid small sums (usually $15 to $30) to provide detailed opinions about everything from their favorite brand names to new product offerings. The data was collected over the phone rather than using a written online survey because that approach allowed for asking follow-up questions. In addition, they were able to capture data from people with literacy issues, people speaking a variety of languages (employees needed to be fluent in at least three commonly spoken languages to get the job), and people with unreliable internet connections.

Newly hired employees went through a 3-day onboarding process that included training about the company's vision, mission, and values as well as specialized training in survey delivery. The training was intensive because surveyors could easily bias results if surveys were not delivered using an appropriately neutral tone. In addition, it took new hires some time to learn the company's data coding system, that is, assigning codes to different categories of responses, which greatly facilitated later analysis. All training was completed by learning specialists at the company headquarters, which was located on the other side of the country from Raul's field office. The training itself was delivered using a combination of lectures that made heavy use of PowerPoint slides, along with detailed written instructions and phone scripts. They were also expected to do *homework*, reviewing policy and procedure manuals in their hotel rooms in the evening. After 2 days of pen and pencil exercises, the new hires spent the last day on mock phone calls, going through survey scripts with each other and getting real-time feedback from their trainers. In a nod to a long-standing company tradition, after the last day of training everyone went to a local Chinese buffet restaurant, then proceeded to a nearby go-kart course for some teambuilding races that would help everyone relax and get to know each other better.

Raul was confident about his new hires, but he was concerned about the training component. One of his hires, a man named Betong, had very limited vision. While he could make out shades of light and dark, he was considered legally blind and used a cane when walking. Raul had hired Betong because he had a pleasant phone manner, a knack for making people open up and share information, and he spoke four different languages that were well represented in their community: English, Filipino, Spanish, and Vietnamese. It had been a struggle to find Filipino speakers in particular, and that skill was highly valued. Raul had been confident that he could accommodate Betong at work using text-to-voice software to enable reading of scripts and voice-to-text software to enable data input. Betong had also demonstrated during the testing phase of recruitment that he could memorize a new phone survey quickly, even when it was multiple pages. Raul had not, however, thought about the week of training that was required. Betong would need to travel, take the training, and participate in activities as an equal member of the team. Raul wondered how best this could be achieved, or if another approach might be needed. He was very unsure of himself, wondering what to do. He decided to talk with Betong directly about his comfort level with travel, making it clear that the answer would not impact his employment, along with consulting the disability accommodation expert who worked in HR at company headquarters. Together they developed a plan.

The Accommodation Plan

Betong expressed some concerns about navigating the airport by himself; however, he was comfortable doing so along with coworkers who were taking the same flight and then going to the same hotel. Since Raul was sending five new hires to training all at once, this was easy to arrange. The company paid for a limo service for all five, which was cheaper than paying for some of them to park at the airport or take individual taxis. The trainer arranged to send the policy and procedure manuals that were usually read in the evenings to Betong in electronic format a week early. This allowed him to use his text-to-voice reader and have extra time because using it was somewhat slower than an average reading speed. Similarly, training scripts and instructions were provided in advance in accessible formats. Betong was paid for 2.5 extra days of self-directed training at home to acknowledge the extra time required for him to review these documents, memorize scripts, and generally prepare. In addition, the trainer made sure they described any visuals that were on the PowerPoint slides during their in-class sessions. Finally, they arranged to have the final dinner at a sit-down Chinese restaurant rather than a buffet, and they planned at attend a trivia night at a local venue instead of go-karting. They ended up retaining that last change for all subsequent training sessions because they found working as a team at trivia night helped bring people together more effectively than racing each other in go-karts!

Had Betong not been comfortable traveling, then remote learning tools could be used, allowing him to join the group sessions online. Alternately, he could be trained individually in the field office. Either option would result in some isolation from his colleagues and deliberate effort would be needed to make him feel socially welcome and integrated into the team.

FURTHER READINGS

French, S. (2017). *Visual impairment and work: Experiences of visually impaired people*. Taylor & Francis.

Müller, A., Engel, C., Loitsch, C., Stiefelhagen, R., & Weber, G. (2022). Traveling more independently: A study on the diverse needs and challenges of people with visual or mobility impairments in unfamiliar indoor environments. *ACM Transactions on Accessible Computing, 15*(2), 1–44. https://doi.org/10.1145/3514255

"Is She Drunk?" Disability and Intersectional Stereotyping at Work

An entrepreneur needs to decide how to address customer complaints that target a worker with a visible disability who is also simultaneously being discriminated against based on stereotypes associated with their Indigenous identity.

The Case

It was a beautiful snowy Saturday afternoon in the second week of December and the Christmas shopping rush was in full swing. Maryanne watched another angry customer turn and stalk away, coat flaring and high-heeled boots clicking aggressively. This customer clearly felt that she had just accomplished something important. Maryanne sighed. It was the fourth complaint about her sales associate and cashier, Winona, in a week. Maryanne knew that the customers were wrong and that the situation was not as it appeared, but the complaints did not have to be fair to negatively impact the reputation of her retail toy and school supply business. She wondered somewhat desperately how she could handle the situation. Perhaps it was time to ask Winona to move into a non-customer-facing role. Would she take a job in the warehouse? And would it be legal, fair, and ethical to even ask her to? If Winona stayed in a customer-facing role, how could Maryanne get the complaints to stop? As owner of the company, she needed to answer these questions and make a decision quickly before things got out of hand.

Maryanne was the owner and CEO of Childcopia, a business located in a community of about 22,500 people in Manitoba. Childcopia started out as a small retail toy store. Since their town and the surrounding rural communities were underserved in the retail market, lacking both indoor malls and a substantial department store, the shop did well almost right away. Over time, Maryanne noticed that many people who were operating home daycares wanted a broader range of supplies such as craft materials, outdoor play equipment, books, and toddler-proof dishes and cups. She expanded beyond traditional retail, becoming a distributor and one-stop shop where small daycares and nursery schools could buy all their supplies quickly and conveniently. Online sales for that component of the business were brisk, and she shipped all over Manitoba, Saskatchewan, and Alberta. The traditional retail component of the business was still important, representing roughly 27% of their revenues and 36% of profits. The remainder of their revenue and profit, however, came from the distribution arm of the business. Maryanne had been required to build a warehouse on land adjacent to the retail store and now had five employees who worked exclusively there, processing, picking, packing, and shipping out the daycare and nursery school orders.

Winona had been hired 4 months earlier when she had first moved to their community from Northern Manitoba, where she had previously lived on reserve lands along with her family and other members of her band. Winona was Anishinaabe. The Anishinaabe were signatories to the historical Treaty 1 that was signed in Winnipeg in 1871 and are formally recognized by the Canadian government as First Nations peoples. Winona's physical appearance made her readily identifiable as an Indigenous person, as did her penchant for wearing contemporary jewelry and clothing that featured traditional beadwork and Indigenous designs. Maryanne had been happy to hire her since she had 8 years' experience working a cash register at a small grocery store in her home community and was available to work days, evenings, or weekends as needed. Winona had also seemed very approachable and friendly during her interview, and customers responded well to sales staff with pleasant dispositions. In fact, Maryanne found that general sociability was one of the things that predicted which sales staff would work out over the long term, so she was pleased to have such an amiable candidate available.

In her first 4 months of employment, Maryanne had been quite impressed with Winona's work performance. She was briefly concerned in Winona's second week of employment when she had noticed that Winona's hands were trembling visibly while she logged into the cash register for her shift. Maryanne had found the trembling strange, but it didn't seem to slow Winona down at all, so she had shrugged it off. Then she saw the same thing 2 days later while Winona was stocking shelves. Concerned, she asked if Winona needed to sit down. "No," Winona had replied as her voice shook and she blushed deep red. "I'm fine. I was hoping nobody would notice." Winona then explained that she had a medical condition called "essential tremor." She experienced sporadic tremors in her hands, usually when she was actively engaged in a task. Sometimes her arms or even her voice would also shake. These tremors had been happening for 10 years, and they were not getting worse over time, nor did they interfere with her ability to function unless she was under extreme stress. (Stress and anxiety made the tremors worse.) Winona did find them embarrassing though so she tried to hide her condition. Unfortunately, the beta-blocking drugs and anti-seizure medications that sometimes helped control symptoms did not work for her. She was unwilling to take the other option, tranquilizers, due to their addictive nature. As a result, Winona just lived with her symptoms.

After hearing the explanations for the tremors and observing her work behavior for the remainder of the initial 4-week probation period, Maryanne felt confident providing Winona with an excellent performance evaluation. She had not regretted the choice because Winona continued to perform well 4 months into her employment period. Winona was an excellent employee. She was very reliable. She usually arrived at work 5–10 minutes early, and she was friendly and pleasant with her coworkers and customers. Winona also learned quickly and had started offering customers appropriate suggestions and advice when they weren't sure what toy to buy for a child. Maryanne especially appreciated how quickly Winona could scan and ring through purchases when things got hectic—that speed had come in handy as weekends began to get busy due to the upcoming holiday season. Their customers, however, had created an unexpected problem.

It had first happened about 6 weeks into Winona's employment. A man who was a long-time customer had come in to find a birthday present for his son, and Winona had helped him select something and then rang it in. As it happened, her tremor flared up twice—once when she was showing him items on the shelves and once when she was giving him his change. He had gone over to where Maryanne was restocking a shelf with stuffed animals and had asked to speak with her confidentially. She stepped outside to speak with him. "I'm pretty sure your cashier is drunk or on something," the embarrassed man blurted out. "She is shaking like she has withdrawal or alcoholic tremors or something. You know a lot of kids come into this store. It just isn't right to have them exposed to that type of thing." He then left hastily before the surprised Maryanne could formulate a response. She was shocked that he had just assumed Winona was drunk or on drugs, but she received a phone call from the warehouse shortly after that, distracting her. Later, when she thought about it again, she figured that the complaint was a one-off and didn't worry much more about it.

It happened again a week and a half later. This time it was a grand-motherly farmer from out of town who was buying books and LEGOs to donate to the local Salvation Army Christmas hamper campaign. Maryanne had been standing near the till chatting with Winona when the woman came up to pay for her purchases. Winona's hand and arm shook slightly as she used the cash register. This customer did not bother trying to be discreet; she looked Winona right in the eye and said out loud, "Well, I guess I should have expected one of you people would be drinking on the job;

that's what you all do." Maryanne, horrified, was shocked into silence as the woman left the store. Once she was gone, Maryanne turned to Winona to share her disbelief but Winona, who seemed flushed with either anger or embarrassment, didn't act surprised. "That happens a lot," Winona said, "I once got kicked out of a shopping mall by security for being so-called drunk just because my arms and voice were shaking badly that day. People see an Indigenous person and immediately stereotype, assuming we are all lazy alcoholics on welfare. You get used to having to ignore it." Maryanne had never felt more awkward in her life, but she managed to stammer an apology for the customer's behavior before heading to her office to think.

Since then, there had been a few similar incidents. Maryanne had asked Winona if she wanted Maryanne to explain about her tremors to customers to avoid the problem of being mistaken for an addict, but Winona had said that her medical history was nobody's business. It was private, and customers' stereotypes about Indigenous people were their problem, not hers. Maryanne tended to agree but already she had friends alerting her to a couple social media posts on Facebook telling people not to shop at her store because she "fostered addicts who threaten our children." She believed those posts represented fringe members of the community, but she could not be sure how far the messages would spread and who would choose to believe it. Her community was very insular and socially conservative, and prejudices of various types had been a problem in the past, undermining certain businesses to the point of bankruptcy. For example, in 2015 an immigrant family from India had moved away after accusing locals of actively undermining their profits by loitering excessively in and around their restaurant and intimidating potential patrons. Similarly, the community had pointedly not celebrated PRIDE Day, a day that was all about equal rights for gay, lesbian, and transsexual members of the community, until 2017. Even in 2017, their first PRIDE parade was formally boycotted by all municipal politicians, including the mayor. Given the social environment in the community Maryanne just couldn't be sure how far this could all go and how much boycotts, if any were started, could impact her business.

Making the situation even more difficult, the holiday shopping rush was now in full swing. That added a lot of stress to the workplace. Winona had also been anxious about the health of an aunt back home. Her aunt had been diagnosed with cancer and could not get appropriate healthcare in her community, so she had been required to drive to Winnipeg for treatment. The entire family was distressed and concerned, and Winona spent hours each night talking with her aunt and others to offer some reassurance. Maryanne figured that it was the combined stress of the busy season and her personal situation that had resulted in the noticeable increase in Winona's tremors recently. Although the tremors still did not impair her work performance, their increased frequency meant that more customers noticed and there were more complaints, including the woman who had just turned on her heels and marched out (without making a purchase, Maryanne couldn't help but notice).

Maryanne had several options for how to proceed but she wasn't sure which option(s) would be appropriate for her business as well as fair, legal, and ethical. As far as she knew, her options included the following: She could just ignore the complaints and continue with Winona in her current role. She could ask again for permission to share Winona's medical information so that customers were more understanding. She thought briefly about discontinuing Winona's employment but was unclear on what legal issues, if any, that may create. She also considered moving Winona to another job where she wouldn't interact with customers. There was a job available picking and packing orders in the warehouse, but it was very different from the job Winona had now. Although both paid a similar hourly wage, the sales job included significant performance bonuses for high levels of sales and upselling. The warehouse job had more regular hours (no evenings or weekends) but also no scheduling flexibility. The cashier and sales associate job consisted of helping customers, operating the cash register, and doing light lifting of a maximum of 10 pounds to restock shelves. The warehouse job was more physically demanding since it required lifting up to 65 pounds fairly regularly and packing up large boxes. It was also not a social job; people worked independently with minimal interaction, so Maryanne wondered whether the extremely sociable Winona would even want it. All in all, Maryanne felt lost. She did not want to be a party to prejudice, but she couldn't afford to lose her business either.

Maryanne's Next Steps

Unfortunately, there is no single choice that represents an ideal outcome. Firing Winona is clearly a very poor choice because it is unethical, creates substantial legal risk, and creates new market and reputational risk if concerned customers find out she acted in a discriminatory manner. While there are positive aspects to changing Winona's job or publicizing her medical condition, both options depend heavily on Winona's feelings and desires, and she is not obligated to accept either option, nor should she be pressured to. Forcing a job change may be considered constructive dismissal in some legal jurisdictions, which is illegal. Barring Winona's free and open acceptance of a transfer or public medical disclosure, the only practical and ethical solution is to retain Winona in her current role, even though doing so creates meaningful risks for Winona's health and well-being and for their sales, especially local retail sales. In such difficult circumstances, Maryanne's strategy should be to retain Winona but also try to mitigate the risks associated with that decision. There are several small things that Maryanne can do to influence public perception. While none magically fixes the problem, collectively they may prove beneficial:

- Post statements on social media denying that any of her employees are impaired at work, and state, "Out of respect for employee privacy, that is our only comment on the matter."

- Address individual incidents on a one-on-one basis, taking offending individuals aside privately to explain that their fears are misplaced without providing medical details.

- Publicly highlight Winona's skill and professionalism by posting plaques naming her employee of the month, putting her in advertising materials using images in which she is competently helping customers, putting a positive employee profile in the local newspaper, and talking about how well her new employee is working out with regular customers who are also social influencers in the community.

- Increase customer awareness of the range of neurological impairments that can cause tremors by fundraising for an associated charity, of course without mentioning Winona.

- Explicitly let Winona know that harassing behavior will not be tolerated, and Maryanne should be informed when it happens.

- Ban repeat offenders who insist on directing racially offensive or harassing comments toward Winona.

- Provide Winona and all other employees with access to paid mental health days.

- Recognize and reward positive work behaviors, and openly praise Winona when appropriate and let her know that she is valued at work.

- Allow Winona to contact elders from her community during work hours should she need emergency emotional support.

FURTHER READINGS

Joseph, B., & Joseph, C. (2019). *Indigenous relations: Insights, tips, and suggestions to make reconciliation a reality*. Indigenous Relations Press.

Pedersen, A., Walker, I., & Wise, M. (2005). "Talk does not cook rice": Beyond anti-racism rhetoric to strategies for social action. *Australian Psychologist, 40*(1), 20–31. https://doi.org/10.1080/0005006051233131729

10

Putting Ideas into Practice

D iversity and inclusion work is never done. Understanding of best practices in inclusion is continually evolving as social scientists develop more refined insight into the underlying psychological processes involved and the relative effectiveness of varied interventions. Employers can educate themselves either by reading original research or by reading research summaries and recommendations published by credible professional licensing and support organizations such as the American Society for Human Resource Managers (SHRM), Canada's Chartered Professionals in Human Resource Management (CPHR), and the United Kingdom's Chartered Institute of Personnel and Development (CIPD).

Engaging in ongoing formal assessment of organizational policies, procedures, and inclusion initiatives should be standard practice, with critical evaluation and continuous improvement as the main goals. Assessors can collect data on subjective impressions, such as whether people feel safe, included, supported, and valued at work; acquired knowledge, such as whether staff can pass a relevant test after receiving diversity training; measurable behaviors, such as whether formal reports of harassment have increased or decreased and whether supervisors observe exclusionary behavior when casually interacting with staff; and outcomes, such as whether equity-seeking employees receive equal pay and are proportionately represented in promotions and whether they are more likely to quit than other employees. Evaluation of such data must be done by persons with underlying knowledge of the organization's history to assist in interpretation. For example, increases in reports of harassment may signal a deterioration in social conditions, an improvement in willingness to report long-standing harassment, or both. Let's discuss some areas in which the current research's understanding of appropriate accommodation is actively evolving, requiring extra efforts on the part of human resource (HR) managers and supervisors to self-educate to ensure best practices are implemented, and then explore a couple examples of putting ideas in practice.

Disability Management Plans

Chapter 7 described disability management plans, which are frequently used in the context of addictions, and in that context, they are sometimes labeled *last chance agreements* because they often require an employee to avoid using the substance to which they are addicted to maintain employment. Disability management plans are intended to provide meaningful support to employees and are not intended to be punitive; however, they are not always implemented in a manner that makes that clear. There are active court cases in several jurisdictions in the United States, Canada, and Europe that challenge the idea of a last chance agreement on the basis that being unable to control an addiction is part of the diagnostic criteria of addiction-based disability, and therefore it cannot be used as a basis to fire someone. Some employers are attempting to avoid the issue altogether by creating policies that require employees to proactively disclose an addiction. Understandably, many employees are reluctant to do so, fearing being stigmatized by such a disclosure.

Employers have been using this as a loophole to fire employees who are found to be impaired at work. They are technically fired for violating the disclosure policy, not for their addiction. A case like this went all the way to the Supreme Court in Canada in 2017, *Stewart v. Elk Coal Company* (2017 SCC 30). The employee, who was involved in a workplace accident while high on cocaine, had their termination upheld by a slight majority of the Supreme Court judges, who said that no discrimination had occurred. A minority felt it was discrimination, but it was justified due to undue hardship related to accommodation needs because the employee was a heavy equipment operator in a mine. One judge wrote an impassioned dissenting opinion claiming the disclosure policy itself amounted to disability-based discrimination, which highlights the potential unpredictable nature of such court cases.

Organizations who plan to use disability accommodation plans for addictions should be careful to investigate the ongoing legal landscape before proceeding. They are also encouraged to remember that disability management plans are intended to be a support tool and should be created and implemented in that spirit.

Workplace Accommodation of Neurodiversity and of Intermittent Impairment

Accommodation of neurodiversity is another area that is evolving. Conditions such as autism and attention deficit disorder are more reliably diagnosed, especially among females. (The previous diagnostic criteria were inappropriately centered on masculine presentations of these conditions, which historically made it difficult to diagnose and support females.) Greater recognition of these conditions has been accompanied by social and political movements to increase acceptance and make workplaces more accommodating. Workplaces are also increasingly valuing neurodiverse employees for their unique skills and perspectives, and formal workplace programs to support and embrace neurodiversity—like EY's program described in Chapter 2—are emerging in large numbers. The amount of research and corporate attention being paid to these workers makes it likely that new understandings will emerge about best practices in accommodation in the future. Researchers are particularly encouraged to study the appropriateness of common recruitment, team building, and onboarding processes and exercises for this population because such programs are often overly reliant on individual social competence and political impression management skills for their success.

Workplace accommodation of intermittent disabilities is also an area where understanding, support, and best practices are developing and evolving. While a number of workers have always had intermittent disabilities, that number is likely to skyrocket as a result of long-haul COVID-19 infections resulting from the global pandemic. This creates pressure to ameliorate strategies for accommodating intermittent disabilities, an area that is not currently well understood. Researchers and practitioners should pay particular attention to accommodations for workers unable to work from home, and workers with inflexible deadlines. Team-based work models and cross-training may mitigate some of the unpredictability associated with intermittent disabilities because they ensure that individual workers have back-up; however, this approach can create social perception issues. Peer responses to the individual with a disability may require monitoring and can be improved with careful management attention to workload impacts, equity, and fairness. Field research should be conducted among those companies that are currently successfully managing workers with intermittent disabilities to establish more detailed best practices.

Peer Attitudes

While the aforementioned issues and evolutions in our understanding are important, the most impactful area that researchers and practitioners can focus on is peer attitudes. Peer attitudes make an enormous difference in accommodation outcomes, job satisfaction, and one's sense of belonging. Direct peer cooperation is often needed to implement accommodation strategies. Yet peers are often influenced by stereotypes about disability, fears (often misplaced) that working with a colleague with a disability creates more work for them, and, in some cases, even distaste or discomfort at being in the presence of someone with a disability. In yet unpublished interviews I (the author) have conducted, one worker who is blind reported that it was commonplace for peers to express resentment and refuse even extremely simple requests for assistance, such as verifying that text in a press release was an appropriate font size. Another worker with a hearing impairment reported that colleagues, when asked to face him when they spoke so he could read lips, would be noncompliant to the point of intentionally covering their mouths. A worker with autism was reported to HR for harmless hand flapping when they became excited by a new product idea because a colleague thought the behavior was "weird" and they should be "made to act normal." This led to the worker with autism suppressing their creativity in later product development meetings to avoid getting over-excited and flapping again. For all three individuals, these types of microaggressions were not outliers limited to one person or even one employer, but rather they represent the majority of their peer interactions both in tone and actual behaviors, that is, peers refused to participate in reasonable accommodations.

In other interviews, other employees with disabilities reported very positive peer experiences. These positive experiences not only made them feel more welcome, but they subjectively felt that their productivity was increased as well. This highlights the critical importance of paying more attention to nurturing positive peer attitudes about colleagues with disabilities and their accommodation needs. Storytelling based diversity training and other methods of creating genuine empathy are needed to address the very real issue of negative peer impacts on the work lives of people with disabilities. This is true everywhere but is especially true when working within national or organizational cultures that still heavily stigmatize disability.

Storytelling-Based Diversity Training

Storytelling-based diversity training is a type of training that promotes perspective sharing through narratives to build inclusion and strengthen team relationships through awareness and empathy. It is best that this training method be delivered by professionals with specific expertise in appropriate pedagogical practices because expert knowledge, high emotional intelligence, and robust communication, counseling, and conflict management skills are needed to successfully lead such sessions. Done incorrectly storytelling training can increase rather than lessen bias (Rose et al., 2016), but done properly, it encourages perspective taking, which is a prerequisite for empathy, and it can even help learners develop new and more inclusive behavioral scripts.

This type of training generally takes three forms. In its simplest form, a speaker from outside the organization with relevant lived experience gives a talk about their personal experiences with opportunities for questions afterward. This is a useful starting point, especially for people who may be uncomfortable with a new approach to diversity training or may not yet trust their employer or coworkers sufficiently to share personal information. It is more effective, however, if people actively participate.

A second form of training involves a heavily structured, guided exploration of relative privilege. This often involves questionnaires and checklists that allow people to recognize and compare privileges they have, such as male privilege, White privilege, cisgender privilege, and the privilege of having a conventionally functioning body. Participants then share stories about what privilege means to them in a manner that helps gently correct problematic behaviors. For example, a person who uses a wheelchair or who has ADHD may be given a safe space to talk about the impact inadvertent barriers and nonconscious bias have on their day-to-day work lives. Their coworkers, who are listening, are then able to better understand the impact of behaviors they might have believed harmless, such as pushing someone's wheelchair without permission or failing to provide written task instructions when asked. They also become aware of nonconscious behaviors, such as the tendency to talk down to or use condescending language and tone when speaking with people with disabilities, as though they were children. This allows for self-directed behavioral correction.

A third form of story-telling-based training is more open ended, allowing people to share personal stories freely as they see fit without the formality of the structured checklists about privilege. For example, an employee who has a disability may feel empowered in an open discussion session to share some of the barriers they face that are invisible to their coworkers, as well as describe how those barriers impact them. This type of open sharing session is very effective at improving diversity outcomes because, when done correctly, it creates genuine mutual understanding. However, employees must be willing to make themselves somewhat vulnerable to fully participate. This format requires a great deal of trust, clear ground rules, and a highly competent facilitator. That level of trust may not be obtainable in the short term within organizations with a history of poor diversity and inclusion, with employees who have had negative experiences with previous employers, or with employees with highly stigmatized differences or disabilities. When done properly, there is early evidence from healthcare settings that storytelling-based training increases empathy while also providing appropriate and actionable behavioral scripts for those looking to overcome their own internalized nonconscious biases (Holdren et al., 2022; Rose et al., 2016).

A Case Study on Peer Attitudes in a Call Center in India

Japinder looked around the call center, wondering what to do to make the workplace more inclusive. The call center, which served a major U.S. technology company, had recently opened in Palani, a town of about 60,000 people in the Jhunjhunu district of Rajasthan, India. As the HR manager, Japinder had hoped to use his influence to create opportunities for workers with disabilities. He had been inspired as a student when he volunteered for the India Inclusion Foundation, an agency that worked to dispel stereotypes and encourage hiring of workers with disabilities. They faced an uphill climb. While the government of India had instituted legislation to encourage the hiring of workers with disabilities, the legislation was not well known and was seldom enforced. Furthermore, many people in Palani shared the viewpoint that disability was something shameful, that it arose because of bad karma from prior lives and therefore people with disabilities were worthy of shunning and scorn (Griffin, 2021). Some families even refused to allow family members with disabilities to leave the house because the family would feel shamed by them. Not everyone shared these attitudes of course; as with any community, there was a range of perspectives. Japinder's neighbor, for example, took great pride in his daughter, who had cerebral palsy, and he could frequently be seen walking alongside her in her wheelchair in the street while bragging to all who would listen about her academic achievements. Japinder knew there were other allies in the community, he just didn't necessarily know who they were.

Japinder had decided to move forward with his initiative to hire workers with disabilities. He used his connections at the India Inclusion Foundation to help with a search and placement process, and he was delighted to get suitable candidates. He had hired three workers. A young woman with Down syndrome named Ira was hired to wheel around a coffee cart, maintain the staff kitchens and bathrooms, and do light cleaning. A middle-aged man named Darsh, whose feet had suffered severe nerve damage due to now cured leprosy and who used a wheelchair, was hired to manage staff scheduling and payroll. Finally, a hearing-impaired employee named Saanvi was hired for the call center but assigned exclusively to text message and chat-based customer inquiries. Japinder had felt very proud of himself, like he was helping change the world. That feeling, unfortunately, did not last.

Darsh lasted 1 week in his new job. After hearing that he was leaving, Japinder asked to speak with him. "What happened," asked Japinder, "I thought you liked the job." "The job itself was fine," Darsh replied, "but I can't handle everyone staring and pointing. They can see my leprosy scars, and some won't even come into the same room with me. I told them I am cured and not contagious, but all they see is a leper. One even asked why I deserved a job while her 'good' brother couldn't find one. I can't take the hostility anymore."

Saanvi lasted almost 3 months before quitting. Japinder was worried she had been treated in the same manner as Darsh. "Nobody is rude to me exactly," said Saanvi. "They invite me out with them after work and we have fun. But I keep hearing about how much easier my job is than theirs because the customers on the phone are more likely to be abusive than ones in chat. Some people complain that I make the same starting wages as every other call center worker. Plus, every time I am proud of myself for my good performance, my supervisor just says, 'Well of course you do well, you have an easy job.' But it isn't easy; nobody values what I do. The supervisor just told me that promotions to Customer Service Rep Level 2 requires good phone *and* chat service scores, which I can never achieve. I'll never be able to grow or be appreciated in this job."

Ira lasted almost 6 months. She did a good job and was well liked. Her father, however, made her quit the job after hearing stories about men being nice to her at work. Due to her cognitive limitations, she was not able to comprehend the predatory sexual nature of the interest a couple of her male coworkers were showing her. Her father, however, had no difficulty understanding the nature of the coworker comments she had shared with him, and he felt she was vulnerable and unsafe working there.

Japinder felt defeated. He thought hiring workers with disabilities would be the hard part. He did not realize that hiring was only the first step to inclusion, and he had failed to consider the impact peers would have on the work experience of his new hires. He knew that before bringing in another round of workers with disabilities, he would need to address peer attitudes and behavioral standards.

After careful consideration of his options, Japinder made a number of changes. He instituted diversity training aimed specifically at stereotypes and bias reduction, and he supplemented it with lunch hour learning sessions. The lunch sessions consisted of spokespeople from the disability community sharing their personal workplace stories to help create empathy. He created a policy about respectful workplace interactions that prohibited bullying and sexual harassment, he then trained staff on it, and when the first incident occurred, he was sure to enforce the policy in a highly visible way. Encouraging bystander reporting, including anonymous reporting, was part of this program. Japinder adjusted the onboarding program to assign supportive mentors who could help with social integration, and he modified promotion criteria in the call center so all employees could be eligible regardless of whether they offered phone- or chat-based support. He even arranged for the company to sponsor a leprosy-related charity, and he used that as an opportunity to educate his workers on the condition. "I think I've fixed everything, and we can hire again," he bragged to his contacts at the India Inclusion Foundation. "Hold up," said his mentor. "You've fixed the problems the former employees had, and that is a good start. But new employees will have new needs. This is an ongoing improvement process that never stops." Armed with this new understanding, Japinder vowed to do a better job with his next round of hires. He went back to the job posting sites to start again.

A Case Study of the Continuous Improvement Process

As Japinder learned, continuous improvement is part of any accommodation strategy. Let's explore an example where a well-intended HR manager is observed getting some things right while simultaneously identifying several unintentional barriers and problems, learning from them, and devising strategies to correct them. The example is fictional but is inspired by real events that occurred in several different companies during hiring initiatives, as outlined to me while conducting yet unpublished research interviews.

Colin Brewer looked over the job ad he had just written for the forensic accountant role. He hoped to hire someone as soon as possible. Colin was the HR manager for a midsize legal firm that specialized in family law and divorce. The firm was attracting more and more high net worth clients, and a forensic accountant was required because it was not uncommon for people to try to hide assets or obscure their true net worth during divorce proceedings. The asset portfolios of the wealthiest couples could be especially complex, and the firm had been paying far too much to hire outside expertise. The firm's partners had decided that they had enough work for a full-time in-house forensic accountant. Colin feared it would be a hard job to fill. There were few qualified forensic accountants on the job market, and the competition to hire them was fierce because government agencies, insurance firms, accountancy firms, and even law enforcement all required their skills. In addition to worries about labor scarcity, Colin also wanted to ensure that the ad was seen by equity-seeking groups. His law firm staff was not terribly diverse, and Colin was aware this was an issue that they should try to address when hiring.

When developing the job ad, Colin had conducted interviews with subject matter experts and determined that, in addition to a professional accounting designation with a supplementary forensic audit credential, a minimum of 5 years' experience in audit was recommended. Critical competencies included the ability to work alone with minimal supervision, attention to detail, analytical skills, and a strong ethical compass. Communication skills were also important. While those were the primary qualifications, Colin also recalled that auditors occasionally traveled as part of their audit work. He recalled one incident in which a forensic accountant the firm hired on contract had been required to go to warehouses in another country and physically count inventory to confirm the existence and extent of the assets held by the spouse of a client seeking a divorce settlement. Such instances were rare because the assets being divided were more often than not stocks, cash, pensions, or property with a clear market value rather than other physical assets, but it did still occur.

Colin considered how to attract the best possible candidate pool. Jobs were usually put on the firm's website, which sufficed for most staff jobs. The firm was well known, and people seeking work in the legal field in their city knew to go to their site. Lawyers were generally recruited as interns out of law school and were then promoted, but that path was not suitable for this role because they needed an experienced professional who would be able to work independently right from the start. Colin thought carefully about the firm's equity targets and decided to post the job in a few unconventional places. Specifically, he decided to reach out to a job board specific to the accounting industry, the local Indigenous Band Office, an agency that helps place professionals on the autism spectrum, and a disability rights not-for-profit. He asked the latter three to distribute the job ad to their members as an email or by posting it in their community meeting spaces. He also placed an ad in a local advocacy publication that catered to the Black community and an online newsletter that catered to the South Asian immigrant community.

Four weeks after placing the job ads, Colin received six résumés. However, two of the candidates did not have sufficient experience, so he considered the other four. Once again, he thought carefully about their equity hiring goals. While the job ad had specified that the firm welcomed applications from equity-seeking members of the community, nobody had identified themselves as such in their application. In hindsight, he was not surprised. After all, the ad had only mentioned that they sought applications from equity-seeking members; he realized that it had not actually provided any direction about how to identify oneself as such, and the online résumé submission form on their website did not offer any prompts to collect the information. "Something to fix for next time," he affirmed to himself.

Since they had only four appropriately qualified applicants, Colin decided to simply interview and test all remaining candidates. Normally, interviews were conducted by a group of three people, which included Colin, the direct supervisor for the role, and one of the senior partners. In this case, since the forensic accountancy role would be central to their future strategy, five senior partners wanted to be involved. Unfortunately, their schedules were poorly aligned, so Colin planned for three sequential interviews rather than a lone panel interview. He sent emails asking all the remaining candidates to come in for the three interviews followed by a selection test, cautioning them that they would need to be onsite for at least 6 hours. Just before sending the messages, he remembered to add a line telling the candidates that the firm valued equity, and should they require any accommodations or wish to identify themselves as an equity-seeking candidate, they were welcome to contact him directly with that information.

As he went home for the night, he thought vaguely about how to better encourage such disclosures in the future. "Maybe we need to put more information about our diversity programming on our website to send a signal of our supportiveness," he mused to himself. "After all, there is nothing there now telling people that we care about these issues and are welcoming." One of the senior partners had a visible disability and used a wheelchair. Colin wondered if using a photo of him on the website that included his chair rather than a headshot might send a subtle message of commitment to inclusion. He decided to ask the senior partner's thoughts on the matter next time he saw him.

When he returned to work the next morning, Colin had email responses from all four candidates accepting the interview. One candidate, Jaya Agarwal, had identified that three interviews and a selection test all on one day may pose a strain on her. She explained that her cystic fibrosis often left her fatigued and that stress made it worse. Since job interviews were inherently stressful, she was concerned. She wanted to know of there would be any time for short breaks, or if she would be required to be actively engaged for 6 hours in a row. She was also concerned that interviewers wearing heavy scents may trigger breathing issues or coughing. At first, these questions concerned Colin. "If she can't conduct interviews and tests for six hours straight, how can she work full time," he thought to himself. "Maybe I should cancel the interview." Then he caught himself. He realized he was making assumptions. First, interviews and tests were much more stressful and intense than day-to-day work, so it made sense that it would be more tiring. Second, people did get breaks throughout the day when working full time. Between coffee breaks and lunch, he realized it would be highly unusual to be expected to work 6 hours with no break. "Maybe I am being too hasty," he wondered. "I shouldn't make assumptions, I should talk to the candidate." Happy with his choice, he replied to her email and proposed that they divide the interviews and test such that they occurred over 2 days rather than 1. He also reassured her that all personnel would be asked to avoid scented products on the days she was there. Finally, he asked if there were any other accommodation needs or concerns. Jaya replied, thanking him and confirming there were no other issues.

The first day of interviews went very well. The morning of the second day, when further interviews were conducted, also went well. Unfortunately, there were problems in the afternoon of the second day when Jaya was supposed to complete her pen-and-paper work sample test, which required her to review some fictional financial records to identify signs of fraudulent activities. The wind patterns had changed over the course of the day and smoke from long distant wildfires has started to permeate the city. It was forecast to get worse over the course of several hours, and a formal air quality warning had been issued. Jaya was concerned about getting home before the smoke worsened because she had advanced air filtration systems in her home that would minimize the negative impact of the poor outdoor air quality. Under the circumstances Colin agreed that she should head home and, once home, she could complete the test while being monitored over Zoom. Since she was free to use online resources (much as she would be when completing her job), there were few concerns about cheating. This was a good solution for all.

After all interviews and tests were complete, Colin looked over the scoring rubrics that each interviewer had completed for the candidates. Each candidate had been seen by six interviewers in total: Colin himself, the four senior partners, and the investigations supervisor to whom the forensic accountant would report. Five of the interviewers had given top scores to Jaya. The other interviewer gave her a very low score. Surprised by the discrepancy, Colin asked the partner who had provided the low score what her thought process was. "I'm not sure," she replied. "It is nothing I can put my finger on, she just seems like a poor fit. Besides, she was rude. I saw her cough something up into a tissue just before the interview started. She thought I didn't notice but who does that? It was gross." Colin was dismayed by this response. He immediately decided that anti-bias training for senior partners was in order before any future interviews. Since he knew that her opinion had been informed by irrelevant and discriminatory criteria, he decided to dismiss her scores for all candidates. As a result, Jaya was the highest scoring candidate and was offered the job, which she happily accepted.

Before Jaya started her job, Colin decided to consult with her about any accommodation needs she might have. He brought a list of questions that asked about her limitations, the work tasks that would be impacted by her limitations, and any accommodations she might need. Before they started their discussion, he reassured her: "This is just a first pass. I understand that there may be issues you cannot anticipate right now, but we can review the plan again shortly after you start." "That is good to know," Jaya replied, "but don't you need a doctor's note to even get started?" Colin considered the question carefully. "I don't think that is necessary at this juncture," he said. "There may be a point in the future in which that is required to get final approval depending on the nature of your accommodation needs, and if you feel it adds value, then we are happy to support that. But since cystic fibrosis is a lifelong chronic condition and not something new to you, I assume that you already have a good idea about your needs, so let's see how far we get without requiring a medical note." Jaya was pleasantly surprised by this trusting and helpful attitude, having previously encountered barriers when she'd had to provide onerous proof before other employers would even consider her needs. That small measure of consideration and trust made her feel more like a human and less like an employee number. She liked her new employer already!

Over the course of their discussion, Colin and Jaya identified that her main limitations were fatigue, sensitivity to certain scents and pollutants (particularly perfumes, smoke, and chemicals), and occasional digestive issues that resulted in excessive trips to the bathroom and a need for a private bathroom to maintain dignity. She also had to be attentive to her diet.

For example, fatty fried foods could worsen her digestive symptoms. While they both agreed that working in the office was preferable most of the time so she could more readily integrate with the broader legal team, they also agreed that flexibility to work at home was easy to arrange given the nature of her job duties. "We can just see how it goes," Colin reassured Jaya. "If coming to the office regularly becomes too tiring, we could even switch you to a regular schedule with, for example, two days in the office a week and three days at home. That would still keep you connected with your team while lessening fatigue caused by commuting." The work-from-home solution would also be available when she experienced digestive issues. Colin also agreed to initiate a company-wide scent-free policy, asking all workers to avoid wearing scented products in the workplace. He consulted with the contract cleaning staff, asking them to replace any scented cleaning products with unscented ones. He also pointed out that the company's existing gender-neutral bathroom was a private bathroom and recommended she use that one when desiring more privacy. Finally, Colin agreed to make a note that if meals were served at meetings or other company events, then the menu needed to include some nonfatty foods. Both Colin and Jaya were happy with their plan.

Colin then began to consider the orientation and training process. Jaya's orientation would only last 1 day because she needed to be introduced to the company culture, policies, procedures, and software, but as an established professional, she did not need much guidance on her job tasks. After the first day she would be assigned a mentor to consult when she had questions. Colin was concerned because orientation was usually conducted by the same senior partner who had downgraded Jaya's interview score. He could neither share Jaya's diagnosis without permission, nor could he even be sure that the knowledge would change the partner's attitude. He decided that another partner, one without preconceived negative ideas, might be more suitable. He did not want Jaya to suffer any unfair political backlash because of this decision. After careful consideration, he decided to propose that a new partner conduct orientation to develop competency just in case the primary training partner was unavailable in the future. This much more politically neutral explanation was readily accepted, and Jaya was able to get a good orientation experience and enter the organization without having unwittingly made a political opponent through no fault of her own.

After working for the firm for several weeks, Jaya and Colin again reviewed their accommodation plan. Jaya noted that despite people not wearing scented products, there were still many chemical scents in the workplace that triggered breathing difficulties and coughing. Some came from other floors in the office tower, occupied by other tenants. Some came from the retail outlets on the ground floor of the building, one of which sold scented products. Some wafted in from the street, including scents and dust from adjacent construction. Jaya requested a special air filtration system for her personal office. The medical-grade filtration system would cost several hundred dollars, unlike her other accommodations, which had been free. After consulting with the partner who approved such expenses, Colin was informed that a medical note would be required before the expense would be approved. Since it would take a week for Jaya to get an appointment to get the note, she was permitted to work from home for that week. She was also reimbursed for the cost because the doctor charged a fee for the service and provision of medical notes was not covered by their benefits plan. After providing her doctor's note, Jaya received her air filtration system within 4 days. But the whole issue had sparked a thought. Colin remembered Jaya's difficulties during her interview when wildfire smoke from forest fires had permeated the city and the offices, and she had struggled with her breathing. What if there is a fire in the office, Colin thought. Will Jaya be able to evacuate down multiple flights of stairs if she can't breathe properly? He did some research and determined that N95 respirator masks, which had come into common usage during the COVID-19 pandemic, also helped filter out harmful particles associated with smoke. He stocked her office with a couple masks, explaining their purpose. With Jaya's permission, he also asked the two colleagues who had offices on either side of her to assist her in the event of an evacuation. Now, if she did experience problems breathing and needed assistance, at least someone would know about it and could help!

Colin went home after the second accommodation meeting feeling good about the work he had done. He recognized there had been a few issues and gaps, and he had taken steps to correct them. He knew that in the future he would identify even more improvements. Yet they were on their way to becoming a truly inclusive organization, and they had gotten a great employee with a scarce skill set who might otherwise have been overlooked. He vowed to continue his efforts the next time he was asked to hire someone. It felt good to make the world a more equitable place while also doing his job well and adding value for the organization.

Moving Forward

Like all organizational initiatives, disability inclusion is best carried out with the support and endorsement of senior management, under the umbrella of consistently applied evidence-based best practices and policies, while being supplemented with training and ongoing cycles of evaluation and improvement. And policies should focus on outlining appropriate processes and not on outcomes. For example, a policy on accommodation should include processes for requesting and granting accommodations but should not delineate which specific accommodations are acceptable. That gives practitioners the flexibility to respond to unique individual needs and avoids overly narrow, legalistic interpretations of accommodation responsibilities. It is also helpful to have a designated person or committee who is ultimately accountable for disability inclusion processes and outcomes because that accountability ensures that the matter will get focused attention in a busy workplace with many competing demands.

Remember that ultimately HR practitioners, supervisors, and managers are not merely trying to obey a law (although that is also important), they are trying to help a fellow human being contribute to their fullest potential. The inclusive design principles discussed in Chapter 8 remind us that disability-related barriers are created by thoughtlessness as much as or more often than by the disabilities themselves. A person-focused approach rather than a legalistic one not only leads to better productivity for the individual with the disability, but it also sends a broad signal of empathy and inclusiveness to other employees. This improves perceptions of support and morale, leading to many positive outcomes such as increases in job satisfaction and reductions in turnover intentions. Furthermore, many free and easy accommodations, such as a switch to positive supervisory practices, providing instructions in writing, or permitting flexible scheduling can be readily extended to entire work teams and are valued by other employees. At the end of the day, including people with disabilities in the workplace is not just about benefitting people with disabilities, it benefits us all.

FURTHER READINGS

Barker, R. T., & Gower, K. (2010). Strategic application of storytelling in organizations: Toward effective communication in a diverse world. *International Journal of Business Communication* (1973), 47(3), 295–312. https://doi.org/10.1177/0021943610369782

Equal Employment Opportunity Commission. (2008). *Applying performance and conduct standards to employees with disabilities.* https://www.eeoc.gov/laws/guidance/applying-performance-and-conduct-standards-employees-disabilities

Equal Employment Opportunity Commission. (2022). *The Americans with Disabilities Act and the use of software, algorithms, and artificial intelligence to assess job applicants and employees.* https://www.eeoc.gov/laws/guidance/americans-disabilities-act-and-use-software-algorithms-and-artificial-intelligence

Government of Canada. (2021). *How to build a disability management program.* https://www.canada.ca/en/government/publicservice/wellness-inclusion-diversity-public-service/health-wellness-public-servants/disability-management/how-to-build-disability-management-program-steps.html

Shrey, D., Hursh, N., Gallina, P., Slinn, S., & White, A. (2006). Disability management best practices and joint labour–management collaboration. *International Journal of Disability Management, 1*(1), 52–63. https://doi.org/10.1375/jdmr.1.1.52

REFERENCES

Brecher, E., Bragger, J., & Kutcher, E. (2006). The structured interview: Reducing biases toward job applicants with physical disabilities. *Employee Responsibilities and Rights Journal, 18*, 155–170. https://doi.org/10.1007/s10672-006-9014-y

Breward, K. (2017). Individual, organizational, and institutional predictors of the granting of employer-sponsored disability accommodations. *Canadian Journal of Disability Studies, 6*(4), 56–91. https://doi.org/10:15353/cjds.v6i4.383

Calkins, J., Lui, J., Wood, C. (2000). Recent developments in integrated disability management: Implications for professional and organizational development. *Journal of Vocational Rehabilitation, 15*(1), 31–37.

Chalmers, S. (2021). *Cystic fibrosis.* Mayo Clinic. https://www.mayoclinic.org/diseases-conditions/cystic-fibrosis/symptoms-causes/syc-20353700

Currier, K. F., Chan, F., Berven, N. L., Habeck, R. V., & Taylor, D. W. (2001). Functions and knowledge domains for disability management practice: A Delphi study. *Rehabilitation Counseling Bulletin, 44*(3), 133–143. https://doi.org/10.1177/003435520104400303

Cystic Fibrosis Trust. (2022). Digestive system and cystic fibrosis. https://www.cysticfibrosis.org.uk/what-is-cystic-fibrosis/how-does-cystic-fibrosis-affect-the-body/cystic-fibrosis-complications/digestive-system

Emens, E. F. (2008). Integrating accommodation. *University of Pennsylvania Law Review, 156*(4), 839–922.

Griffin, J. (2021, June 17). Disability is possibility: A mission to bust myths in India. *Guardian.* https://www.theguardian.com/global-development/2021/jun/17/disability-is-possibility-a-mission-to-bust-myths-in-india-photo-essay.

Holdren, S., Iwai, Y., Lenze, N. R., Weil, A. B., & Randolph, A. M. (2022). A novel narrative medicine approach to DEI training for medical school faculty. *Teaching and Learning in Medicine, 35*(4), 457–466. https://doi.org/10.1080/10401334.2022.2067165

Hursh, N. (2003, January 20). Benchmarking: What works in disability management. *Business and Health, 1,* 7.

Kettler, R. J. (2012). Testing accommodations: Theory and research to inform practice. *International Journal of Disability, Development, and Education, 59*(1), 53–66. https://doi.org/10.1080/1034912X.2012.654952

Kristman, V. L., Boot, C. R., Sanderson, K., Sinden, K. E., & Williams-Whitt, K. (2020). Implementing best practice models of return to work. In U. Bültmann & J. Siegrist (Eds.), *Handbook of disability, work, and health* (pp. 1–25). Springer.

MacDonald-Wilson, K., & Fabian, E. (2008). Best practices in developing reasonable accommodations in the workplace: Findings based on the research literature. *Rehabilitation Professional, 16*(4), 221–232.

Rose, R., Chakraborty, S., Mason-Lai, P., Brocke, W., Page, S. A., & Cawthorpe, D. (2016). The storied mind: A meta-narrative review exploring the capacity of stories to foster humanism in health care. *Journal of Hospital Administration, 5*(1), 52–61. https://doi.org/10.5430/jha.v5n1p52

Appendix: Checklists for Practitioners

What Checklists Can and Cannot Do

The checklists presented in this appendix can help ensure that practitioners do not overlook important considerations when designing and carrying out human resource management processes with employees with disabilities. Importantly, they are not a substitute for professional legal or medical advice, and there are some differences in the legal rights of employees based on jurisdiction. Each country has its own employment laws, and furthermore, employment law is often handled at a state or provincial level in some nations (e.g., the United States and Canada), so there are variations within countries as well. There is no substitute for professional legal advice from a practitioner who is knowledgeable about a specific jurisdiction. In addition, there is no substitute for professional medical advice regarding functional limitations associated with an individual worker's disability.

The checklists presented differ significantly from the typical ones offered by not-for-profit agencies and HR consultancy groups. Most checklists in existence related to disability and employment are designed to either make sure the employer has complied with the letter of the law or to identify the functional limitations and accommodation needs of employees who have a specific condition (e.g., selecting from a pre-existing list of limitations and accommodations for limb differences, Crohn's disease, or anxiety).The checklists provided in this book, by contrast, encourage holistic conversations that put the person first, treating them as a complex human being, not just a generic diagnosis. These lists encourage real collaboration and creative problem solving by acknowledging that there isn't a set solution that will work for each diagnosis or type of functional limitation, or in every setting. This collaborative approach helps change the mindset from a narrow "what do we have to do to comply with the law" focus to "what do we have to do to help this person and our organization thrive," which serves everyone better—employer, employee, and the community at large.

Both traditional types of checklists have significant disadvantages and limitations. Lists that focus solely on legislative compliance encourage decision makers to concentrate narrowly on whether they have done anything wrong, legally speaking. The goal, on both a conscious and nonconscious level, becomes merely getting the process right as defined by eliminating legal liability. That defensive mentality can distract practitioners, preventing them from focusing on the real goal: helping a worker to be able to perform to their full potential. Outcomes are less favorable under such conditions. The existence of this dynamic was supported (although not definitively proven) by the results of a study of 5,418 Canadian workers with disabilities who had requested accommodations from their employer (Breward, 2017). Logistical regression was used to identify which individual, organizational, and institutional variables impacted whether a worker received their needed accommodations. The research also found that when an industry was federally regulated, the regulated status had no significant impact on accommodation granting even though these industries are subject to equity-based legislative requirements above and beyond those required for provincially regulated employers. Furthermore, being unionized reduced the rate of accommodation granting, likely due to a focus on prioritizing rigid compliance with collective agreements over accommodations when the two were perceived to be in conflict (e.g., as relates to amending job descriptions or standard work hours). It is worth noting that subsequent studies have found inconsistent results, with some researchers finding that unionization improved accommodation outcomes (e.g., Lippel, 2020) while others found either the opposite or mixed effects (e.g., Lee, 2001; Wu et al., 2023).

Checklists that feature a list of functional limitations and accommodations associated with a given disability are also problematic. The HR practitioner and worker with a disability are expected to go through the list item by item, identifying the items that are relevant in their context to develop an accommodation plan. These lists do have their good points. When well developed, they can help ensure that entire categories of barriers are not overlooked, enabling a more comprehensive accommodation strategy. They can also help employers anticipate and remove barriers before they occur. But there is a three-fold problem. First, the lists may be incomplete, especially if they were originally developed with a specific industry, work setting, or occupation in mind. Incomplete lists can result in needs being overlooked and going unaddressed. Some employers may treat the list as the last word and authority on the matter. As a result, they may perceive needs that do not appear on their list as illegitimate, engendering resistance to the accommodation process. Second, even when they are comprehensive, these lists encourage over-generalization. Many practitioners erroneously assume that every limitation on the list will be relevant to every person with a given diagnosis. This over-generalization is a problem because the list of impairments associated with a given disability can be somewhat intimidating, creating the impression that employers will face burdens that are overstated and exaggerated. For example, a typical list of potential functional limitations associated with autism will include a very wide range of physical, emotional, sensory, social, and behavioral impairments because that condition is highly variable. Any one individual with autism is unlikely to experience all (or even most of) the limitations listed, and most employees will require one, two, or a few accommodations, not the dozens upon dozens that are theoretically possible. Third, checklists discourage the kind of individual assessment and attention that is necessary to help a real person rather than a theoretical diagnosis. Every workplace is unique, and every worker is unique. Frank conversations about the realities of the work setting and the worker's experience of barriers are more likely to result in creative win-win solutions when compared to limiting to strategies that appear on a premade list developed without the organization's specific context in mind.

The checklists that appear in this Appendix seek to retain the positive aspects of traditional checklists (enabling comprehensive assessments) while mitigating their weaknesses. They seek to foster creative problem solving, help workers with disabilities feel authentically heard and supported, and enhance positive supervisory practices centered around respect and active listening. The need for storytelling is built right into this approach, which should enhance empathy and mutual trust and enable the identification of novel accommodation solutions while simultaneously discouraging solutions that simply check the boxes and do not actually function for the workers they are intended to support. As such, the checklists presented can, when used appropriately, reduce employer risk, enhance worker well-being, and even contribute to a broader culture centered around respect and mutual understanding. One of the most notable differences between these lists and traditional lists is that the functional limitations and accommodations are not narrowly tailored to specific medical conditions. They refer to *conversational areas* rather than diagnosis-specific limitations and accommodation strategies. As such, the same lists can be used for all types of disabilities.

Job Analysis Checklist

Job analysis is the process used to outline key tasks and determine the knowledge, skills, abilities, and other traits (KSAOs) required for a given role. It also determines which requirements are critical (the bona fide occupational requirements, or BFORs) and which are secondary. That is important because accommodation legislation requires adjustment of secondary aspects of a job to accommodate disabilities but not BFORs. The result of this process is a job description and specification. In addition to using basic best practices (described in Chapter 2), there are specific considerations when conducting a job analysis or reviewing a previously completed analysis to ensure inadvertent disability-related barriers are not actively created. They include the following:

☐ Ensure that all identified KSAOs are actually required for the job (most should be directly related to the job tasks).

- Consider whether less directly task-related KSAOs are required for a legitimate purpose (e.g., respectful conflict resolution may be a competency that is expected of all employees regardless of whether it is a formal part of their job description).

- Consider whether inclusion of general (i.e., non-task–related) KSAOs makes sense for this role, or whether criteria were included because they are *standard* for the company or industry. If there is not a legitimate purpose for a KSAO to be included, remove it from the job description and specification.

☐ Consider whether the job has changed in any significant way over time such that previous criteria may no longer be valid.

☐ Assess all the different ways a given task could be completed versus how the task has been completed in the past. Keep in mind that inflexibility in task completion can create undue barriers (e.g., if occasional lifting of heavy boxes is required, perhaps a device could be used to assist rather than relying on human strength).

Recruitment Checklist

The recruitment process consists of posting job ads or otherwise advertising a job and collecting a pool of applications. To complete these tasks without creating inadvertent disability-related barriers, consider the following:

☐ Job posting includes a formal job description and job specification that has been validated using appropriate scientific job analysis techniques.

☐ Job is posted in a manner that enables members of various disability communities to perceive it (e.g., if billboards and transit bus ads are used, ensure there is a complementary strategy to allow people who are vision impaired to become aware of the opportunity).

☐ When posting online, the job board used complies with WCAG (Web Content Accessibility Guidelines) standards for accessibility, including external job board services and the employer's own website.

☐ Consider outreach recruiting, including actively pushing the job posting out to not-for-profit agencies and publications that serve the disability community.

☐ If the primary recruitment method is job fairs or crowded in-person networking events, provide a mechanism for people unable to participate in such events to hear about and apply for the job.

☐ Allow interested parties to make inquiries about the job in both verbal (i.e., phone) and written formats, and clearly indicate these formats in the job ad.

☐ In jurisdictions in which it is permitted, ensure the job ad explicitly encourages people from equity-seeking groups to apply.

☐ Provide an optional mechanism for people applying to identify that they are members of an equity-seeking group. (Note: Asking about being a member of an equity-seeking group is only legal when the information is used to support employment-equity goals. Otherwise, asking about disability status during hiring processes is both inappropriate and illegal. Chapter 1 covers legal parameters.)

☐ Ensure a formal, objective, consistent grading rubric is used when screening applications and résumés.

☐ Advise all personnel involved in applicant screening of which aspects of the job are critical, representing BFORs, and which are secondary, and make sure this information is made clear in the job posting. (Note: Designations of primary and secondary aspects should be derived from formal job analysis processes.)

☐ If artificial intelligence (AI) is used to screen applicants, test it for bias and seek one that is specifically programmed to avoid biases related to disability (and other equity-related characteristics).

Employment Testing Checklist

Employment testing may occur at multiple stages in the selection process and can take many forms, such as skill and knowledge tests, personality tests, and situational judgment tests. Regardless of when it occurs, ensuring the following can minimize disability-related barriers:

☐ All selection tests are testing KSAOs that have a clear connection to the job description and specification.

☐ All selection tests are verified by a third party, such as a professional psychology or HR association, as being valid and reliable. (Note: Some very large organizations may have in-house HR personnel capable of proper scientific validation of their own custom tests; however, this is a highly specialized skillset that generally requires advanced degrees beyond the bachelor's level.)

☐ The nature of the test(s) is clearly described in advance such that applicants could reasonably anticipate whether they will have accommodation needs.

☐ There is a clear mechanism communicated to all applicants by which they may request disability-related accommodations for selection tests.

☐ Avoid imposing time limits on tests unless there is a compelling job- or compentency asessment-related reason for them.

☐ If using multiple tests, ensure they are spaced out in a manner that does not create undue exhaustion or fatigue.

☐ Online tests must be on WCAG compliant sites that permit access for people with a range of disabilities. The tests themselves should also be WCAG compliant.

Job Interview Preparation Checklist

Job interviews often have the most influence in determining who is ultimately hired. Structured interview protocols should always be used. Being attentive to the following can help minimize barriers for the disability community:

Basic Interview Preparation

☐ Explicitly ask candidates if they have any accommodation needs related to the interview, and if so, confirm whether those needs have been addressed.

☐ Verify all interviewers have received formal anti-bias training within a reasonable time frame, generally 2 years ago or less.

- Anti-bias training should have included content specifically related to combatting stereotypes about disability.

- Anti-bias training should have also explained neurodiverse differences in communication style and body language.

☐ Whenever possible, use multiple interviewers to lessen potential for emergence of specific nonconscious biases.

☐ When there is more than one interviewer participating in the process, ensure the interview team is diversified as much as possible.

☐ Review interview questions to ensure that they are job related and free from bias.

☐ Ensure all candidates are asked the same questions in the same order.

☐ Ensure there is a formal scoring rubric for each interview question that includes a rating scale and behavioral anchors, and all candidates are scored using the same rubric.

☐ Verify that the scoring criteria avoids awarding or taking away points for irrelevant things that are not job related and may be impacted by disability (e.g., amount of eye contact or posture).

☐ If using AI to conduct interviews, ensure the program is designed to avoid bias related to disability. This means, among other things, that it avoids making attributions based on interpretations of micro expressions, eye contact, and posture, and it does not negatively score candidates with speech impairments, stutters, or other communication barriers.

Online Interviews

☐ Do not assume, based on the demographics of the applicant pool, that all candidates will have ready access to a computer, reliable internet connection, and a private, quiet space to participate in interviews. If a candidate lacks these resources, have a plan in place to accommodate them. (Recall that disability and poverty are correlated, so this may be a bigger barrier in the disability community.)

☐ Train interviewers to avoid making assumptions based on personal items that may appear in the background of the interview (e.g., equipment to address disability-related needs or books on shelves).

☐ Ensure the application selected (e.g., Zoom, Skype, Discord) can be downloaded for free by the candidate and that it permits closed captioning as needed and has a chat option for people with verbal communication issues.

In-Person Interviews

☐ The workplace needs to be physically accessible for people with sight and mobility impairments, including people who use wheelchairs.

☐ Ensure transportation to the interview site is available for people unable to drive their own vehicles, and, if on a mass transit route, that public transport is accessible to all, including wheelchair users and people with visual impairments. If not, offer a solution such as a funded taxi or online interview (especially when the interview location differs from where they will be expected to work).

☐ Hold the job interview in a quiet, distraction-free location.

☐ Advise interviewers to avoid wearing scented products such as perfume and cologne.

☐ Avoid conducting interviews over meals.

☐ Offer seating that accommodates a range of body types comfortably.

☐ If written materials will be offered to the candidate during the interview, they are available in suitable formats based on any identified accommodation needs.

Orientation and Training Checklist

The orientation and training process sends important messages about organizational culture to newly hired workers. Sending a message of inclusion can be accomplished through attentiveness to the following:

- [ ] Ask all successful candidates about accommodation needs after having signed their offer to hire. Because many workers with disabilities will be hesitant to identify disabilities prehire due to fears of discrimination, asking after they have been hired, even if they were previously asked, is important.

- [ ] If accommodation needs are identified, alert the instructor or manager who will perform orientation and training and provide appropriate resources and training.

- [ ] Present orientation and training materials in an appropriate format based on the needs of learners. (For example, people with vision and hearing impairments may need alternate formats for written materials and lectures, respectively.)

- [ ] Deliver training in a format and at a pace that minimizes potential for fatigue, exhaustion, and becoming overwhelmed.

- [ ] Provide learners with some training materials in advance, when possible, so they have more time to familiarize themselves with the content and to structure questions. (Note: This is not intended to create homework or self-study of content that is not covered by the instructor, but rather it is an opportunity to get an advance look at what the instructor will cover.)

- [ ] If orientation demands the use of skills that will not be required for the actual job, ensure it will not pose any barriers. (For example, some orientation programs engage in physical challenges such as a team building exercise, while others demand advanced social skills that may not be needed for the worker's paid role depending on job description.)

- [ ] Include diversity topics in orientation, including anti-bias training and information about what to do if one is experiencing bullying or harassment.

- [ ] When addressing diversity-related topics during orientation, ensure the instructor does not treat a person with a visible disability as a spokesperson for the entire disability community.

☐ Include time for workers to get to know their coworkers, share personal stories, and connect on an individual level during orientation. This can help mitigate nonconscious bias through knowledge and familiarity.

☐ Orientation and training should avoid social time that revolves around alcohol consumption, in favor of alternate social activities.

☐ Assign a formal mentor for ongoing support and direction for new hires.

Accommodations Screening Questionnaire

The HR practitioner or manager should go through this questionnaire with new hires after the offer to hire has been signed and before the employees start their employment so that needed accommodations can be in place on the first day. It should be reviewed after a couple weeks of employment so that any unanticipated barriers may be addressed. A quarterly review for the first year may be helpful, and then annual reviews may be sufficient in most but not all contexts. Changes in job role, work tools, processes, or medical status should trigger a new review. Note that this questionnaire does not ask about a medical diagnosis at any point. That is by design because employers in the overwhelming majority of jurisdictions are entitled to information about functional limitations and accommodation needs but are not entitled to detailed diagnostic information or private medical information.

When going through this questionnaire, asking about the relative frequency and duration of symptoms and the worker's ability to anticipate onset of symptoms is helpful. Some limitations may be ongoing (e.g., a person in a wheelchair will never be able to climb stairs), while others may be sporadic (e.g., grasping tasks may be difficult only during flare-ups of rheumatoid arthritis). The frequency with which the limitation is experienced and the predictability with which it occurs may impact which accommodation strategies are considered most desirable:

☐ Thinking broadly, what limitations should your employer be aware of that may have an impact on your work-related needs? Consider each of the following areas:

   • Physical limitations related to strength, stamina, mobility, agility, or use of limbs

- Physical limitations related to sensory perceptions including hearing and seeing

- Cognitive limitations related to memory, focus, ability to prioritize tasks, or ability to identify steps in a process

- Sensory limitations related to difficulties tolerating noise, light, scents, or other stimuli

- Communication-related limitations

- Social interaction–related limitations

- Emotional, anxiety, and stress management–related limitations

- Any other limitations not already identified

☐ Based on the limitations identified, which job tasks are problematic or difficult for you? To ensure nothing is overlooked, employers should not only review a list of job tasks but should also discuss with you the following:

- Appropriateness of workspace, including location, furniture, lighting

- Appropriateness of work tools, including hand tools, computer and electronic devices, and software

- Appropriateness of work processes

- Appropriateness of work hours and scheduling

- Appropriateness of training delivery and day-to-day information distribution methods

- Appropriateness of performance management and supervisory processes

☐ What accommodations and resources could best address the issues identified in Sections 1 and 2 of this questionnaire? Remember to consider all options, including innovative ones that do not appear on this list. Accommodations are limited only by the creativity of the employer:

- Technical devices and physical tools (e.g., software, braille readers, and specialized hand tools)

- Minor changes to job descriptions, particularly for secondary aspects of the job

- Scheduling flexibility, including flextime and, if requested, reduced hours

- Work-from-home options

- Ergonomic assessments and workstation customization (e.g., special desk and chair)

- Structural changes to a building (e.g., installation of a wheelchair ramp)

- Direct human support (e.g., having access to a personal assistant)

- Reductions of sensory stimuli through workstation placement and design

- Amendments in supervisory practices (e.g., methods of providing instructions and feedback, interaction style, and degree of direction provided about prioritization of tasks)

- Adjustments to policies and procedures

- Social consideration from peers and managers (Note: This may require training to achieve. For example, coworkers are generally more open to neurodiverse styles of communication if they have been trained on neurodiversity.)

- Access to quiet, calming spaces

- Access to a coach or advisor

- Access to counseling resources, often through an employee assistance plan or part of many standard benefit packages

☐ Based on the limitations identified, which workplace tasks that are not directly job related are problematic or difficult for you?

- Issues with completing personal care tasks due to inappropriate facilities or service offerings (e.g., toileting and accessing appropriate food services)

- Issues with social tasks, such as remembering colleagues' names or understanding political relationships in the workplace

- Issues with accessing training or informational resources needed for development and career advancement

- Issues with getting to work or finding sufficient transportation options

- Experiencing any bullying or harassment from peers

- Peers creating inadvertent barriers due to lack of understanding or awareness of your accommodation needs and the nature of those barriers

Health and Safety Program Checklist

Health and safety program planning and implementation should consider the unique needs of workers with disabilities. This is true across the board but is especially true for emergency evacuation plans. The employer health and safety committee should consider the following:

☐ Ensure that there is a clear and reasonable evacuation path for workers with disabilities. This may require taking steps such as ensuring that a worker who uses a wheelchair is given an office on the first floor because elevators may not be available during an emergency or having policies limiting hallway clutter that are regularly enforced.

☐ Identify and train *buddies* who are assigned to help vulnerable workers during an evacuation. For instance, a colleague who works in an adjacent cubicle may be assigned to help a worker with a severe vision impairment to exit the building.

☐ If there are employees who are deaf or extremely hard of hearing, ensure there are emergency alert signals that do not rely on sound.

☐ Develop and implement, in cooperation with senior executives, anti-bullying, anti-harassment, and diversity programs. Psychological safety is part and parcel of their responsibilities.

☐ Verify that maintenance services critical to safety are carried out. This may include snow removal on outdoor wheelchair ramps or any other maintenance related to accessibility supports.

☐ Provide training, if needed, on how to respond to specific medical situations. For example, if a worker is known to have epileptic seizures, having colleagues who work directly with them trained in how to respond to a seizure is prudent. Note that permission should be obtained from the affected worker before sharing any medical information.

The worker's immediate supervisor or manager should consider the following, although they are encouraged to consult with the health and safety committee or other subject matter experts for guidance:

☐ Ensure that work tools and workspaces are ergonomically appropriate based on the unique needs of the worker with the disability.

☐ Confirm that all personal protective equipment, such as safety goggles, hearing protection, respirators, and harnesses for working at height, is appropriate based on the unique needs of the worker with the disability. Finding replacements when specific protective equipment is unsuitable.

☐ Monitor social behaviors in the workplace, being attentive to signs that workers are being bullied or harassed by colleagues and following up when there are concerns.

Team Building Activity Checklist

Team building activities are a frequent problem area for individuals with disabilities because many of the conventional activities that are popular in the business world are not particularly disability friendly. When designing team building activities, employers should keep the following in mind:

☐ Avoid events centered around the consumption of alcohol.

☐ Avoid events centered around intensive physical activity, such as wilderness retreats and ropes courses, especially when physical activity is not normally part of the job description of the workers involved. If physical activities are going to be conducted, make sure employees attending are aware of the requirements beforehand so they can identify accommodation-related needs in advance.

☐ Avoid events that require a specific type and size of body to participate. (Go-kart racing is a good example of an activity to avoid.)

- [ ] Ensure events have a mix of activities, including some quieter activities that make fewer sensory demands and some noncompetitive activities.

- [ ] Encourage activities that involve sharing stories and getting to know each other personally, but do not force disclosures from those who are hesitant.

- [ ] Be clear about expectations, such as whether participation is mandatory or optional, how long the activity will last, and the goals of the program. Avoid surprises!

- [ ] If the team building activity lasts more than 3 hours, have a quiet place where attendees can retreat as needed without experiencing social sanctions.

- [ ] If food is served, make every reasonable effort to offer foods that accommodate all dietary needs without singling out individuals as *different*.

Individual Disability Management Plan Checklist

Individual disability management plans are most frequently used for two purposes: managing return to work for injured workers and managing addictions in the workplace. There are slightly different concerns dependent on the purpose for which it is being used. Disability management plans are an evolving practice, and legal precedents are still being established in many jurisdictions, especially as relates to addiction management. Since this is an evolving area of law, it is especially critical that employers seek qualified legal advice before proceeding.

Injured Workers Returning to Work

When an injured employee is recovering and, later, returning to the workplace, employers should ensure the following:

- [ ] A medical professional has provided a relevant assessment so return to work plans are realistic and medically appropriate.

- [ ] There are clear expectations for when, how, and how often workers will update their employer while on leave.

☐ There is a clear return to work path that permits workers to come back incrementally as they heal and strengthen. (For example, offer light duties, part-time work, work-from-home options, or other accommodations to the returning employee.)

☐ A specific individual is designated to reasonably keep the worker informed about workplace developments, enabling ongoing engagement and a sense of belonging.

☐ It is clear what the worker should do if, after attempting a return, they find they overestimated their current abilities and need to adjust their duties, and the disability management plan avoids penalizing a situation like this.

Workers With Work Performance-Impacting Addictions

When an employee with a work performance-impacting addiction returns to work, the employer should ensure the following:

☐ A medical professional has provided a relevant assessment.

☐ If participation in a formal treatment plan is a condition imposed in the disability management plan, the treatment was recommended by a physician or other qualified medical professional rather than a manager, business owner, or HR professional.

☐ The proposed treatment plan considers the individual's disability. (For example, Alcoholics Anonymous may not be suitable for some people with extreme social anxiety because it is an inherently social model of treatment.)

☐ The employer has provided funding or other resources required to access a treatment plan. (Even in countries with socialized medicine, addictions treatment for adults is not always covered by the government.)

☐ If participation in a formal treatment plan is not a condition imposed in the disability management plan, other supports and resources are offered to the worker to enable their return to work.

☐ Behavioral expectations are clear, including identification of the types of behaviors that could result in further actions by

HR. (For example, if the disability management plan is related to alcoholism, it is specifically mentioned that being under the influence on the job is prohibited, even if the drinks are not actually consumed in the workplace.)

REFERENCES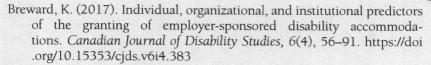

Breward, K. (2017). Individual, organizational, and institutional predictors of the granting of employer-sponsored disability accommodations. *Canadian Journal of Disability Studies, 6*(4), 56–91. https://doi .org/10.15353/cjds.v6i4.383

Lee, B. A. (2001). The implications of ADA litigation for employers: A review of federal appellate court decisions. *Human Resources Management, 40*(1), 35–50. https://doi.org/10.1002/hrm.4014

Lippel, K. (2020). Regulatory contexts affecting work reintegration of people with chronic disease and disabilities: An international perspective. In U. Bültmann & J. Siegrist (Eds.), *Handbook of disability, work, and health. Handbook series in occupational health sciences* (Vol. 1). Springer. https://doi.org/10.1007/978-3-030-24334-0_18

Wu, J. R., Iwanaga, K., Grenawalt, T., Mpofu, N., Chan, F., Lee, B., & Tansey, T. (2023). Employer practices for integrating people with disabilities into the workplace: A scoping review. *Rehabilitation Research, Policy, and Education, 37*(1), 60–79. https://doi.org/10.1891/ RE-21-25

Bibliography

Balser, D. B., & Harris, M. M. (2008). Factors affecting employee satisfaction with disability accommodation: A field study. *Employee Responsibilities and Rights Journal, 20*(1), 13–28. https://doi.org/10.1007/s10672-007-9062-y

Bartram, T., Cavanagh, J., Meacham, H., & Pariona-Cabrera, P. (2021). Re-calibrating HRM to improve the work experiences for workers with intellectual disability. *Asia Pacific Journal of Human Resources, 59*(1), 63–83. https://doi.org/10.1111/1744-7941.12230

Beatty, J. E., Baldridge, D. C., Boehm, S. A., Kulkarni, M., & Colella, A. J. (2019). On the treatment of persons with disabilities in organizations: A review and research agenda. *Human Resource Management, 58*(2), 119–137. https://doi.org/10.1002/hrm.21940

Blanck, P. (2020). Disability inclusive employment and the accommodation principle: Emerging issues in research, policy, and law. *Journal of Occupational Rehabilitation, 30*, 505–510. https://doi.org/10.1007/s10926-020-09940-9

Brucker, D. L., & Sundar, V. (2020). Job crafting among American workers with disabilities. *Journal of Occupational Rehabilitation, 30*, 575–587. https://doi.org/10.1007/s10926-020-09889-9

Cavanagh, J., Bartram, T., Meacham, H., Bigby, C., Oakman, J., & Fossey, E. (2017). Supporting workers with disabilities: A scoping review of the role of human resource management in contemporary organisations. *Asia Pacific Journal of Human Resources, 55*(1), 6–43. https://doi.org/10.1111/1744-7941.12111

Chan, F., Tansey, T. N., Iwanaga, K., Bezyak, J., Wehman, P., Phillips, B., Anderson, C. (2021). Company characteristics, disability inclusion practices, and employment of people with disabilities in the post COVID-19 job economy: A cross sectional survey study. *Journal of Occupational Rehabilitation, 31*, 463–473. https://doi.org/10.1007/s10926-020-09941-8

Chaudhry, I. S., Paquibut, R. Y., & Tunio, M. N. (2021). Do workforce diversity, inclusion practices, & organizational characteristics contribute to organizational innovation? Evidence from the UAE. *Cogent Business & Management, 8*(1), 1947549. https://doi.org/10.1080/23311975.2021.1947549

Ellinger, A. E., Naidoo, J., Ellinger, A. D., Filips, K., & Herrin, G. D. (2020). Applying blue ocean strategy to hire and assimilate workers with disabilities into distribution centers. *Business Horizons, 63*(3), 339–350. https://doi.org/10.1016/j.bushor.2020.01.009

Fisher, S. L., & Connelly, C. E. (2020). Building the "business case" for hiring people with disabilities: A financial cost-benefit analysis methodology and example. *Canadian Journal of Disability Studies, 9*(4), 71–88. https://doi.org/10.15353/cjds.v9i4.669

Flower, R. L., Hedley, D., Spoor, J. R., & Dissanayake, C. (2019). An alternative pathway to employment for autistic job-seekers: A case study of a training and assessment program targeted to autistic job candidates. *Journal of Vocational Education & Training, 71*(3), 407–428. https://doi.org/10.1080/13636820.2019.1636846

Guevara, A. (2021). The need to reimagine disability rights law because the medical model of disability fails us all. *Wisconsin Law Review, 2021*(269). https://ssrn.com/abstract=3957584

Gould, R., Harris, S. P., Mullin, C., & Jones, R. (2020). Disability, diversity, and corporate social responsibility: Learning from recognized leaders in inclusion. *Journal of Vocational Rehabilitation, 52*(1), 29–42. doi:10.3233/JVR-191058

Habeck, R., Hunt, A., Rachel, C. H., Kregel, J., & Chan, F. (2010). Employee retention and integrated disability management practices as demand side factors. *Journal of Occupational Rehabilitation, 20*(4), 443–455. https://doi.org/10.1007/s10926-009-9225-9

Harpur, P., & Blanck, P. (2020). Gig workers with disabilities: Opportunities, challenges, and regulatory response. *Journal of Occupational Rehabilitation, 30*, 511–520. https://doi.org/10.1007/s10926-020-09937-4

Kendall, K. M., & Karns, G. L. (2018). The business case for hiring people with disabilities. *Social Business, 8*(3), 277–292.

Khayatzadeh-Mahani, A., Wittevrongel, K., Nicholas, D. B., & Zwicker, J. D. (2020). Prioritizing barriers and solutions to improve employment for persons with developmental disabilities. *Disability and Rehabilitation, 42*(19), 2696–2706. https://doi.org/10.1080/09638288.2019.1570356

Kwan, C. K. (2020). Socially responsible human resource practices to improve the employability of people with disabilities. *Corporate Social Responsibility and Environmental Management, 27*(1), 1–8. https://doi.org/10.1002/csr.1768

Lefever, M., Decuman, S., Perl, F., Braeckman, L., & Van de Velde, D. (2018). The efficacy and efficiency of disability management in job-retention and job-reintegration. *A Systematic Review,* 501–534. https://doi.org/10.3233/wor-182709

Lejeune, A. (2023). Fighting for sheltered workshops or for inclusive workplaces? Trade unions pursuing disability rights in Belgium. *Disability & Society, 38*(2), 228–246. https://doi.org/10.1080/09687599.2021.1921702

Lindsay, S., Leck, J., Shen, W., Cagliostro, E., & Stinson, J. (2019). A framework for developing employer's disability confidence. *Equality, Diversity, and Inclusion: An International Journal, 38*(1), 40–55. https://doi.org/10.1108/EDI-052018-0085.

Lindsay, S., Osten, V., Rezai, M., & Bui, S. (2021). Disclosure and workplace accommodations for people with autism: A systematic review. *Disability and Rehabilitation, 43*(5), 597–610. https://doi.org/10.1080/09638288.2019.1635658

Lund, E. M., Wilbur, R. C., & Kuemmel, A. M. (2020). Beyond legal obligation: The role and necessity of the supervisor-advocate in creating a socially just, disability-affirmative training environment. *Training and Education in Professional Psychology, 14*(2), 92–99. https://doi.org/10.1037/tep0000277

Lysaght, R., Krupa, T., & Gregory, A. W. (2022). Employer approaches to recognizing and managing intermittent work capacity. *Equality, Diversity, and Inclusion: An International Journal, 41*(5), 739–759. https://doi.org/10.1108/EDI-02-2021-0046

Macfarlane, K. A. (2021). Disability without documentation. *Fordham Law Review, 90,* 59–102. https://dx.doi.org/10.2139/ssrn.3781221

Maestas, N., Mullen, K. J., & Rennane, S. (2019). Unmet need for workplace accommodation. *Journal of Policy Analysis and Management, 38*(4), 1004–1027. https://doi.org/10.1002%2Fpam.22148

Mark, B. G., Hofmayer, S., Rauch, E., & Matt, D. T. (2019). Inclusion of workers with disabilities in production 4.0: Legal foundations in Europe and potentials through worker assistance systems. *Sustainability, 11*(21), 5978. https://www.mdpi.com/2071-1050/11/21/5978#

Nevala, N., Pehkonen, I., Koskela, I., Ruusuvuori, J., & Anttila, H. (2015). Workplace accommodation among persons with disabilities: A systematic review of its effectiveness and barriers or facilitators. *Journal of Occupational Rehabilitation, 25*, 432–448. https://doi.org/10.1007/s10926-014-9548-z

Østerud, K. L. (2023). Disability discrimination: Employer considerations of disabled jobseekers in light of the ideal worker. *Work, Employment, and Society, 37*(3), 740–756. https://doi.org/10.1177/09500170211041303

Raghavan, M., Barocas, S., Kleinberg, J., & Levy, K. (2020, January). Mitigating bias in algorithmic hiring: Evaluating claims and practices. In *Proceedings of the 2020 conference on fairness, accountability, and transparency* (pp. 469–481). https://doi.org/10.1145/3351095.3372828

Richard, S., & Hennekam, S. (2021). When can a disability quota system empower disabled individuals in the workplace? The case of France. *Work, Employment, and Society, 35*(5), 837–855. https://doi.org/10.1177/0950017020946672

Richard, S., & Hennekam, S. (2021). Constructing a positive identity as a disabled worker through social comparison: The role of stigma and disability characteristics. *Journal of Vocational Behavior, 125*, 103528. https://doi.org/10.1016/j.jvb.2020.103528

Schloemer-Jarvis, A., Bader, B., & Böhm, S. A. (2022). The role of human resource practices for including persons with disabilities in the workforce: A systematic literature review. *International Journal of Human Resource Management, 33*(1), 45–98. https://doi.org/10.1080/09585192.2021.1996433

Schur, L. A., Ameri, M., & Kruse, D. (2020). Telework after COVID: A "silver lining" for workers with disabilities? *Journal of Occupational Rehabilitation, 30*, 521–536. https://doi.org/10.1007/s10926-020-09936-5

Shrey, D., Hursh, N., Gallina, P., Slinn, S., & White, A. (2006). Disability management best practices and joint labour–management collaboration. *International Journal of Disability Management, 1*(1), 52–63. https://doi.org/10.1375/jdmr.1.1.52

Solovieva, T. I., Dowler, D. L., & Walls, R. T. (2011). Employer benefits from making workplace accommodations. *Disability and Health Journal, 4*(1), 39–45. https://doi.org/10.1016/j.dhjo.2010.03.001

Su, H., Wong, J., Kudla, A., Park, M., Trierweiler, R., Capraro, P., Heinemann, A. W. (2023). Disability phenotypes and job accommodations utilization among people with physical disability. *Journal of Occupational Rehabilitation, 33*(2), 352–361. https://doi.org/10.1007/s10926-022-10078-z

Syma, C. (2019). Invisible disabilities: Perceptions and barriers to reasonable accommodations in the workplace. *Library Management, 40*(1/2), 113–120. https://doi.org/10.1108/LM-10-2017-0101

Tang, J. (2021). Understanding the telework experience of people with disabilities. *Proceedings of the ACM on Human-Computer Interaction, 5*, 1–27. https://doi.org/10.1145/3449104

Topping, M., Douglas, J., & Winkler, D. (2023). They treat you like a person, they ask you what you want: A grounded theory study of quality paid disability support for adults with acquired neurological disability. *Disability and Rehabilitation, 45*(13), 2138–2148. https://doi.org/10.1080/09638288.2022.2086636

Toquero, C. M. D. (2020). Inclusion of people with disabilities amid COVID-19: Laws, interventions, recommendations.

Multidisciplinary Journal of Educational Research, 10(2), 158–177. https://doi.org/10.17583/remie.2020.5877

Trewin, S., Basson, S., Muller, M., Branham, S., Treviranus, J., Gruen, D., Hebert, D., Lyckowski, N., & Manser, E. (2019). Considerations for AI fairness for people with disabilities. *AI Matters, 5*(3), 40–63. https://doi.org/10.1145/3362077.3362086

Waddinton, L. (2008). When it is reasonable for Europeans to be confused: Understanding when a disability accommodation is "reasonable" from a comparative perspective. *Comparative Labor Law & Policy Journal, 29*(3), 101–124.

Williams-Whitt, K. (2007). Impediments to disability accommodation. *Relations Industrielles, 62*(3), 405–432.

Zhu, X., Law, K. S., Sun, C., & Yang, D. (2019). Thriving of employees with disabilities: The roles of job self-efficacy, inclusion, and team-learning climate. *Human Resource Management, 58*(1), 21–34. https://doi.org/10.1002/hrm.21920

Index

Fetal alcohol spectrum disorders (FASDs), 119, 134, 136–139
Fetal alcohol syndrome (FAS), 137
Fingerprint-based biometrics, 86
Fiske, S. T., 54
Flexible scheduling, 10, 88, 91, 104, 125, 156, 162
Forbes Magazine!, 112
Formal recognition programs, 56
Full-time work, 2–3

Glassdoor, 26
Glick, P., 54, 63
Granger, B., 127

Hand tools, 181
Hard of hearing (HoH), 79–81
Health and safety program, 261–262
Hearing impairments, 79–83
HoH. *See* Hard of hearing (HoH)
Human resources (HR), 11, 21, 71, 95, 152, 231
  managers, 74
  neurodiverse workers. *See* Neurodiversity
  recruiting team, 152
  representatives, 71
  and software applications, 182
Hyper-masculine cultures, 63

Implicit association test (IAT), 49–51
Inclusion, psychological aspects, 4, 47–48
  hyper-masculine cultures, 63
  inclusive cultures, 64
  nonconscious prejudice, 48–57
  organizational culture, 59–62
  peer attitudes, 64–66
  personal biases, 57–58
Inclusive design
  accessibility, 172–174
  echolocation accommodations, 175–176
  interior design, 177–180
  mental health and well-being, 176–177
  policies and procedures, 185–187
  social environment, 187–188
  vision impairment, 174–175
  work tool and software design, 180

Indeed, job-posting service, 26
Indirect discrimination, 7, 8, 21, 29, 113, 153
Individual disability management plans, 263–265
In-group members, 51–52, 55, 59, 66
In-person interviews, 256
Integrate Autism Employment Advisors, 110
Integrated Threat Model of Prejudice, 54, 55
Interior design
  color design, 178–180
  furniture and shelving placement, 178
  privacy design considerations, 178
  signage design, 177
Intermittent disabilities
  accommodations for workers, 153–163
  categories, 147–148
  special considerations, 149–153
  team warehouse setting, 191–195
International Dyslexia Association, 110–111
International legislative environments, 12–16
Intersectional stereotypes, 53
Invisible Knapsack exercise, 56
Irritable bowel syndrome, 31

Japanese Sign Language (JSL), 80
Job analysis, 24–25, 251–252
Job interview preparation
  basic, 255
  in-person, 256
  online, 255–256
Job-posting services, 26
Job satisfaction, 34, 38, 47, 155, 176, 245
Job-seeking, 4, 25
Job sites, 33–34

Kalev, A., 61
Knowledge, skills, abilities, and other traits (KSAOs), 9–10, 24, 25
Kutcher, E., 28